A
NATURALIST
GOES FISHING

Casting in Fragile Waters from
the Gulf of Mexico to
New Zealand's South Island

JAMES McCLINTOCK

St. Martin's Press
New York

To my mother,
Helen Muriel Ganopole

www.stmartins.com

Fish illustrations by Annabelle DeCamillis.

A part of the events related in Chapter 2 appeared in a different form in *Sierra* magazine.

Library of Congress Cataloging-in-Publication Data

McClintock, James, 1955–
    A naturalist goes fishing : casting in fragile waters from the Gulf of Mexico to New Zealand's South Island / James McClintock.
        pages   cm
    ISBN 978-1-137-27990-3
    1. Fishing. 2. Endangered ecosystems. I. Title.
SH441.M442   2015
    799.1—dc23
                                                                                    2015011419

ISBN 978-1-137-27990-3 (hardcover)
ISBN 978-1-4668-7925-6 (e-book)

Design by Letra Libre, Inc.

Our books may be purchased in bulk for promotional, educational, or business use. Please contact your local bookseller or the Macmillan Corporate and Premium Sales Department at (800) 221-7945, extension 5442, or by e-mail at MacmillanSpecialMarkets@macmillan.com.

First Edition: October 2015

10   9   8   7   6   5   4   3   2   1

CONTENTS

1

CHANDELEUR ISLANDS

Redfish

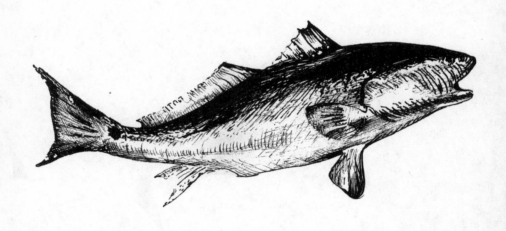

T he bull redfish was probably close to forty pounds, large by Chandeleur Islands standards. The fish had beaten the odds—one of the last survivors of twenty-five million eggs spawned by its mother over a single breeding season. The vast majority of the eggs had not been fertilized or had been carried by currents to shallows warmed by Louisiana's afternoon sun. Some had been tossed by waves onto the shore to dry among the detritus. Those that had developed into larvae were largely consumed by zooplankton and juvenile fish.

The redfish had grown quickly in its first year—reaching a foot in length by gorging itself on the rich beds of polychaete worms buried in their homemade tubes in the soft sand or by chasing down small crustaceans that darted in and out of sea grass blades. By three years of age, the fish probably weighed an impressive eight pounds and had shifted its diet to big blue crabs—its favorite—along with penaeid shrimp, small croakers, mullet, menhaden, and lizardfish.

As the seasons piled up, the big male attained "bull" status, defined in measure as thirty-five inches or longer from nose to tail. Its foraging range and feeding habits became routine, so much so that the white, pink-tailed plastic jig attracted the fish's attention. After the slightest hesitation, the tantalizing herky-jerky movement of the lure triggered an irreversible burst of neuromuscular activity. The bull redfish struck.

"Fish on!" I yelled in the general direction of my fishing buddy and younger brother Pete, who was seated behind me in our twelve-foot skiff. Pete smiled despite the lightly falling rain and a southwest wind that stirred the water in the shallow cut between the islands. A deep tug followed by strong head wags ruled out a speckled seatrout or ladyfish. "I think it might be a big red!" I shouted. Pete reeled in his line and stowed his pole using the clips on the aft side of the skiff. We both knew the fish would dictate the terms of the fight. If one didn't take immediate action, a fish this size hooked on medium tackle strips a good bit of line from the reel and invariably escapes, either from the line-breaking tension caused by setting the drag in a desperate attempt to turn the fish or, just as often, from running smack out of line.

Pete reached back, grasped the engine's throttle in his left hand for balance, and used his right hand to pull-start the twenty-five-horsepower outboard. The engine, still warm from a recent run, sputtered to life after a few quick tugs. Knowing that from his position Pete couldn't see in which direction to head the skiff, I stood at the bow, fishing pole in hand, and pointed in the general direction the fish had surged. Clicking the engine into gear, Pete gently gunned the throttle and nudged the skiff forward as I reeled line. After what had seemed an interminable stretch of anticipation, we were underway, the big fish holding tight to the bottom, still hooked, still unseen.

Les Îles de Chandeleur lie thirty miles off the coast of Louisiana, delineating the southeasternmost corner of this decidedly Cajun territory. A portion of the Breton National Wildlife Refuge,[1] the fifty-mile chain of uninhabited islands is a naturalist's dream. The landscape consists of low-lying, densely vegetated barrier islands built of sediments washed down the Mississippi long before the Army Corps of Engineers began to dam up the river. In stark contrast to the lack of relief of the islands, the sky and the horizon are as immeasurable as any I have seen in Florida, Montana, or Wyoming. The grandeur sets the stage for jaw-dropping sunrises and sunsets, and during the summer, afternoon thunderheads open up. Thousands of once-endangered brown pelicans[2] and magnificent frigate birds nest among black mangroves, the frigates often soaring in huge spirals, effortlessly riding the thermals until they are but specks in the sky.

I have visited these islands with eleven friends to fish for speckled seatrout and redfish just about every summer or fall for the past fifteen years. Some in our group have been coming more than twice as long, a testament to the addictive nature of this annual pilgrimage.

Each year, we drive from Birmingham, Alabama to Biloxi, Mississippi, squeezed into sedans and vans brimming with fishing gear. Arriving at Point Cadet Marina, nestled under the belly of the Golden Nugget Biloxi Casino (formerly the Isle of Capri Casino, which was heavily damaged in 2005 by Hurricane Katrina), we board the *VI*, an oddly named, 127-foot live-aboard ship owned by Southern Sports Fishing Inc. and captained by Robbie Thornton. Between the twelve of us, more than sixty rigged fishing poles are secured between paired holes cut in wooden boards lining the underside of the open ceiling on the outside back deck. Tackle boxes are slid below benches. Beer is iced down in large coolers. Duffle bags stuffed with toiletries and clean clothes are tossed on bunks below deck (so as to best lay claim to sleeping quarters farthest from noisy engines or those who snore). By late evening, alarm clocks set, we settle into our bunks. Around midnight, Robbie fires up the ship's engines, and the first mate unmoors the ship. Four hours later, the ear-jarring racket of anchor chain disrupts our sleep. Alarms ring. Half asleep, we climb from our bunks to dress, pulling on long-sleeved fishing shirts. Sipping dishwater coffee, we shovel down breakfast while the captain and first mate lower our skiffs by crane from the ship's upper deck, plopping each into the still-dark waters of the Gulf of Mexico. The small skiffs, each provisioned with gas, net, cooler, and life jackets, form a bobbing line against the early dawn sky, an umbilicus connecting our ship to the sea.

"He's running again!" I warned Pete over the whine of reel drag and rumble of engine idle. We had followed the fish for close to forty minutes. Hard rain, stiff winds, and a falling tide had conspired and left us wet and chilled. The only good news was that I had caught a glimpse of the fish. It was definitely a big red, its upper body carpeted in a mosaic of coppery red scales. The fish had to be at least three feet long, with a broad muscular girth that spoke to its bulldog strength. The fish slowed. Maybe it was tiring. I lifted my rod tip and pulled back slowly and steadily and reeled in line as my rod descended. Again and again, lift, pull, reel. With mounting excitement, Pete and I watched the fish's tail fin break the surface near the skiff. Then, as if punctuating the end of a sentence with a deft tail kick, the bull red broke free and vanished.

Ken Marion, a professor of freshwater and marine ecology at the University of Alabama at Birmingham, has been visiting the Chandeleur Islands to cast his line into its fish-laden waters for almost four decades. Long before I joined in on these fishing trips, Ken and some of the others in our current fishing group first chartered a ship to the Chandeleurs to fish for speckled seatrout and redfish and to get away from the routines of office and home. They also wanted to take advantage of great birding and revel in the raw, untamed scenery. The fishing trips became so popular that for a while the group chartered the ship in both the summer and spring of a given year. When I asked Ken to estimate, all told, the number of times he had visited the islands to fish, he told me he had to be closing in on his fiftieth trip. Ken had probably accumulated enough speckled seatrout stories to fill a good portion of this chapter. But when I asked him, he told me that one story back in the mid-1990s stood out.

Ken and his longtime skiff-mate, Bruce Cusic, a dentist and nature photographer, were easing toward the end of a long summer day of Chandeleur fishing that had begun well before dawn. A scorching mid-July heat draped the islands in a thick blanket of impossibly muggy air. It was so unbearably hot that Ken and Bruce had had to periodically fire up the skiff's engine and throttle their boat full tilt over the grass flats to cool themselves. Early evening found the two fishers adrift in a slack tide forty yards off of a narrow cut in North Island. Hundreds of laughing gulls nesting on the island filled the sky, some circling directly overhead, others returning low across the water with small fish and crustaceans to feed to their nesting chicks. The beehive of gulls generated a cacophony of chatter that did little to distract the two fishers from the stomach-churning odor of guano baking in the warm, moist marsh mud. Despite the slow fishing that the Chandeleurs are known for during late afternoons and early summer evenings, Ken and Bruce continued to cast their medium-weight rods with spinning reels spooled with translucent green, eight-pound test line toward the shore. Ken was fishing one of the lures most favored by Chandeleur fishers, a white, three-inch plastic grub with a flattened red tail weighted with only the smallest of split shots. Because of its flattened tail this plastic bait is sometimes referred to as a stingray grub. The plastic bait is generally fished by casting it close to shore and using one's wrist action to generate a repetitive up-and-down motion of the pole while reeling to "hop" the grub through the water and back to the skiff.

Ken cast his line in a long high arc toward the mouth of the cut in North Island. The grub landed in the water and sank as the line continued a trajectory seemingly destined for the water's surface. A laughing gull, gliding low on its return to the island, never saw what was coming. Midair, Ken's descending fishing line settled over and wrapped around one of the gull's wings, abruptly dropping the bird to the water. Now, sitting on the water with its wing entangled in line, the gull was clearly unhappy. Ken recalls his immediate thought was *Oh, shit! Now I have to untangle a pissed-off gull!* Bruce started the engine and ever so slowly edged the skiff toward the ensnarled gull to avoid further startling the shocked bird. Suddenly, the gull jerked down into the water. Ken and Bruce watched in astonishment as the gull's head and wing jerked down below the water's surface and then, immediately upon return to the surface, jerked down again. Ken puzzled over whether the gull was injured or panicked. What could be causing the bird to display such odd spasms? As the skiff neared the gull, the answer was revealed in a flash of silver in the clear blue-green water below the bird. A speckled seatrout had taken Ken's grub. The gull had become a bobber— a feathered fishing bobber.

Bruce eased the skiff the final few feet toward the gull-turned-bobber and the now-hooked speckled trout. Ken grabbed the handle of the three-foot-long fishing net and lifted it from the floor of the skiff. Placing the mouth of the net down into the water, he slipped it under the gull and lifted the entangled bird up and into the skiff.

After placing the bird on the skiff's floorboards, Ken firmly grasped the gull's torso and wings, avoiding the reach of its sharp beak. The gull calmed and allowed itself to be untangled from the still-intact fishing line. Ken gently lifted the freed bird over the side of the skiff and placed it into the water. Acting a little embarrassed by the incident (anthropomorphism aside), the gull slowly swam off, twisting its head and neck to periodically peek back toward the skiff. Now, Ken could return his attention to the speckled seatrout that with any luck was still hooked to the end of his line. Retrieving his fishing rod, he reeled in slack line recovered from the entangled bird and fought the fish. The speckled seatrout was the largest he had hooked in the twenty years he had fished the Chandeleur Islands up to that very moment, and all twenty years since. Probably measuring twenty-eight or more inches and weighing a good seven or eight pounds, the fish was truly massive by Chandeleur standards.

As fishing etiquette dictates in a two-person skiff, while Ken fought his fish, Bruce prepared to net Ken's record trout. Ken knew that despite the fish holding in the water above a thick grass-bed of *Ruppia,* there was an outside chance the fish could dodge into the weeds and break free. Suddenly, it all came to a head. With one final desperate lunge, the massive speckled seatrout forced itself deep into the weeds. Despite the vanishing act, the sustained tension on his line convinced Ken that he still had the fish hooked. Alas, when Bruce forced the fishing net down into the *Ruppia,* it came back up with Ken's stingray grub attached to nothing more than a pile of weeds.

The silver-colored speckled seatrout (*Cynoscion nebulosus*)—called *truite gris* in Louisiana French or, in English, speckled trout, spotted seatrout, or just "speck" for short—is largely named for the generous sprinkling of black dots that cover the dorsum, upper sides, and the dorsal fin and tail.[3] The fish bears no direct kinship with the familiar trout caught by fly and spinner fishers in mountain streams and lakes around the world. Indeed, speckled seatrout are members of the drum family, the same taxonomic group that claims the red-fish. Members of the drum family generally produce grunting noises using specialized sonic muscles; speckled trout, like redfish, are no exception. Scientists suspect that these noises are used in fish-to-fish communication.[4] Because the grunts are made by sexually mature male seatrout, they are likely to play a role in reproductive behaviors such as attracting and courting egg-bearing females. I have heard specks grunt as I dropped keepers into my skiff's live-well in the Chandeleurs and in Alabama's Fish River. Similar to that of redfish, the grunting is faint out of the water, but like most sounds produced by marine animals, the sounds carry much greater distances under water.

Most speckled seatrout spend at least some portion of their lives in an estuary. Marine ecologists refer to such fishes as "estuarine-dependent" species. Accordingly, the health of coastal estuaries is critical to the fish's survival, much as healthy productive estuaries are central to sustaining rich populations of blue crabs and oysters. Speckled seatrout occur along the Atlantic coast of the United States from Florida to Massachusetts (they are called spotted weakfish along the northern Atlantic coast) and also throughout the Gulf of Mexico, including, of course, the Chandeleur Islands. Despite the fish's broad geographic distribution, fisheries scientists have learned from tagging studies that speckled seatrout don't wander much.[5] They are homebodies. Some individuals spend their entire lives within just a few miles of the estuary where their parents released egg and sperm. Animal species that don't migrate and have resident populations often exhibit a high degree of genetic relatedness. Speckled seatrout are no exception. By examining the DNA sequences of seatrout sampled from different geographic regions, fishery geneticists have found that populations in the Atlantic are genetically distinct from those in the Gulf of Mexico and that even within a given ocean some populations exhibit genetic differences. The degree of genetic differentiation seen so far is insufficient to divide speckled seatrout into distinct subspecies or new species, yet these genomic changes indicate that as subpopulations of speckled seatrout continue to evolve further, taxonomic differentiation is likely to occur. There can be advantages to variation in genomes between populations of a given species. For instance, if a pathogenic virus or bacteria were to infect one population of speckled seatrout, those fish that compose genetically unique populations elsewhere may prove more resilient and ultimately provide stock to replenish disease-impacted populations.

Young speckled seatrout grow up quickly. Female fish reach a sexually mature twelve to fourteen inches in a single year and are an impressive sixteen to eighteen inches long by the time they turn two years of age. Combine a rapid growth with the ability to produce up to 350,000 eggs per spawn over five months of annual spawning (and thus millions of eggs per fish per year), and you have a species of game fish that when properly managed can replenish its populations with gusto. In a sort of evolutionary trade-off with rapid growth and early reproduction, speckled seatrout have a relatively short life span that rarely exceeds twelve years. Speckled seatrout are resilient in the sense that, unlike other species of fish that gather to spawn in a specific location, seatrout spawn wherever they occur: weed beds, sand and shell bottoms, and around oil and gas platforms. This spawning flexibility pays dividends because, should a given habitat type become inhospitable, the fish can spawn elsewhere.

Despite the ability of speckled seatrout to rapidly replace their own populations, fishers lament that specks caught in the Chandeleurs are on average smaller than they used to be. There is some truth to these fish stories. The generally smaller fish caught today are almost certainly the result of increased recreational fishing pressure. My fishing friends tell me they would happily up the legal size of keeper specks in the Chandeleurs from the current twelve inches to fourteen inches. Anyone who doubts that specks and reds caught in the Chandeleur Islands and the adjoining coastal marshes of Louisiana have on average gotten smaller over the decades need look no further than the fading fishing photographs that adorn the walls of Louisiana Gulf Coast seafood restaurants. The old, funkier local restaurants are best for good samplings of photographs. Black-and-white Polaroid photographs that predate the 1963 onset of the use of instant color Polaroid film are particularly telling. Fathers and sons proudly pose holding stringers of seatrout and redfish. The scientific evidence is incontrovertible: fish in the black-and-white Polaroids are larger than those in the color Polaroids, and about twice the size of the fish in digital color images posted on restaurant walls since the early 1990s.

Speckled seatrout are weaklings when it comes to sudden environmental change. For example, scientists have discovered that speckled seatrout don't spawn successfully or even at all when seawater temperatures fall below seventy-three degrees Fahrenheit.[6] Sudden cold fronts that can rapidly drop seawater temperatures routinely stun and ultimately kill juvenile and adult seatrout. In December 1983, 623,000 speckled seatrout died in a single Texas freeze. Another 759,000 seatrout were killed in two subsequent record Texas freezes during the winter of 1989. The two freezes were so brutal that fishery biologists estimated 17 million finfish died in Texas bays, crippling the state's recreational fishery for three years. Similar massive die-offs have occurred in other regions of the northern Gulf of Mexico. While I have never experienced a seatrout die-off in the Chandeleurs or other regions of the northern Gulf of Mexico, my former doctoral student Steve Beddingfield and I witnessed tens of thousands of dead green sea urchins washed up along the shores of Saint Joseph Peninsula State Park on the Florida Panhandle in mid-March 1993. The urchins had been killed by a cold front with subfreezing temperatures that rapidly cooled the shallow bay. We spent many long, cold hours in a stiff north wind measuring the diameters of skeletons of the thousands of dead urchins that littered the shoreline and published a short scientific paper documenting the freeze-related die-off.[7]

Seatrout are similarly vulnerable to rapid declines in salinity that may occur in coastal waters during heavy rain events or when estuaries are flushed with large volumes of freshwater from terrestrial runoff or engorged streams and rivers. Ironically, the nickname for speckled seatrout along the northern Atlantic coast, spotted weakfish, is a term that is fitting not only for its etiological origins in the fish being a weak fighter (the notable exception being specks in the six-pound-and-up category), but also for its accidental description of a fish that has a weak ability to withstand sudden change. As global climate change continues to favor weather events characterized by great extremes of temperature and excessive periods of drought or flooding, speckled seatrout will face ever greater challenges.

Although weak, speckled seatrout are aggressive ambush predators. I know from experience. One memorable day in the Chandeleur Islands, I cast a top-water plug into dawn seas that perfectly mirrored the orange-pink sky. Slowly rotating the handle of my bait-casting reel between quick staccato lifts of my rod tip, I danced my lure across the sea's surface. Halfway back to the skiff, a big speckled seatrout exploded on my lure. And no sooner had I begun to reel in the speck than a second big speck erupted on my plug and engulfed the other treble hook. Now, gripping my pole with both hands, I was fighting two specks hooked on the same cast and to the same lure. Having not anticipated fighting *two* fish, I heard the squeal of my line signaling a call to action. Holding the deeply bent rod with my left hand, I released my right hand from the rod and awkwardly reached across my left wrist to tighten the drag knob using my right thumb and forefinger. With the drag recalibrated, I reeled between runs and let the disparate swimming directions of the two fish work against one another. The two big specks joined the others in our cooler.

When speckled seatrout are larvae, they are less than three-quarters of an inch long and feed on tiny zooplankton, including crustacean copepods and the larvae of snails and clams. As they grow into juveniles, the fish switch to a diet of larger prey such as amphipods and especially juvenile penaeid grass shrimp that populate sea grass meadows or the submerged stalks of emergent salt marsh cordgrass. Once the seatrout become adults, they feed on a variety of finfish, including anchovies, sheepshead minnows, mullets, croakers, gobies, and menhaden. Some of the bigger specks even cannibalize the young of their own species. Despite marine ecologists considering speckled seatrout a top carnivore, they really do not belong at the apex of coastal food webs. Indeed, speckled seatrout fall prey to a host of larger predators, including mangrove snapper, gaff-topsail catfish, Spanish and king mackerel, barracuda, bluefish, and alligator gar. I have watched small schools of specks dart frantically under my fishing skiff while being chased by powerful jack crevalle ten times their size. No wonder specks "school," a common behavior displayed by many species of fish that lowers the chances of any given individual being eaten.[8] Schooling may also deter predators who perceive a much larger and more formidable superorganism. Only when speckled seatrout are older than six years of age do they become fully or semi-solitary. Mostly big females, these fish are nicknamed "gator" or "sow" trout by fishers or are sometimes called "rogue" trout, a nickname Ken used to describe the massive speck hooked below his feathered gull bobber.

No matter how well the specks are biting, ignoring gathering clouds in the Chandeleurs is risky. Many a fisher has learned this the hard way. On a typical summer day, moisture is lifted upward into the atmosphere during the morning hours. By early afternoon, towering cumulus clouds can climb so high you get a kink in your neck from looking up at their summits. Perhaps the immensity of the Chandeleur landscape makes approaching thunderstorms so difficult to gauge in time and space. I have learned to be extra vigilant, and even well-seasoned Chandeleur fishers are conservative. My friend Rob Angus, an aquatic biologist, bluegrass musician, and fly-fishing enthusiast, told me he had witnessed two fishing buddies learning their lesson about Chandeleur thunderstorms on a muggy July afternoon in the mid-1990s.

Rob and his skiff-mate Rick Remy had sensed trouble when a light wind suddenly picked up and rippled the surface of the Chandeleur Sound. Late-afternoon thunderheads thickened the near-distant sky. The two fishermen reeled in their lines and hightailed it back to the mother ship *Becuna* at full throttle. Once back aboard ship, Rob and Rick were immediately joined by the fishermen from all but one of the six skiffs that had been sprinkled throughout the

islands after an on-board lunch. George Vedel and his skiff-mate
Dave Tyner were catching fish and decided to stay put a little longer.
The short delay could have cost them their lives. By the time George
had motored their skiff within sight of the *Becuna,* a fast-moving
squall had erupted. Sixty-knot winds drummed up white caps and
three-foot waves. Rob and the other nine fishermen watched from
the shelter of the canopy over the *Becuna*'s back deck as George tried
repeatedly to position the bouncing skiff behind the ship. The gale-
force winds slammed into the small skiff, pushing the bow violently
to one side and then the other as water splashed in over the gunnels. Rob recalls that the two frightened fishermen looked as if they
were "riding the skiff like it was a bucking bronco." Flat-bottomed
fishing skiffs are not designed to handle rough seas. Powering the
skiff into the approaching seas becomes a trade-off between making headway and taking on water. The more water that entered the
skiff the lower she rode. It was a negative-sum game. Dave made yet
another in a series of desperate attempts to toss the skiff's bowline
to the first mate. At long last, much to George and Dave's relief, the
mate caught the bowline and man-hauled the bouncing skiff in tight
to the *Becuna.*

   In 1980, when Rob settled in to his career as a biology professor at the University of Alabama at Birmingham, he discovered that
fly-fishing wasn't an interest of his new fishing partners. Rob had
fly-fished off and on when a graduate student at the University of
Connecticut and had enjoyed the art of casting a fly line despite not
catching many fish. For twenty years, Rob fished the rivers and lakes
of Alabama and the northern Gulf Coast and Chandeleur Islands
with spinning and casting rigs. Then one day around 2000, Rob decided it was time to buy himself a fly-fishing outfit. His first year in
the southeastern United States using a fly pole was pretty much a
bust. He fly-fished for bass and bream in the lakes and for specks and
reds in the Chandeleur Islands. But he caught little. In retrospect,
Rob thinks this is because fish generally don't bite within a forty- to
fifty-foot perimeter of a boat. He thinks they are just too spooked by

the boat. After a year of practice, Rob began to cast beyond the spook perimeter of his boat, and fish started to take his flies. Before long, there were days when Rob said he caught as many fish as a fishing buddy using a spinning or bait-casting rod and reel.

Rob learned to work eight-weight fly line, tied off to a nine-foot leader line and a three-foot tippet. With each false cast of his nine-foot rod, he pinched line between thumb and forefinger to strip line from his fly reel and send it shooting forward by parting line from fingers. When Rob fly-fished for specks in the Chandeleur Islands, he'd use floating line and surface flies such as popping bugs and crease flies. Popping bugs are made out of balsa wood, and the bugs come in a variety of shapes. They have a concave face that when pulled along the water's surface makes a popping noise. To a fish, this sound can be an invitation. Crease flies look like minnows and are made of Styrofoam folded over a hook. Rob's favorite sinking fly is one called Lefty's Deceiver Fly, a minnow-shaped fly made of a deer's "buck-hair" and a hen's feather. The fly is fished with sinking fly line. Rob learned to tie his own flies and modified Lefty's Deceiver by substituting the hair of his family collie, Fergus. Rob would collect hair from Fergus's brush and then wrap the individual hairs around one another to create a fuzzy thread. The thread was then wrapped around the shank of the hook. The final step in tying the fly was to take a small hen feather and use the dog-hair thread to secure the feather to the top portion of the shank just below the hook's eye. Rob told me this upper portion of the feathered shank is called a hackle, but he didn't have a clue why. Later, I found out the feather hook shank is called a hackle because it resembles the feathers on the neck or saddle of a bird. One of Rob's fishing buddies, David Diaz, nicknamed Rob's homemade fly the "soft hackle Fergus fly." Fergus eventually passed away but lives on in spirit in a fly storage box in Rob's garage.

Despite the excitement of the chase when fighting a red so big the boat has to follow it—just like Pete and I had done in the Chandeleur Islands—sight fishing for reds (or any other fish for that matter) with a fly or spinning pole is arguably even more thrilling. The argument for biologists like myself, Ken Marion, and Rob Angus goes like this: not only do you end up with a fish but you combine the thrill of watching a top predator detect, consider, chase, attack, and consume your bait. Captain Tristan LeCour, a fishing guide who works out of southern Louisiana, is an expert in the art and science of sight fishing. Rob told me he met up with Captain LeCour to fish for reds in salt marsh waters early one fall morning at the marina in Port Sulphur, a little town just up the road from Venice, Louisiana and only sixty miles southwest of the Chandeleur Islands. The first element of sight fishing for redfish is just that, sighting the fish. The second element of sight fishing is making sure the fish doesn't sight you. Redfish will surely spook and tear off out of sight. As Captain LeCour poled the flats boat through the shallow water, Ron stood on the bow and systematically searched the surface of the water for telltale movements. Before long, he was rewarded with a redfish lying very still in water so shallow the upper tip of its tail fin stuck out of the water. Rob's thirty-foot cast dropped the slow-sinking minnow-shaped fly within five feet of the fish. With an impressive muscular burst of acceleration, the red exploded on the fly. Setting the hook was nothing more than an afterthought.

On a subsequent trip in the winter of 2005, Captain LeCoer met up again with Rob and Dave for a weekend of redfishing near Port Sulphur. The first day, the wind blew so hard it was difficult to sight the fish, and only a few were caught. The second day, the fishing trip was completely blown out. So, instead, Rob and Dave drove south down state Highway 23 toward Venice. The highway was a mess. Hurricane Katrina had roared through on August 29, 2005, and four months later, debris was still spread everywhere: old tires, broken pieces of furniture, glass shards, rusty sedans and pickup trucks. Houses and mobile homes on either side of the road were peeled open, eviscerated by hurricane-force winds and flooding caused by a breached levee, tidal and storm surge, and rain-flooded marshlands. The few homes and businesses that had survived lay shuttered and sadly desolate. When Hurricane Katrina ripped into the Chandeleur Islands, different components of the islands' habitats were severely damaged.[9]

The main Chandeleur island stretches about fifteen miles in length and is by far the biggest of the islands. The long, narrow, crescent-shaped barrier island wraps roughly northwest-southwest and serves as the primary buffer against the storms of the open Gulf and thus protects the smaller New Harbor islands to the northwest. These smaller islands are home to lush submerged sea grass meadows, emergent salt marshes, and semiterrestrial terrain with forests of stunted mangroves. The surf zone, beach, and sand dune communities of the main Chandeleur island are home to a variety of plants, marine invertebrates, fish, and seabirds. While the surf zone appears devoid of marine life, this is simply because most of the animals live buried in the sandy sediments. Here, some live in detrital and sand tubes glued together with various natural adhesives. Others burrow into the sand using appendages as varied as the shovel-shaped telson of the mole crab and the muscular foot of the surf clam. Tiny animals called meiofauna live in a mysterious world between the sand grains. So small and inconspicuous are these myriad invertebrates that, when discovered, marine biologists were surprised to find they included several major taxa and hundreds of species. Jason Cox, one of the crew members on our ship who has grown up visiting the Chandeleurs, told me that a special breed of raccoon is historically known to frequent the sand beaches of the main Chandeleur island. The raccoons look like a cacomistle, a raccoon-like mammal that ranges from Mexico down into South America. They are smaller than typical raccoons, tall and skinny (almost looking emaciated) with sun-bleached red hair. Presumably, the island raccoons reached the Chandeleurs by rafting on debris across the sixteen miles of open water between the islands and nearest salt marshes of Louisiana. One day Jason and his dad ran into a group of island raccoons on the beach of the main Chandeleur island that had chewed open bottles of drinking water that floated ashore in a crate. The raccoons, lapping the water up, growled at the two men, protecting their precious discovery. Freshwater is scarce on the islands between rains. The raccoons get most of their water from a diet of fish and crabs caught in the marsh tide pools and carrion that washes up on the sandy beaches. When I pressed Jason on whether raccoons could survive the sixteen-mile float, he told me the story of an old fellow who lost his fishing boat and floated the sixteen miles on his cooler. Certainly, Jason said, if he could do it, so could the raccoons.

I became familiar with the various types of fish that live in the surf along the main Chandeleur island. On my first trip to the Chandeleurs, I discovered that some of the fishermen brought along surf-casting outfits. Beaching or anchoring their skiffs on the lee of the main Chandeleur island, the fishermen would hike across the island to the open Gulf and spend hours fishing for big reds in the rolling surf. Some of the surf-fishers returned to the ship with an impressive bounty. Tempted, I purchased a surf-casting outfit and brought it along on my next trip. Wading out waist deep in the surf, I cast a hook the size of a golf ball baited with a big chunk of catfish flesh caught on light tackle the previous night off the back of our ship. With my twenty-pound line tied off to a hefty six-ounce pyramid surf-casting weight, I was able to both cast a long distance offshore and sufficiently weigh down the bait with a sinker designed to dig into the sand. This kept my bait from being repeatedly beached by the strong long-shore drift. I caught hardhead catfish, whiting, and stingrays. When the redfish were running, my bait didn't rest on the bottom for long. By the time I had cast, set the gear of my surf-casting spinning reel, and retreated backward a few steps to shallower water, a series of abrupt jerks on my line would signal a hungry red. An exciting battle would ensue. Sometimes, I beached the fish. But often a big red proved too powerful, and I would stand helplessly, ankle-deep in the surf as the fish spooled my line and broke off.

It didn't take long to discover that sharks also roamed the surf zone. I caught several small Atlantic sharpnose sharks. Later, I learned that in the years preceding my Chandeleur trips, some

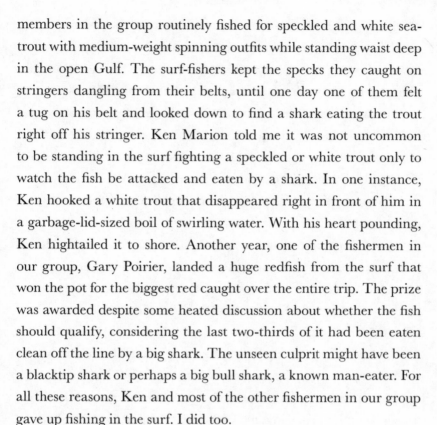

members in the group routinely fished for speckled and white sea-trout with medium-weight spinning outfits while standing waist deep in the open Gulf. The surf-fishers kept the specks they caught on stringers dangling from their belts, until one day one of them felt a tug on his belt and looked down to find a shark eating the trout right off his stringer. Ken Marion told me it was not uncommon to be standing in the surf fighting a speckled or white trout only to watch the fish be attacked and eaten by a shark. In one instance, Ken hooked a white trout that disappeared right in front of him in a garbage-lid-sized boil of swirling water. With his heart pounding, Ken hightailed it to shore. Another year, one of the fishermen in our group, Gary Poirier, landed a huge redfish from the surf that won the pot for the biggest red caught over the entire trip. The prize was awarded despite some heated discussion about whether the fish should qualify, considering the last two-thirds of it had been eaten clean off the line by a big shark. The unseen culprit might have been a blacktip shark or perhaps a big bull shark, a known man-eater. For all these reasons, Ken and most of the other fishermen in our group gave up fishing in the surf. I did too.

Black skimmers, American oyster catchers, and three species of terns—the common, royal, and least tern—nest on the sandy beaches of the main Chandeleur barrier island. My favorite is the diminutive least tern, whose twenty-inch wingspan, black-capped head, and jerky erratic flight pattern easily distinguish it from the two larger species. The terns gather to breed in sparse colonies in the spring; they then court and lay eggs on the exposed beach. There is no nest, just two or three eggs laid simply, side by side, their mottled appearance a nod to the evolution of cryptic coloration against a backdrop of sand and gravel. The parents take turns incubating the eggs, and, when they hatch in about three weeks, the two adult birds tend to the young. I've watched skimmers off New Harbor Island circle our fishing skiff just above the sea's surface, trolling for small fish by running the extra-long lower mandible of their black, orange-based bill along the sea's surface. Similarly colored black-and-white oyster catchers rarely eat oysters. They use their sleek, bright mandarin-orange bills to dig into the wet sand in search of polychaete worms (*polychaete* refers to many—poly—hairs—chaete—that line a series of skin flaps along each side of the worm) and small clams and snails. Skimmers, oyster catchers, and terns are intimately linked to low-lying coastal habitats for their roosting, nesting, and wintering. Accordingly, the birds are collectively called obligate coastal species. This inherent fidelity renders the birds especially vulnerable to the impacts of global climate change, in particular rising sea levels and intensifying coastal storms.

The rolling sand dunes built up by beach sand blown landward provide a transitional backdrop to the surf-swept beaches of the main Chandeleur island. The dunes provide a fortification against storm-driven seas that would inundate the smaller New Harbor islands in Chandeleur Sound. The picturesque sea oat *Uniola paniculata* is the most well known of the perennial grasses that stabilize the frontal dune system by trapping wind-blown sand.[10] Bright green seaside elder bushes with lavender blooms dot the frontal dune and interdune meadows and help accumulate sand. Further inland, the longitudinal valley and back-dune regions are sprinkled with such plants as running beach grass and Gulf bluestem. The dune plants, while also vulnerable to the same issues of a changing climate that threaten shore birds, are uniquely adapted to survive in foot-burning sand and salty spray. Many have thickened leaves for water retention or waxy leaves for salt resistance. Collectively, these plant communities are the glue that sustains the structural integrity of sand dunes long constructed by the flow of offshore sand and sediments washed down a once free-flowing Mississippi. The Chandeleur beach and sand dunes in turn protect the neighboring salt marsh and mangrove communities along with the sea grass meadows that attract the speckled seatrout and redfish that keep bringing fishers back.

The vast meadows of flowering sea grasses that carpet tropical and subtropical coastal beaches, lagoons, and bays, as well as the shallow waters of protected regions of the Chandeleur Islands, are at first blush surprising to most everyone except a botanist. The concept that flowering plants can spend their entire lives submerged in seawater seems abstruse. Similar to terrestrial plants, sea grasses have roots, stems, and blades and seasonally flower and seed.[11] Because the underwater grasses require sunlight to photosynthesize, they populate clear water. Indeed, the clarity of sea grass habitats in the Chandeleurs is remarkable. I have enjoyed countless hours casting my line over grass flats that resemble a crystalline aquarium. At times, this aquarium can be so enchanting a polite silence falls over me and my fishing partner. We watch tiny grass shrimp dart between blades of sea grass and schools of small fish being chased by bigger fish and so on, constructing the links of the food chain. Sea grass meadows are more than an esthetic retreat. In the Chandeleurs, as elsewhere, sea grasses play a key role in providing oxygen to sediments and water, as well as food and nurseries for marine invertebrates and fish, and in trapping and cycling nutrients. Coastal sea grasses improve the quality of the seawater. The dense meadows of grass filter out excessive nutrients and slow down the flow of sediment-clouded water sufficiently to clear the water of particles. The grass beds also help to attenuate wave action and stabilize sediments, protecting shorelines. Scientific studies have shown that sea grass meadows denuded by mechanical damage from dredging, anchoring, siltation, pollution, and the impacts of climate change (erosion due to rising sea level, increased storms, and increased ultraviolet radiation) result in a depletion of economically important shellfish and finfish.

Salt marshes line the protected shores and bays of the New Harbor islands, protected from the open Gulf by the main Chandeleur island. The island marshes are but microcosms of the vast salt marsh systems of Texas, Louisiana, Mississippi, western Alabama, and Florida. Despite their small size, the marshes are bountiful ecosystems in their own right and help fortify each delicate island.[12] Wading ashore, my fishing skiff anchored on the edge of an island salt marsh, I stop briefly to watch an American egret's stealthy wade as the marble-white bird stalks its next meal. A male red-winged blackbird sings *conk-a-reeeee*. The salt marsh in front of me is bursting with ecoservices: a nursery for marine life, a sieve to clean the water and recycle nutrients, and a means of protecting this island from an encroaching sea. I step gingerly into the squishy black mud between the tall stalks of marsh cordgrass (*Spartina alterniflora*), the dominant species of salt marsh plant in the Gulf of Mexico. Crouching, I dig blindly into the black ooze in search of the tips of the valves of two- to three-inch-long ribbed mussels (*Geukensia demissa*). Eventually, I locate and forcefully pull a mussel free of the byssus threads that anchor it in the mud, feeling the ribbed shell with fingertips tainted by the smell of rotten eggs. Transparent ghost (glass) shrimp dart along the interface between the blades of *Spartina* and the shallow water's edge. Wading on into clear water, I discover blue crabs as tiny as a child's fingernail, yellow-striped hermit crabs sporting various-sized oyster drill and whelk shells, comb jellies, and a healthy dose of larval and juvenile fish. In addition to protecting Louisiana's islands and coastal parishes from storm surge, the salt marshes provide essential nursery habitat for shrimp, crabs, and fish. Countless microalgae and miniscule invertebrates weave food webs, nourishing the nurseries that seed commercial and recreational fisheries. Like an immense sieve, the coastal marsh strains pollutants from tidal creeks, rivers, bays, and tributaries, while rich bacterial communities break down and recycle organic particles in the sulfurous black pudding that is marsh mud.

Several of the Chandeleur Islands host large expanses of stunted three- to four-foot red mangrove trees. Similar to sea grasses and salt marsh cordgrasses, the prop roots and pneumatophores (special breathing roots that grow upward out of the mud) of mangrove roots and branches above the sediment provide a three-dimensional habitat that protects the young of marine invertebrates and fish from predators.[13] The roots dug into the island help stabilize the sediments against the erosion of a rising sea. On one of the inner New Harbor islands, the mangrove trees are home to one of the largest nesting rookeries of magnificent frigate birds in the Gulf of Mexico. With both sexes black-feathered with hooked bills and a wingspan of six to seven feet, the birds are true to their scientific name, *Fregata magnificens*.[14] The male sports a pouch in the throat region that is inflated when mature males congregate during mating season to attract prospective females. I have watched these mating displays while quietly drifting in a fishing skiff just a few feet from a frigate perched on a shoreline mangrove. The male first rocks back on its tail and vibrates its wings and then tosses its head backward to disclose a brilliant red throat pouch so fully inflated as to appear on the brink of popping. A deep drumming vocalization accompanies this generous display. I found this robust sexual display rather humbling. To a female frigate, it must be tantalizing.

Magnificent frigate birds are masters of the air. As oceanic birds, they virtually live on the wing for extended foraging trips. Some ornithologists have deemed frigate birds the ultimate gliders, capable of suspending themselves in the air for hours on end without the slightest movement of wing. Even when nesting on the Chandeleur Islands, frigate birds spend the vast majority of their time soaring. On a warm afternoon, I have watched frigates ride the thermals in ever higher spirals, a phenomenon that Ken has fondly dubbed a "tornadic frigate vortex." Frigates, with angular wings and forked tails, are exceptional acrobats that possess an arsenal of foraging tactics. These include surface-dipping in flight for squid and airborne flying fish; settling to the sea surface to consume small fish, jellyfish, and crustaceans; and feeding onshore on carrion, turtle hatchlings, and seabird eggs and chicks. My favorite foraging tactic of the frigate is kleptoparasitism. This awkward term describes predators that force other animals to abandon what they are eating so that the predators can consume what is left behind. In the case of frigates, this means chasing another bird until it drops its prey and swooping in to scavenge the stolen food. Sadly, magnificent frigates are not immune to falling victim to long-line fishing by getting snared on the baited hooks, and they drown.

The Chandeleur Islands are dying: neither in the manner of the traditional millennial life span of barrier islands—whose essential nature is to form and reform so as to be recast—nor on the time scale of the death sentence handed down by damming the Mississippi River. Today, the islands display accelerated erosion, perhaps exacerbated by a global rise in sea level already challenging low-lying islands around the planet. In 2012, the Intergovernmental Panel on Climate Change (IPCC) predicted that sea levels will rise by one and a half to three feet by century's end. With the integrity of its barrier islands compromised, coastal Louisiana's salt marshes, long dissected by oil-boat channels and desperate for new sediments, are increasingly vulnerable to the ever more powerful storms predicted in a warming future. Marine invertebrates and fish of the Chandeleur Islands are facing mounting challenges. The luxuriant sea grasses that surround the shrinking islands are the most obvious. Equally challenging are separate but related issues of global climate warming and ocean acidification, a seawater acidifying process that occurs when atmospheric carbon dioxide dissolves into the sea.[15] Both owe their ontogeny to fossil fuels, which when burned release carbon dioxide into the atmosphere. Marine organisms in the Gulf of Mexico are adapted to live near the upper threshold of their thermal tolerance. As climate warming increases summer seawater temperatures, key marine organisms may become stressed. "CJ" Brothers, one of my graduate students in the biology department at the University of Alabama at Birmingham, recently found that when the green sea urchin (*Lytechinus variegatus*), an important member of the sea grass communities of the Chandeleurs, is exposed to a temperature just two degrees warmer than the current summer average, it drops its spines, fails to right itself, and ultimately dies within a period of nine days.[16]

Ongoing ocean acidification, which has increased the acidity of the world's oceans by about 30 percent since the Industrial Revolution, impacts the same species of sea urchin. Dr. Roberta Challener, who recently completed her doctorate in my research laboratory, discovered that skeletal development was hindered in larval sea urchins when held under laboratory conditions that mimicked ocean acidification.[17] Impacts of ocean acidification are not limited to skeletons. Some fish lose their sense of smell when exposed to near-future conditions of ocean acidification, rendering them vulnerable to predators as they search for their home reef. When warming is combined with ocean acidification, the challenges facing marine organisms can become even greater. For example, sea urchins may devote critical energy to calcification while at the same time suffering a compromised immune system triggered by temperature stress. In this example, energy may be squandered on calcification rather than invested in a life-saving response to a potentially fatal disease.

Commercial fishers do not harvest the sea urchins that graze on the sea grasses of the Chandeleur Islands or elsewhere in the Gulf of Mexico, which is good news for green sea urchins whose relatives have largely been overfished to support a billion-dollar roe industry in Japan. Both speckled seatrout and redfish are protected from commercial fishing in the Breton National Wildlife Refuge. Nonetheless, some states allow speckled seatrout to be netted in small numbers and sold in local fish markets. Redfish have a long history of intense commercial fishing. The large commercial nets used to capture redfish were far too effective; in some instances, helicopters tipped off commercial fishing boats to the whereabouts of huge aggregations of big males gathered to attract females. Recreational overfishing of young redfish added to the problem. By the late 1970s, redfish were in serious decline.[18] This trend was exacerbated in the early 1980s when New Orleans chef Paul Prudhomme turned blackened redfish into an overnight sensation. Caught up in the blackened frenzy, I experienced a scary episode involving a red-hot iron skillet and my first redfish fillet. Apparently the moisture content of my fillet was high enough to cause it to mildly explode when I dropped it into sizzling oil—splattering my bare chest with 600-degree oil droplets. Ultimately, President George W. Bush issued an executive order on October 20, 2007, making it illegal to market redfish caught in federal waters and encouraging states to limit recreational fisheries through tighter catch quotas and size limits.[19] Today, redfish populations have rebounded, and despite the lack of a commercial fishery, one can still fry up a redfish fillet caught recreationally or farm raised.

The surf and sand beach communities of the main Chandeleur island were first to show the telltale signs of the approach of Hurricane Katrina. Perhaps the terns had noticed the ever so slight shift in the tides, intensifying their erratic flights and shrill cries. With the hurricane still a day out, the barrel-shaped surf rose to a height that would have attracted skilled surfers. Yet, as the winds built from the south, the once graceful waves were soon a jumble of white-capped, closed-out slop. Rain bands encroached on the island and a tremendous storm surge pushed ashore. The surge followed paths of least resistance, breaching sections of the island that were narrow or had low-lying dunes. Streams became rivers whose currents washed away vast amounts of sand and sediment along with countless meiofauna, mole crabs, ghost crabs, and once dune-stabilizing plants. Katrina moved on toward New Orleans on August 29, 2005, leaving the barrier islands a shamble. In a fraction of the time it takes the Army Corps of Engineers to dredge a channel, the main Chandeleur island had been effectively cut to ribbons. Coastal geologists later estimated that 85 percent of the surface area of the Chandeleur Islands had vaporized in a single day. Recovery from Hurricane Katrina, as after other hurricanes in the 1980s, 1990s, and 2000s, has been especially tough. The fresh cuts I have witnessed post-Katrina in the main Chandeleur island have allowed the gulf waters to accelerate erosion. A spot check by geologists three years after Hurricane Katrina revealed 50 percent of the shoreline had continued to erode.

The dense sea grass meadows that carpeted the extensive flats on the lee of the crippled main Chandeleur island were next in line to absorb the wrath of Hurricane Katrina. Hundreds of square miles of meadows and their myriad inhabitants were buried in displaced sand and sediment. No longer able to exploit the energy of the sun, the sea grasses were fated to slowly decompose. Most mobile marine life—swimming crabs and fish—may have avoided being smothered or beached and escaped to live another day, but countless sea urchins, sea squirts, and sponges lay buried among the dying sea grasses. Salt marsh and mangrove communities of the once protected New Harbor islands were similarly dissected by the hurricane. Just as the violent surge had reduced the outer barrier island to a shell of its former self, a similar fate befell the smaller islands. One small sand island was swept off the map.[20] Others were considerably reduced in surface area, the surge sweeping away tons of uprooted salt marsh cordgrass and, to a lesser degree, mangroves that had grown along the shore's edge. In some areas, salt marsh cordgrasses and mangrove trees that had not been uprooted now lay submerged. They too would slowly decompose. Coupled with the immediate loss of nesting habitats for red-winged blackbirds, green herons, magnificent frigate birds, and brown pelicans was the more serious loss of tidally submerged habitats to support the nurseries of gulf marine invertebrates and fish. The nearby Mississippi River, long dammed, offered no hope of a lifeline replenishment of sand and sediment.[21] The summer of 2006, a year after Hurricane Katrina, our annual fishing trip to the Chandeleurs had to be canceled for the first time ever. The damage to the islands, the danger of submerged hazards, and the demise of the speck and red fishery were so severe that the fishing captains and their ships were staying away. When we did return the next summer, we found the islands vastly diminished. If the trend continues, in just a few decades fishers may not be able to enjoy a Chandeleur sunrise while casting for speckled seatrout and redfish.

2

MANITOBA

Lake Trout

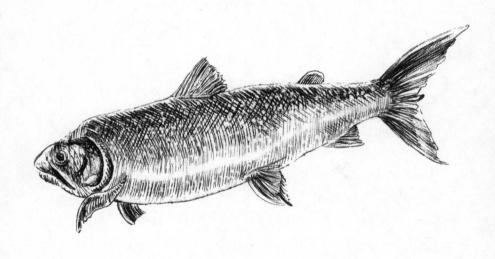

"**W**e're screwed," our Cree aboriginal fishing guide Ralph Thomas uttered under his breath as he peered at the windblown surface waters of Lake Nueltin. Many miles north of our Manitoba fishing lodge, the one-inch prop nut securing the propeller to our twenty-five-horse Mercury outboard had come off and sunk to the lake bottom. We were stranded near the mouth of a broad river that flowed into the lake from the northwest—our nearest refuge the sandy driftwood-strewn bank of a small deserted island. We had come all this way hoping to hook a trophy fish. Now, we heard only the rustle of birch leaves in the breeze.

Two days earlier, my longtime friend and colleague Ken Marion, a skilled fisherman and recently retired professor of ecology at the University of Alabama at Birmingham, and I had traveled almost two thousand miles to join a cadre of ten fishermen for four days of some of the best lake trout and pike fishing in the world. We had landed in an explosion of dust on a dirt runway a short boat ride from our destination, Nueltin Lake Lodge. Once off the plane, we strolled a quarter mile to a dock where welcoming staff ferried us and our luggage across an inlet. A metal chimney pipe emerged from one side of the dark-brown, V-shaped roof of the one-story cedar-log lodge. It smelled of burnt firewood and the morning pancakes and bacon that were cooked in the adjoining kitchen. From its perch on a hill of sandy soil, the lodge commanded a sweeping view of a stunted black spruce forest and a deep-blue lake that stretched a mile or two before disappearing from view around a bend to the northeast. Nueltin Lake, one of the largest lakes in Canada, stretched northward from our lodge some 120 miles. Composed of a seemingly endless series of bays, tributaries, narrows, and small islands, the lake boasts 715 square miles of fishable water.[1]

Ken and I met Ralph when he dropped by our cabin to introduce himself. He wore sunglasses and a dark-blue Lake Nueltin baseball cap over his close-cropped hair. Surveying the tackle strewn about the cabin, Ralph seemingly sized up our fishing potential and quickly departed after setting a time to meet at the dock. Later, as Ken and I situated ourselves and our gear in our aluminum fishing boat, I overheard Ralph speaking with one of the guides in his native Cree-Montagnais, a subfamily of the Algonquian languages.[2] Once under way, I yelled at Ralph over the noisy two-cycle engine, asking him about his family origins. "I am Scottish," he yelled back. "My great, great, great-grandfather was a Scot."

Ralph had grown up in northern Manitoba and had guided fishing clients for the past seven years for the owners of Nueltin Lake Lodge. To make ends meet, Ralph also had recently fished commercially for lake trout on Wollaston Lake using gill nets. In addition, he guided hunters visiting the lodge during the fall caribou and bear seasons. Ralph explained that he was first and foremost a trapper, following in the footsteps of both his father and grandfather— trapping wolf, bear, mink, fox, beaver, rabbit, muskrat, martin, and lynx for their pelts. As each of Ralph's seven children reached teenhood, he took them into the wild to teach them to trap. He said the weeks and months spent deep in the spruce forests helped keep his kids from "getting in trouble."

The next morning, excited about heading back out to the lake for our second day of fishing, we got our first taste of Ralph's outdoor resourcefulness. After polishing off a hearty early morning breakfast, packing up our fishing gear, and making our way from our cabin back down to the dock, we settled once again into our boat. "Did you bring your rain gear?" Ralph asked matter-of-factly from his seat just in front of the outboard engine. The question, of course, was prophetic. Heavy rain was falling at a steady pace by midday; little streams of cold water dripped off our rain hoods and threatened to soak through our rain pants. Whenever we traveled between fishing sites, Ken and I lowered our hooded heads, preventing the raindrops from stinging the exposed skin of our faces. When Ralph, who did not wear a watch, finally asked what time it was, I rapidly fired back, "It's after one!" I was starving. I could almost taste the pan-fried fish fillets that Ralph was to render from the two twenty-five-inch-plus pike flopping around next to his feet. "Shore lunch," he finally said.

Ralph seemed unconcerned about building a wood-fueled fire on a soggy shoreline. After filleting the fish while staying seated in the back of the boat, he pulled a brown six-by-eight-foot ground tarp from the covered boat box built into the front hull. Tying four arm-length pieces of woven yellow rope to the grommets set in each corner of the tarp, he briefly eyed the surrounding spruce trees. Climbing a three-foot-high bank of dirt, Ralph reached up and tied off the first of the four ropes to the upper reaches of a spruce; then, moving to another slightly smaller tree, he bent down the pliable upper trunk, tied on another rope, and let the spruce spring back upright. Ralph located two more suitable trees and finished the job. The elevated tarp formed a slightly slanted roof about eight feet off the ground. Pooled rainwater trickled off the corners. Ralph removed a single-bit axe from the boat box and disappeared into the woods. The sharp reports of an axe biting into dead spruce echoed across the lake water. Ten minutes later, Ralph returned to our makeshift shelter with three-foot logs. He set the firewood down under the rain canopy and used the heel of his boot to kick out a fire pit in the soft dirt. Small, dead branches below an umbrella of live spruce provided kindling. Ralph lit a match. Soon the sap-laden spruce crackled into flame, and the logs piled on top of the kindling burned red hot. I used a stick to lift the tarp to prevent the intense heat from melting the tarp's plastic. Ralph produced a massive cast-iron skillet from the boat box, wiped it clean with a handful of lime-green moss plucked from the shoreline, and set the heavy pan on top of the flames. Thirty min-utes later, we stood together along the shore, the rain now a drizzle against the tarp, and wolfed down hot, hand-cut fried potatoes, corn-meal-coated pike seasoned with salt and pepper, and can-simmered corn and baked beans.

The third day, Ken and I awoke to distant rain-thickened clouds and a light north wind. Once our boat had cleared the dock, Ralph accelerated northward. Our destination, Ralph declared, was the Putahow River. The name, Putahow, meaning "little fish," is thought to have its origins in the river's bounty of grayling, a small rainbow-colored fish with a sail-like dorsal fin. The day before, several fishermen at the lodge had caught trophy-sized (thirty-five-inch-plus) lake trout at the mouth of the river. Surely, Ken and I surmised, the river mouth was our morning's fishing destination. We were wrong. After an hour racing due north at full throttle, we turned to the west and entered the mouth of the Putahow. Ralph cut the engine and let our forward momentum gently ground our boat onto the sandy shore of a small island. Lifting the motor's foot out of the water, Ralph locked the engine in its upright position and used a small wrench to unscrew the prop nut. "I'm putting on my beat-up prop," he said, sliding the prop off its bolt and replacing it with another one from the floorboard under his feet. A mile or so upriver, Ken and I discovered Ralph's reasoning for the prop replacement. Here, over the span of a football field, the river climbed a couple of hundred feet, the smooth water transforming into churning white water speckled with protruding boulders. Wasting no time, Ralph stood up in the rear of the boat, carefully sized up the rapids, and gunned the engine. "You can't stop," I heard Ralph yell over the collective roar of the engine and cascading white water as we bolted upstream like a water bug skittering from one whirlpool to the next. Ken and I held tight, grinning despite the gut-wrenching whack of prop against rock.

Past the white-water assault, Ralph guided the boat along the shore through placid water for half an hour as Ken and I fished for pike. Standing in the boat, we cast silver spoons up against the shoreline. Several pike exploded from the weeds and attacked our spoons. Ralph netted the fish and with gloved hands expertly re-moved the hooks from sharp-toothed jaws before tossing the lively fish back into the water. "We go now," Ralph said, the three words all too familiar by now, meaning it was time—no questions asked—to change fishing locations. Ken and I nervously eyed the next stretch of white water; the boiling river climbed steeply upstream three hundred yards before disappearing around a bend. This set of rapids appeared even more challenging than the first set: faster, shallower, and more boulders to negotiate. I couldn't imagine Ralph would actually attempt the climb. Yet, tempted by either the storied upstream fishing or perhaps the challenge of summiting the rapids, Ralph had other ideas, and up we went. In retrospect, Ken and I were relieved that the attempt failed—our prop grounded in the shallows. Ralph tilted up the foot of the idled engine, and as we drifted backward into deeper water, he quickly dropped the foot back into the water, swung the engine hard right, and gunned the boat, bow first, downriver. Despite the challenge of steering a boat at the full mercy of the rapids and a moment of panic when our boat became temporarily grounded midstream on a large flat boulder, we reclaimed the safety of calmer water. "Want to try again?" Ralph asked enthusiastically. Ken's eyes gave Ralph the answer. He headed back down the first set of rapids.

Close to an hour had passed since we had begun our search for the prop nut lost to the lake bottom. Ralph, all six feet plus, lay perched on the bow, his upper torso dangling precariously, in one hand the fishing net, in the other the paddle. Using the handled end of the paddle, he awkwardly poled the boat a few feet upstream and eyed the lake bottom four feet below. For the umpteenth time, he plunged the net to the bottom, scooping up only mud and small pebbles. "No good," he said finally. The nut, perhaps stripped, had spun off the prop shaft as Ralph shifted the engine into reverse. We drifted slowly to the sand beach of the small island at the river mouth where we had first switched props. The island was topped with a small hill, and at the base of a rock-strewn slope stood a stand of birch trees swaying in the breeze. The birch gave way to a sparse forest of black spruce. Overhead, a cloud-studded blue sky remained free of rain. Suddenly, Ralph interrupted our thoughts. "We'll sail home," he announced.

Ken and I made eye contact. Surely Ralph was joshing. Despite there being a wind from the north, how could we sail a sixteen-foot motorboat ten miles or more? But Ralph, even after sensing our confusion, was not about to explain. He tore into the boat box and removed his axe, several short pieces of frayed rope, and our brown plastic tarp, somewhat thinned in its center from serving as a rain shelter over our lunch fire the previous day. Ralph jumped off the boat and tossed the tarp and the rope onto the shore. "You two better untwine all the rope," he said. "We're going to need all we can get." Ralph turned and disappeared into the black spruce forest, axe in hand.

Twenty minutes later, Ralph emerged from the woods carrying a ten-foot-long spruce tree over his shoulder. Ken and I had finished unraveling the sections of rope, and the strands lay in sloppy coils near our feet. Much of the rope was rotten, and when unfurled, the individual strands broke easily. Ralph tossed the tree onto the ground and with several sharp blows of his axe finished trimming off the last of the branches. The ten-foot tree trunk, now destined to be our "mast," was about five inches in diameter at its base and tapered to two inches at the crown. Laying one of the eight-foot edges of the tarp next to the tree trunk, Ralph pulled a folding knife from his pocket, grabbed several rope strands, and after cutting the rope into appropriate lengths and poking holes in the tarp with his knife, dropped to his knees and proceeded to attach the tarp to the mast at two-foot increments. Ralph's second excursion into the forest produced two shorter lengths of spruce. Crouching, he attached one five-foot spruce pole to the lower edge of the tarp to serve as a boom and the other between the top of the mast and the end of the boom, completing the triangle of the sail. After Ralph had attached the edges of the tarp to the two poles and folded down the one loose corner left on the tarp, he stood up and eyed the crude sail lying on the shore.

Ralph stared into the boat's bowels; a prolonged silence spoke to his deep concentration. "I have to cut my boat," he said, finally. Removing the boat's one-inch-thick plywood floorboard, Ralph used his axe to cut a hole a little larger than the base of the mast in the central portion of the floorboard that fit up against the benched seats. After replacing the floorboard, Ralph returned to the shore to retrieve the mast and boom with its tarp sail. He lowered the bottom end of the mast through the hole he had cut in the floorboard. Remarkably, the four inches of space between the floorboard and the bottom of the boat provided a secure base for the mast. Ralph tied odds and ends of rope around the lower portion of the mast and connected the ropes to the starboard and port sides of the boat. When he had completed securing the guy lines, Ralph tested the structural integrity of the mast and sail by pivoting the boom ninety degrees, first to the right and then to the left. The mast stood firm.

"We go now," said Ralph.

Ken and I obliged by climbing into the "sailboat." Ralph took the five-foot-long fishing net and jammed the handled end up into the lower right-hand pocket of the sail at the far end of the boom. He nodded to Ken. "You hold this," he said. Ken sat down, propped himself against a boat seat, and, using both hands, grasped the net handle. Now, he could control the position of the boom. Ralph pushed our boat off the beach, climbed in, and perched himself on the bow. He used the oar to pole the boat one hundred feet along the shore until we reached the end of the island and the open water of the lake. Captain Ralph ordered me to take control of the propless engine shaft—now our de facto tiller. I swung the steering arm of the outboard motor back and forth and felt the boat's delayed and sluggish response—like trying to sail in molasses. Ralph directed Ken to adjust the boom so that the sail was ninety degrees to the boat, a sailing configuration known as a "broad reach" that best fills the sail when sailing straight downwind. With a ten-knot wind out of the north, Ralph gestured toward a small spruce-covered island to the south. With no sound but that of the tarp fluttering in the cool breeze and the gentle sloshing noise of water sliced by the bow, I set course for the first of what would be a long series of way-marks. When we reached our last mark, the narrows, a section of the lake where all the other boats would be returning from their day's fishing, we would have topped four hours under sail.

I stood by at the tiller, took a deep breath, and took it all in: the sensation of the breeze against my face, the smell of the fresh subarctic air, the sensation in my legs of our boat cutting through rippled water. Two professors who had dipped into their savings to catch trophy fish might be upset about losing a day of fishing to a lost prop nut. More well-heeled sportsmen would have had their feathers ruffled. Yet above me lay an immense sky with a horizon rimmed by clusters of clouds—some appeared as paint-dabbed cotton balls, others more elaborate, like sculpted works of art. One reminded me of the profile of the head of a bear cub: a perfect set of ears, one wide-open eye and a short snout. Thousands of black spruce lined the lake's banks and carpeted the islands, their gnarled, weather-beaten crowns naked except for haphazard patches of pine-needle green. On a nearby ridge, a lone tree towered above the others, as if a sentinel defying the odds of surviving the poor soil and long subarctic winter. Arctic terns called out to one another, their flight paths woven of sharp dives and turns. Ralph passed around a Tupperware with a few cream-filled vanilla cookies, our last remnants of shore lunch. I chewed slowly, savoring the sweetness of the cream. This was my moment, standing at the helm, doing three knots by the grace of tarp, twine, and spruce.[3]

Once we sailed into the narrows, it wasn't long before we were rescued by the occupants of a motorboat on its way back to the lodge. Ralph dismantled our sail, and Ken and I climbed into the rescue boat. Ralph threw a line to the guide in the rescue boat, and he settled into our former sailboat as it returned to the dock under tow. The next morning, our last at the lake, Ralph didn't say much. Guiding our boat to the northeast, he darted down long tenuous leads in the lake ice before heading deep to the south. We had traveled for a solid two hours before Ralph finally slowed the engine. Here, the lake waters swirled in circles like fields of spiderwebs—deep, strong currents generated by a narrow gap through which the lake was forced to flow. It was the perfect place for large fish to ambush smaller prey attracted to nutrients concentrated in the swirling currents. "Nobody has fished here for years," said Ralph.

As Ralph set the boat in motion, I released line from my bait-casting reel and watched my pink six-inch single-hooked spoon drop into the water and out of sight. After I had spun off about 150 to 200 feet of line, I rotated my reel handle clockwise to set the gear and hand-tugged the line to check drag. Ralph slowly accelerated the engine to a steady trolling speed, fine-tuned from many years of experience, and guided the boat in a broad circular pattern over the swirling blue-green water. Given the weight of my spoon, coupled with the length of line I had released and the speed of the boat, I estimated that my lure was trolling behind the boat at a depth of about thirty feet. No more than five minutes had gone by when my pole suddenly bent deep, instigating a reflexive "Got one!" I jerked my rod tip upward and felt a reassuring tug that indicated the barbless hook was set. Ken cranked in his spoon to keep our lines from tangling. Ralph and Ken watched as I stood and wrestled with the big fish, sporadically gaining line only to hear it stripped back in that quintessential squeal of reel-drag that resonates with fishers everywhere. After what seemed like fifteen minutes but was probably less than ten, I glimpsed a flash that couldn't be explained by anything other than a huge lake trout. Following the trajectory of my fishing line, I could just make out the mosaic of light-yellow pencil-eraser spots carpeting the greenish-brown skin of the fish's head, trunk, and tail. As the fish tired, the tail thrusts translated to shallower and shallower tugs on the fishing pole tightly gripped in the palm of my left hand.

Ralph lifted the aluminum fishnet off the floor of the boat, leaned over the gunnel, submerged the mouth of the net in the water, and nudged it under the big trout. Gripping the net handle with both hands, he lifted the fish and placed it on the carpeted floorboards. The trout, which I estimated to measure about thirty-six inches and to weigh a good twenty-five pounds, cooperated as Ralph removed the hook from its massive jaw. Ralph hoisted the fish by its lower jaw and handed it to me so Ken could snap a couple of photographs with my camera; then I bent over and eased the tail and rear trunk of the fish back into the water. As the fish floated in the water I let go of its lower jaw and slipped my hand down under its belly. For a moment, the huge trout lay completely motionless in the water, my hand cradling its soft yellow-white underside, which ended with a swoosh of big tail. Over the next hour and a half, Ken and I reeled in twelve lake trout, half of them among the biggest either of us had ever caught or will likely ever catch again.

The scientific name for lake trout is *Salvelinus namaycush*. The species name is derived from *namekush,* a term coined by the Southern East Cree. Other common names for lake trout include lakers, tongue trout, mackinaw, and lake char, the latter because the fish belongs to the salmonid group called char. Lake trout like deep, cold water and are slow to grow and die.[4] The species is unique in that individuals can be either planktivores, eating copepods, mysid shrimp, and other aquatic invertebrates in lakes with few forage fish, or piscivores (fish eaters). The latter lifestyle results in fish growing considerably larger. Judging by the size of the lake trout in Lake Nueltin, the lifestyle most definitely is one that includes fish in the diet. The record for a lake trout caught in Manitoba was a fish caught by Eldred Zobl in 2001 that measured fifty-four inches.[5] Not surprisingly, the fish was caught in Lake Nueltin. Lake trout caught for sport are rarely weighed; rather, their length is measured. However, some information about the weight of trophy lake trout is available. According to records maintained by the International Game Fish Association, the largest lake trout ever caught on hook and line weighed a whopping seventy-two pounds and measured fifty-nine inches. Lloyd Bull caught the record fish on August 19, 1995 in Great Bear Lake in the Northwest Territories of Canada.[6]

We were never supposed to have fished with Ralph. Ken had initially made a reservation for us to fish Lake Nueltin in June 2011, an entire year prior to our catching big lakers with Ralph. Ken had visited Lake Nueltin twice in the 1990s and both times fished out of the Narrows Camp, a small lodge and cluster of cabins on an island accessible by float plane and managed by the Gurke family, who own and operate Nueltin Lake Lodge. Accordingly, we had planned to stay at the Narrows Camp. By doing so, we would avoid the more expensive guided trips based out of the fancier main lodge. Ken felt confident he could serve as our guide, despite admitting that getting lost on the lake had crossed his mind on past trips to Lake Nueltin. The countless coves, arms, bays, and shorelines of the massive lake could be confusing. After a long day of fishing, the geographic features of the lake began to all look alike. Ken informed me that despite handheld GPS units not being readily available on his two earlier trips, we would have a GPS; he would be cautious about how far we ventured from camp. All would be well. We were excited about our upcoming fishing adventure at the Narrows Camp; that was, until the phone call.

Shawn, Garry Gurke's son, was on the other end of the line when Ken answered. Garry had discovered Lake Nueltin in 1982, waited patiently for five years for a ramshackle fish camp to come up for sale, and then bought the place and devoted his life to building a world-class fishing operation, including several lodges and a dirt runway for wheeled aircraft. The latter had required weeks of remote over-land travel, driving large earth-moving tractors through hundreds of miles of roadless wilderness to reach the lake. Shawn apologized to Ken. For the first time in the thirty years that his family had owned and operated Nueltin Lake Lodge, a combination of severe drought and low winter snow-pack had starved the creeks and streams feeding the massive lake. The water level in the lake was so low that the Gurke family would have to cancel the entire summer fishing season. The change in weather and climate was unprecedented. But the end result, continued Shawn, was that the fishing boats couldn't reach the docks at the lodges and camps; the float planes risked landing on water with hidden hazards, and the dirt runway that served the wheeled aircraft that transported all their guests was so dusty it had been declared unsafe by the Canadian Civil Aviation Directorate.

Losing the revenue from an entire summer fishing season was going to be a huge economic hardship for the Gurke family and their sportfishing company. Their budget operated right on the edge. The company depended on revenue generated from up-front reservations to cover ongoing costs of food, building and maintenance supplies, salaries for facilities staff, cooks and guides, and the chartered flights that brought in supplies and moved guests back and forth between the main lodge at Lake Nueltin and the international airport in Winnipeg. Shawn asked Ken if the two of us would consider allowing his family business to hang on to money we had each put down as a down payment toward our scheduled fishing trip. In exchange, at no additional cost, he would bump our fishing package up to the level of a guided trip, and we could stay in the main lodge the following summer. After deliberation, Ken and I decided this offer sounded like a pretty good deal. We could help the Gurke family make ends meet and take advantage of Shawn's offer of a guided trip and the great meals we had heard about at the main lodge.

The severe drought in Manitoba that shuttered lake trout and pike fishing at the Nueltin Lake Lodge is unlikely to remain an isolated event in a rapidly warming world. Climate scientists predict that as arctic environments continue to warm, droughts and other climate extremes will become more common. The black spruce that are the mainstay of the boreal forests that line the banks and surrounding hillsides of Lake Nueltin are increasingly vulnerable to the impacts of climate change. Black spruce, much like other subarctic and arctic trees, are subject to stressors that interact with one another in a complex and synergistic manner.[7] In August 2010, I accepted an invitation to participate in a four-day workshop at a retreat in Maryland hosted by the U.S. National Academy of Sciences.[8] Our charge was to identify and prioritize a set of questions to help the general public, elected officials, and scientists better understand the impacts of climate change on polar ecosystems. Among the twenty-five participants in the workshop, one scientist's presentation still stands out in my memory.

The presentation was given by Glenn Juday, a professor of forest ecology in the International Arctic Research Center at the University of Alaska Fairbanks, who studies the impacts of climate change on Artic boreal forests. Juday pointed out that while global warming will allow some trees to take up more greenhouse gases, in regions of increasing temperature and drought, the white and black spruce and birch that comprise the dominant tree species of boreal forests are facing increasing constraints.[9] Rapid environmental changes are outpacing the ability of the trees to migrate or adapt. In one stunning example, our speaker informed us that among more localized high-altitude trees, some species are literally being pushed off the tops of mountains to certain taxonomic death. Juday continued to explain that the vast high-latitude, drought-stricken boreal spruce forests are becoming more vulnerable to fires and to infestation by a host of native and invasive insects, most notably the spruce bark beetle and spruce budworm. Spruce beetles live, feed, and reproduce in the layer of living tissue, or phloem, between wood and bark, a key layer that carries essential nutrients to the various parts of the tree. When adult spruce beetles emerge each spring, they attack the bark of uninfected host trees and, if sufficient in number, effectively strangle the host tree, cutting off the movement of life-giving nutrients. It is as if a carotid artery were blocked—the tree dies in one to two years. Spruce budworms are spread from tree to tree by the adult moth. The tiny green eggs hatch, and the resultant worm-like larvae feed on the tree's needles, unopened buds, and flowers. Spruce beetles and budworms have already killed off hundreds of millions of acres of drought-stressed spruce trees. Thankfully for Lake Nueltin, spruce beetles and spruce budworms tend to prefer white over black spruce. But this may change as white spruce die off. Juday shared with our workshop participants alarming photographs, images capturing vast expanses of arctic terrain carpeted with dead forests of spruce and birch. In a complex interplay of climate-related factors, the professor suggested, warming is promoting more beetle infestation; beetle-weakened trees become more vulnerable to drought, and resultant dead trees provide tinder for more intense forest fires. Sadly, climate modelers and foresters now predict that the average amount of area burned per decade in the western boreal forests of North America is projected to increase 350 to 550 percent by century's end. Unfortunately, the eastern boreal forests surrounding Lake Nueltin are unlikely to remain far behind in the race toward more frequent and intense forest fires.

The spruce forests of Lake Nueltin are essential to the health of the lake ecosystem and its sport fisheries. The spruce's roots help stabilize the soil and prevent sediment runoff from spilling into the lake, and in life, death, and decay, the spruce forests exchange key nutrients with the soil.[10] The spruce trees are also critical to the water cycle by passing moisture from soil to the atmosphere through a process called transpiration. But Lake Nueltin's black spruce forests are vulnerable because the north-central region of Canada is predicted by climate scientists to be a "hot spot of vulnerability" to climate warming and because the forests populate a transitional zone between boreal forests and tundra.[11] Species living in transition zones are among the most vulnerable to climate change because they live close to the limits of their environmental tolerance. The vast black spruce forests surrounding Lake Nueltin serve an important role in providing habitat for caribou, moose, black bear, wolverine, fox, mink, lynx, river otter, weasel, and migratory bird species that include eagles, loons, osprey, cranes, plovers, terns, and a diversity of waterfowl. The forest's trees take up carbon dioxide from the atmosphere for photosynthesis and store vast amounts of carbon in roots, trunks, branches, and needles. Boreal forests compose an impressive 22 percent of global carbon storage, storing twice as much carbon as tropical forests per acre. Without the boreal forests, greater amounts of Earth-warming carbon dioxide will remain in the atmosphere.

Black spruce trees frame the Thlewiaza River where it cascades two hundred feet down a forty-degree rocky slope and into Lake Nueltin a few miles from the main lodge. At the confluence of river and lake, golf-cart-sized submerged boulders carve the river's currents, which spiral into eddies and boil the water's surface. Close to the Arctic Circle, daylight stretches deep into the summer evenings. So in the evenings, Ken and I took the boat out to fish on our own. The spot where the Thlewiaza River entered the lake was a popular place to fish; it was almost impossible to get lost getting there and getting back. Even better, lake trout and pike hung out in the currents, preying on smaller fish schooled up to feed on the worms, aquatic insect larvae, and other assorted invertebrates washed downriver. Ken knew from his previous visits that Arctic grayling (*Thymallus arcticus*) were in the streams and rivers feeding the lake and regions of lake near moving water. Arctic grayling are smaller than lake trout or pike but, in their own way, equally alluring. Measuring on average about twelve to fourteen inches, grayling have iridescent rainbow-colored scales that are almost as spectacular as the elongated dorsal fin that is like the sail on a sailfish.[12] Splashes of pink, red, orange, and yellow grace the pectoral and ventral fins and gill plates, and the dorsal fin has columns of oblong, deep-red dots. The fish breed in rocky streams and rivers, and territorial males attract and court females by flashing the colors of their big dorsal fins. The male's dorsal fin also pins the female as the two fish vibrate against one another and release eggs and sperm. Arctic grayling ambush minnows in the rapids or seek out insects, crustaceans, or fish eggs in slack-water eddies. Ken told me that grayling were fantastic to catch on ultralight tackle. They must be, I thought to myself: the Lake Nueltin website called the fish "ballistic" fighters. Even more convincing, Ken told me one morning he had become so enraptured in catching feisty grayling off the Narrows Camp dock that he had chosen to fish despite clouds of mosquitos attacking an ankle laid bare by an overlooked sock. Ken's mosquito-bitten ankle swelled up to the size of a grapefruit. With great anticipation, Ken and I set out one evening from the lodge to try our luck. We had no idea that we would both catch record fish but never glimpse a grayling.

Ken settled into Ralph's seat adjacent to the outboard engine while I untied the bow and stern lines from the cleats screwed down to the lodge's wooden dock. Earlier, we had each methodically packed up our fishing gear, walked down the dirt road to the dock, and placed our five-foot ultralight fishing poles on the floor of the boat at the base of the gunnels opposite one another. Each rod was fitted with a small spinning reel spooled with four-pound test line and tied off to a one-sixteenth-ounce black rooster-tail lure with a silver spinner blade and single hook. An experienced boater, Ken pulled out the choke knob and gave the engine's pull cord a firm yank. The motor sprang to life, and after shutting off the choke and making a few deliberate steering maneuvers, Ken headed us at half throttle out of the cove and along the right bank of the lake. We soon rounded a point and were greeted by an impressive view of the Thlewiaza River cascading into Lake Nueltin. Several fishing boats were already sprinkled in the midst of the churning white water, the fishers having repeatedly motored to the base of the cascading river and then cut their engines to drift-fish the two hundred yards of downstream white water. Ken chose not to drift-fish. Rather, he maneuvered our boat just to the right of the river, where an eddy created a countercurrent that held us temporarily in place without anchoring. The loud roar of white water was deafening, and I had to catch Ken's eye to point out a bald eagle perched on a branch of a dead spruce. The tree's trunk was lodged in a jumble of river rocks that oddly repositioned the tree upright, as if given a second lease on life while providing a perfect vantage point for an eagle that shared our interest in fish.

Ken and I retrieved our ultralight rods from the floor of the boat and freed the tiny hooks from the rod eyelets. Flipping open the bails of our spinning reels, we cast off the side of the boat that faced the cascading river and watched our spinners plop into the deep-green swirling water. When we reeled and cast, the feather-light rods made a whipping sound each time they sliced air. The four-pound test line was so thin it vanished in the water, making our rooster tails look like they spun themselves back to the boat. No more than ten casts into fishing, something big walloped my rooster tail. The ultralight rod bent deep, and my spinning reel exploded drag. This was no grayling. *Don't overreact,* I warned myself. I knew there was no way that my ultralight rod and reel and its four-pound line were going to allow me to muscle a fish this size to the boat. The rod could snap as easily as the line. "Keep it out of the rocks!" Ken exclaimed. I had landed fish in the past that outweighed the capacity of my gear, but that was on eight- or twelve-pound line, not on four-pound test. Nonetheless, so far so good: I seemed to be slowly gaining on the fish; with each run, I was working the fish in a little closer. Finally, Ken and I got a glimpse of what had taken my rooster tail—a big pike. As the fish rolled, I caught a flash of silver from the blades of my rooster tail, its tiny hook embedded in the massive jaw. Ken lifted the fishing net off the floorboards and waited patiently for me to work the fish in close or, more likely, for the line to snap. An anxious swipe of the net might spook the big fish. This is a classic fishing mistake, and one that I myself have made on occasion. The most recent incident was in early October 2013 when a friend of mine, Adam Vines, was about to boat a ten-pound largemouth. The bass panicked when it sensed the lunge of my net and broke off just inches from the boat. Ken dipped the net into the water. In one smooth motion he slid the net gracefully under the pike and hauled the fish out of the water. With the netted fish on the boat's floorboards, I used a pair of needle-nose pliers to pry the tiny hook from the fish's lip. The pike, its olive green body covered with light markings, measured almost thirty inches, and while there was no fish scale, we estimated it weighed twelve or more pounds. The fish was far and away my personal record on an ultralight rig.

The northern pike (*Esox lucius*) is an aggressive predator.[13] Even the etymology of the common name *pike* has a sharp edge: the resemblance of the fish to a long spear or pole weapon called a pike, used by foot soldiers during the early Middle Ages. The renowned twentieth-century poet Ted Hughes captures the malevolent nature of this, his prized fish, in his tense visual poem "Pike." "Killers from the egg: the malevolent aged grin," Hughes writes of the pike.[14] There are a slew of other common names for northern pike, but among my favorites are those that speak to the fish's speed and aggression—nicknames like snot rocket, snake, slough shark, gator, and Mr. Toothy. Big pike, like the one I caught on my ultralight fishing rod, are mostly piscivores, and when food is scarce, the fish are known to include their own in their diet. Ken and I witnessed pike ambushing and attacking behavior as Ralph maneuvered our boat along the crystal clear, shallow waters of a tributary of Lake Nueltin. Casting our silver spoons up against the weedy bank, we watched big solitary pike repeatedly explode from cover, accelerate like drag racers, and intercept our spoons halfway back to the boat. One of the benefits of having Ralph with us was that with gloved hands he removed our lures from the pike's razor-toothed jaws. Despite pike generally not being eaten because of their reputation for being a bit too bony, one of the best lakeshore lunches Ralph cooked up featured fresh pike fillets. The mild-tasting, pan-fried meat melted in our mouths.

Buoyed by my unexpected success at the cascading juncture between the Thlewiaza River and Lake Nueltin, Ken and I continued to cast our rooster tails. The next fish was Ken's, and from the onset, it fought even harder than the big pike I had just landed. Guiding his taut line around the stern, Ken followed the fish as it moved back and forth from one side of the boat to the other. This tactic kept his fragile four-pound line from rubbing against the hull or wrapping around the engine's transom; either would have broken off the fish. Ken was convinced his catch was another big pike until his line bore deep and hugged the bottom. Pike tend to be surface fighters. Complicating the battle, our boat drifted free of the security of the eddy and was caught up in the current. Ken's challenge expanded from fighting a fish to doing so while maintaining his balance in a bouncing boat. Ten minutes later, both fish and Ken were battle-worn. I dipped our big fishnet into the lake and scooped a massive lake trout up and onto the boat's floorboard. Once again, the hook of a tiny one-sixteenth-ounce rooster-tail lure was tugged free from a massive fish jaw. The huge lake trout measured thirty-nine inches from tip of jaw to tip of tail, and crowned Ken's lifetime personal record. The fish equaled the trophy lake trout we would both catch on much heavier tackle later that week in Ralph's secret spot.

I knew something important was up one morning when Ralph suddenly slowed the boat and abruptly changed course. Ralph did not deviate lightly from fishing. We headed toward the right bank of Lake Nueltin and two points that delineated a half-mile-wide channel that mouthed a big bay. Here, swimming with great determination in the midst of the channel, was a female moose or "cow." Keeping our boat at a distance of about thirty feet, Ralph slowly trailed the moose as she swam toward the opposite point. The big paddling cow looked comical, with only her head and the hump on her back above the water and the two oversized ears projecting at seventy-degree angles from the top of her head moving about like adjustable antennae. The brown hair on the hump was still dry and stuck straight up, just like it does when moose display hackled aggression. But there is nothing funny about what is happening to moose populations in Manitoba. Hunters are working harder to find these kings and queens of the boreal forest (moose are the second-largest land mammal in North America), and so are the wildlife biologists studying their population ecology. The eastern subspecies of moose that dwells in the boreal forests surrounding Lake Nueltin are experiencing the same changes in the environment and associated biotic stressors that are causing problems for the other five subspecies in North America. For one thing, climate warming has caused a huge surge in winter tick populations. *Infestation* is too benign a term to describe an adult moose serving as home to more than 100,000 blood-sucking ticks. Standing in the shallow waters of Lake Nueltin to feed on submerged vegetation is no remedy for tick-infested moose as the ticks form air bubbles that prevent them from drowning. Moose with such heavy tick loads can actually experience anemia caused by blood loss. Kristine Rines, a wildlife biologist who is directing studies of tick-infested moose populations in North America, laments, "Anemic, infested animals are being transformed into ghost moose." Sadly, the term *ghost moose* has become so common it has taken root in the moose vernacular.[15] Ghost moose are moose whose carpet of winter ticks has caused such ferocious itching that it has rubbed itself all winter long in an effort to remove the ticks. The rubbing breaks the hair follicles, revealing the inner white portion of each hair and, combined with hair loss, gives the moose a ghostly pale-white appearance.

Nueltin lake trout and pike are but distant evolutionary relatives of moose. Nonetheless, both fish depend indirectly on moose to balance the ecology of the boreal forests that sustain the lake. The role of moose in the ecology of boreal forests is so critical that wildlife biologists rank the impact of moose browsing as a "keystone ecological process" with both direct and indirect roles in forest food chains. As a single moose eats up to forty pounds of plant material per day, moose populations have important impacts on the composition and abundance of low-lying understory plants, the morphology of leaves and branches of shrubs and saplings, and the rate at which carbon is cycled within the forest ecosystem. Moose also contribute valuable nutrients to the soil through their copious fecal pellets.[16] Some of these nutrients find their way into lake waters and help sustain the invertebrates and small fish that provide forage for lake trout and pike. As climate scientists predict moose populations to be increasingly thinned by climate change, this loss of moose could trigger what ecologists deem "cascading effects" throughout the ecosystem. My favorite example of a cascading effect is one I can identify with personally, having grown up surfing along the California coast and later becoming a marine biologist. Humans decimated Pacific sea otter populations for their pelts in the early to mid-nineteenth century, causing a cascading effect on kelp forests along the Pacific coast of North America. Without sea otters as top predators, populations of kelp-eating sea urchins exploded, and the undersea forests were reduced to barren seafloors. The kelps were lost, and so were countless marine invertebrates and fish that lived exclusively among the kelp forests. The loss of a key species—be it otter or moose—triggers a cascade of events that can ultimately decimate a forest—be it kelp or spruce.

As the cow moose swam up against the shore, she found her footing and stood up. Pausing briefly to catch her breath, the cow glanced over her shoulder at the three of us in our fishing boat and shook water off her matted fur like a big dog. Then, striding confidently up and onto the firm forest soil, the moose vanished into a stand of spruce. Ralph gazed after the moose. To me, the moose was a symbol of a sustainable ecosystem. And, despite growing environmental pressures, there are hints of anthropogenic optimism: take, for example, the promise of a sustainability ethic that encompasses a successful catch-and-release sport fishery on Lake Nueltin and a Cree father who still leads his teenaged children into the Manitoba wilderness, one by one, to best appreciate the balance of nature.

3

CAHABA RIVER

Spotted Bass

Ken Marion and I had canoe butt. We had been drifting and paddling in Ken's old sixteen-foot Mohawk canoe for over four hours, fishing a six-mile stretch of central Alabama's Cahaba River. Remarkably, we had yet to see another soul despite the river being within a few miles of the one million residents of the Birmingham greater metropolitan region. The oppressive heat and humidity of an Alabama summer day was softened by the shade of oak, pignut hickory, and loblolly pine, and a thin blanket of river-cooled air stirred from an early afternoon breeze. Rounding yet another in a long series of bends in the river, I watched the great blue heron we had been following down the river lift off from an oak blow-down and then, once again, fly farther downstream. Ken steered the canoe toward a sandbar sprinkled with river-polished pebbles and waist-high water willow. "Time for a break," he said. The sound of the underside of the bow of the Royalex canoe grating the riverbank signaled it was time to unfold my cramped legs. Grasping opposing gunnels with each hand, I lifted my right leg up and over the right side of the canoe. With one felt-soled river boot planted firmly on the river bottom, I swung my other leg up and out of the canoe. Standing, I stretched my arms skyward and arched my upper torso backward to temporarily relieve the deep ache in my lower back. It was time to stroll along the shore, to limber up my muscles, to get the blood flowing.

"Stop!" Ken yelled abruptly. I froze, scrutinizing my immediate surroundings. There, just a step in front of me, a golf-ball-sized flash of white. As my eyes focused on the snake, recognition of its white-throated mouth opening and closing triggered a symphony of reflexes: chills shooting the length of my spine, a crisp sharpening of my peripheral senses, and a tensing of the muscles integral to flight.

The deadly cottonmouth was reared up to a height about half the distance between my knee and my ankle. I watched the snake's jaws open and close, each mouth gape providing me a glimpse of white upper palate, the same palate that had first caught Ken's attention. Another gape—another flash—another warning. *One more step*, I thought. I had been looking ahead at the next bend in the river. One more stride and I would have stepped on the snake. Had the cottonmouth sunk its two protracted fangs into my ankle, a soup of hemolytic and neurotoxic enzymes would have been injected into my leg. Despite the near proximity of Birmingham, Ken and I were a worrisome distance from help. We had no cell phone, no shortwave radio, no means whatsoever for calling in a medical emergency.

Ken would have had to make a tough decision: lay me down in the canoe and negotiate portages across long stretches of shallow rocky terrace or leave me on the bank of the river where I had been snakebit and paddle for help. In either case, it would have taken several hours to get in touch with medics and locate and transport me to a nearby hospital, where, with any luck, there would be a waiting injection of pit-viper antivenin. In the meantime, my ankle would have swollen profusely, accompanied by an intensifying, sharp burning pain with bouts of vomiting.[1] My ankle would have turned gray, green, and blue, a kaleidoscope that would have spread quickly up my leg and across my limbs and body. More serious, my reaction to the venom would have caused shallow breathing and a drop in blood pressure, the latter rendering it nearly impossible for Ken to find my pulse. First dizzy, then unconscious, I might have died.

Cautiously, I lifted one foot and took a slow, deliberate, backward step from the upright cottonmouth. Another step and the big snake relaxed, dropping its olive body and large triangular head to the ground. Ken and I watched as the snake slithered up and over a pile of driftwood, disappearing among a tangle of tree roots emerging from the river-washed bank.

The Cahaba River is a living diorama, home to a lush garden of small herbaceous plants and shrubs whose leaves and flowers buzz with flies, bees, and wasps. Cabbage and sulfur butterflies and tiger, purple, and black swallowtails dance in the cool morning air among the foliage and back and forth across the water's surface. In warmer months, ephemeral dobsonflies, caddis flies, stone flies, and mayflies take briefly to the air. Longer-lived dragonflies patrol shallow grass-lined pools and shoals, preying on mosquitoes and midges. The longest free-flowing river in Alabama, the Cahaba River has its headwaters in the southern reach of the Appalachian Mountains near the city of Birmingham.[2] The river flows 194 miles, first to the southwest and then the southeast before joining the Alabama River and emptying into Mobile Bay on the northern Gulf of Mexico. Ichthyologists estimate that, per mile, the Cahaba River is home to the highest diversity of freshwater fish in North America.[3] Moreover, the river supports an astounding diversity of invertebrates, especially freshwater clams and mussels,[4] so much so that biologists consider the cornucopia of molluscan life evidence of a geographic center of evolution. In addition, on hot summer afternoons, teenagers gather where the river is carved deep. Sunburnt youngsters swoop off the banks on tree swings and drop like ripe figs into the cool river water.

Recovered from my encounter with the cottonmouth, Ken stood in the shallows and steadied the canoe as I repositioned myself in the front seat. Reseated, he pushed his oar into the sand and pried our canoe free of the riverbank. Retrieving my fishing pole from the floor of the canoe, I cast a plastic green pumpkin-seed weenie worm embedded on the shank of a 1/0 worm hook with a one-eighth-ounce slipping weight. Flipping my spinning bale closed, I tightened line and paused to see if there were any telltale *tappity-tap-taps* of a bass attracted to the splash of the worm. I lifted the tip of my rod and cranked my reel twice, initiating an alternating pattern of pole lifts and reel cranks that bounced and wiggled my worm over the river bottom. My next cast overshot, and Ken steered the canoe over to the bank, where I unwrapped my hook from the low-lying branch of a hickory tree.

Back on the river, the great blue heron up ahead made another foray farther downstream, and Ken cast his favorite lure, a spinner bait with silver blades two inches long and a chartreuse skirt. Ken's spinner bait landed with a *kerplop* an inch from the trunk of a tree-fall in water deep enough to hold a fish. An Alabama spotted bass exploded on Ken's spinner bait. The sheer force of impact eliminated the need to set the hook. Ken's pole bent deep as the three-pound bass struggled to dodge back under the submerged tree. Ken horsed the spotted bass away from the tree, and the fish leapt, hovering a split second at the apex of its trajectory, an indelible snapshot frozen in time. Gravity returned the fish to the river. Ken reached down and used thumb and forefinger to gently pinch the lower lip of the spent bass. Hoisting the fish shoulder high, he admired his catch with the gaze of a keen fisher and the nose of a naturalist who appreciates the earthy smell of fresh bass. "Good fish," he finally said, his tone of voice belying a hint of the timeless gloat of men who catch fish together. Ken leaned over the gunnel and submerged his bass in the river, gently pulling the fish along by its lower lip to force cool, oxygenated water through its mouth and across the gills. The fish perked up and swam off.

The Cahaba River is home to a plethora of Alabama spotted bass. This is much to the delight of those who fish the river. Bass fishers in the southeastern United States know from experience that spotted bass are, pound for pound, stronger fighters than largemouth bass. I would offer up a simple algebraic formula that calculates "fight equivalence" for the spotted and largemouth bass: X lb spotted bass = $2X$ lb largemouth bass. Accordingly, a two-pound spotted bass fights at a rod-bending equivalence of a four-pound largemouth, and so on. Give me the option of fighting the same-sized fish and I would favor the spotted bass up until the largemouth approaches my personal catch record of seven pounds. At this point, given my modest record for a largemouth bass, I would have to lean toward reeling in the largemouth over the spotted bass. However, my formula-driven decision gets trickier as the largemouth approaches a weight of twelve pounds because a six-pound spotted bass is closer to the world record of ten-and-one-third pounds than a twelve-pound largemouth is to the world record of twenty-two-and-a-quarter pounds.

That the fisher with the current record for a largemouth bass has a thread that ties him to the Cahaba River caught me by surprise. George Perry caught the fish on a Creek Chub Fintail Shiner crank bait on June 2, 1932, while fishing with a friend on Montgomery Lake, a now silted-in oxbow lake on the Ocmulgee River near Jacksonville, Georgia.[5] As anyone who has looked into the story knows, Perry's fish is somewhat controversial. His catch predated the International Game Fish Association requirements for an officially certified record. Nonetheless, the fish was grandfathered into the record books. Perry took the bass to J. J. Hall's General Store in Helena, Georgia, where the fish was measured with a tape measure and then walked down the street to the post office to be weighed on a postal scale. Perry's fishing buddy, Jack Page, disappeared without a trace; no photos were taken of the fish, and since it was 1932 and money for food was tight, the big bass was eaten for dinner by Perry's family the day it was caught. Perry spent the remaining forty-two years of his life as a mechanic and pilot living a quiet rural life in Georgia. One of his greatest loves was flying. On January 23, 1974, Perry took off by himself in a Cessna 182 from a rural airport in Georgia and headed for Birmingham, Alabama. When heavy thunderstorms clouded his approach to the Birmingham airport, Perry radioed the air traffic controller and was directed to use his instruments to follow a landing path set by the controller. Tragically, the vectored route led him directly into the heart of a violent thunderhead, and Perry lost control of the Cessna. George Perry died instantly when his plane crashed into the side of Shades Mountain just a few miles south of downtown Birmingham. On a clear day, you can stand on the summit of Shades Mountain, not far from Perry's plane crash site, and see the valley where the Cahaba River meanders through Mountain Brook, Hoover, and Helena just a few miles to the southeast. Perry would have flown over the Cahaba River just moments before he crashed.

Largemouth bass prefer the quieter waters of lakes and reservoirs or the sluggish currents and pools of wide rivers. This behavior is in large part why largemouth are comparatively rare on the upper Cahaba River. Nonetheless, one of my fishing buddies, Rob Angus, provided indisputable evidence that a small number of largemouth bass survive and even flourish in the upper Cahaba River. When I say small number, I do not do so lightly. Ken, Rob, and I have collectively fished the Cahaba River for a cumulative number of years that exceeds a century and, to my knowledge, Rob's largemouth catch has been by far the biggest any of us has ever caught on the river. Rob was canoeing with Ken the day of the big fish. He tossed a green pumpkin-seed weenie worm on eight-pound test line next to a downed tree and hooked into what Ken said had to be a largemouth that was no less than eight pounds. Unfortunately, Ken and Rob did not have a fish scale or camera with them that day. The ensuing battle is worthy of honorary mention in the historic lore of Cahaba River fishing; there is no good scientific explanation as to how Rob got the big bass to the canoe.

Once hooked, Rob's record largemouth tore across the entire span of the river. With Ken screaming, "Keep it out of those sticks!" and Rob thinking, *Yeah, sure*, the big fish dove into a thicket of tree branches submerged along the opposite bank. Dodging between branches, the bass attempted the tried-and-true escape technique of wrapping line on structure and pulling free of the hook. It is heartbreaking to watch a big fish employ this technique. Fishers know most of the time the bass vanishes, and a frustrated fisher breaks off or untangles empty line. When I asked Rob how he managed to beat such long odds, he explained that despite feeling a tightness of line that convinced him the big bass had wrapped itself on the tree, the fish had miraculously backtracked out of the branches following a path that untangled the line.

In 2008, with one final computer keystroke that triggered the release of issue number 1861 of the journal *Zootaxa*, a new species of bass was born. The Alabama bass (*Micropterus henshalli*) was awarded species status based not only on its physical attributes but also on unique differences in the sequencing of its DNA.[6] As this new species of bass from the Mobile Delta River Basin was culled from the much broader spotted bass taxon (*Micropterus punctulatus*) that spans the Mississippi River Basin and all the states along the Gulf of Mexico, many fishers refer to the new Alabama bass as the Alabama spotted bass. Having lived in Alabama for the past twenty-eight years, I would argue the state of Alabama is long overdue a namesake bass. This particular bass, a member of the hard-fighting spotted bass group, is a good fit for the state of Alabama. My reasoning goes that the Alabama spotted bass fights as hard as Alabamians do to catch bass. It's a serious fish for a serious bass-fishing state. Case in point: Alabama fishers invest big money in state-of-the-art bass-fishing gear and in glittered bass boats equipped with steering-wheel-gripping 150-horsepower outboard engines. Moreover, Alabamians are serious about going to extremes to catch bass. For example, some fishers are known to rise at ungodly hours on steamy summer mornings to fish for bass long before dawn breaks on Alabama's multitude of waterways and reservoirs. Alabamians compete in big-time bass tournaments with purses the size of the annual budget of a rural Alabama town.

The Alabama spotted bass makes its living as an opportunistic ambush predator that feeds on fish, crayfish, and aquatic insects. Yet despite anecdotal claims by fishers that the bass will eat anything that moves, fisheries biologists have yet to observe the Alabama spotted bass (or spotted bass more generally) eating a reptile. In contrast, its cousin, the largemouth bass (*Micropterus salmoides*), has been documented eating such reptilian appetizers as juvenile musk turtles, baby alligators, eastern newts, and even a striped crayfish snake that was as long as the largemouth bass from whose stomach the big snake was removed.[7] Ironically, neither the largemouth bass nor any members of spotted bass have ever been observed eating a lizard, despite plastic lizards having long been one of the more popular bass baits sold in the United States.

On a late June morning in 2014, while canoeing the upper Cahaba River with my friend Scott Snyder, I vindicated the companies that have long sold packages of plastic lizards to bass fishers. This vindication came to fruition when I hooked a fourteen-inch Alabama spotted bass on a plastic weenie worm along the riverbank where tree branches hung low over the water and a partially submerged tree lay with its roots exposed. As a matter of routine, I grasped the fish by its lower lip and lifted it shoulder high to peer into its mouth to see how best to remove the hook. At this moment, I came face to face with a lizard: a six-inch five-lined skink. The lizard was clearly in the process of being eaten by the fish because, despite the lizard's head protruding from the bass's mouth, its midbody and blue tail were lodged deep in the fish's gullet. The skink was dead, most likely drowned. At long last, here was indisputable evidence, soon to be published as a natural history note in the science journal *Herpetological Review*,[8] that bass do, in fact, eat lizards in the wild. Corporate lizard-bass-bait producers will celebrate this news and the ethical credibility it brings to their plastic product.

I was intrigued with how this skink had fallen prey to the bass. Perhaps the lizard had been climbing on a tree branch suspended over the edge of the river and had slipped and fallen into the water to be attacked and eaten by the bass. Or, given the dexterity and natural climbing ability of lizards, more likely the skink had been sunning itself on the edge of a log protruding slightly above the waterline and a movement to snatch an insect had caught the bass's attention. I could envision the bass ambushing the lizard by leaping out of the water to snatch its prey off of the log. The blue tail of the five-lined skink has long been considered a warning coloration to predators. Bright colors in the animal kingdom can be associated with the presence of a nasty cocktail of distasteful or deadly chemicals. However, the putative chemical defense did little to protect the skink from the attacking bass, and neither did the skink's ability to sever the skin, nerves, muscle, blood supply, and bone of its tail, leaving behind a flopping, wiggling distraction.

Back on the Cahaba River, Ken negotiated our canoe between two tire-sized boulders and plunged his oar deep to center the canoe above the approaching rapids. At the base of the rapids, the canoe slid quietly into an emerald green pool, and Ken back-paddled so we could fish. I cast my line back up the rapids and watched my plastic worm bounce back down and disappear into the bubbling white water where the current entered the pool. A hard pull signaled a fish had taken my worm. The fish I'd hooked is my favorite among the three types of bass that frequent the upper Cahaba, a redeye bass, whose scientific name, *Micropterus cahabae* (recently distinguished from *Micropterus coosae*), speaks to its limited occurrence within the Cahaba River system.[9] This beautiful elongate olive-brown bass lives in clear rocky runs and pools lined with water willow and other aquatic plants of the upper Cahaba. In the spring, adults move into pools or small tributary streams to spawn eggs and sperm into twenty-inch saucer-shaped nests formed by mature males who hold their lower jaw near the bottom and rotate in a circle in the coarse gravel. Adult males guard the fertilized eggs for a week, and the newly hatched young swim in tight, protective schools. True to their name, redeye bass are easy to identify given their distinct red eyes and reddish pectoral and tail fins. Populations are sparse, and as the smallest member of the bass family, they measure only fifteen or so inches as adults. Despite their small size, the fish are scrappy fighters on light tackle. They grow extremely slowly, taking up to ten years to reach just a foot in length. In the meantime, they make their living preying on aquatic insects and, to lesser degrees, ambushing crayfish and small fish. I've caught redeyes on plastic worms, crayfish crank baits, and a minnow-like jointed Rapala. The small bass can be remarkably aggressive. On occasion, I've reeled in a hooked redeye that slammed my crank bait despite the lure measuring a full third of the fish's body length.

The rapidly flowing waters of rocky shoals along the upper Cahaba River are also home to the illustrious Cahaba lily.[10] Featured in coffee table books and in commercial prints by noted nature photographers, as well as in such storied magazines as *Smithsonian* and

National Geographic, the Cahaba lily has come to symbolize a wilderness
ethic whose historical roots are grounded in the longest free-flowing
river in Alabama. The Cahaba lily, also called the shoal lily or shoals
spider lily, grows to a height of about three feet in dense stands on
rocky, tiered shoals of a few of the remaining free-flowing rivers of the
southeastern United States that cross the fall line, descending from
the hills to the coastal plain in Alabama (Cahaba River), Georgia
(Flint River), and South Carolina (Catawba River). The lily has strin-
gent requirements to survive and flourish; most notably that the river
currents must be swift, and there must be lots of direct sunlight. The
lily plants propagate by bulbs that become lodged in between rocks
within the shoals; a single bulb may produce a population of clonal
plants that share the same genetic makeup. In the spring, locals and
tourists flock to see the few remaining stands of lilies bearing their
spider-shaped, ivory-white blooms. Biologist Larry Davenport—or
"Mr. Cahaba Lily" as he is known to friends, students, and faculty at
Samford University in his hometown of Birmingham—is the world's
foremost authority on the lily. Larry told me that the best time to see
the lilies bloom is between Mother's Day and Father's Day. The cel-
ebration of the lily transcends tourist visits to rivers to see the blooms.
Today, there are no less than three spring festivals that celebrate the
lily, the foremost being the Cahaba Lily Festival in West Blocton, Alabama, which just celebrated its twenty-fifth anniversary. Hundreds
of people of all ages, ethnicities, and walks of life attend the festival,
which features food, live music, wildflower education, and presenta-
tions by representatives from various environmental agencies. Similar festivals have sprung up in South Carolina, including the Lily
Fest at the Landsford Canal State Park near Catawba and the Rocky
Shoals Spider Lily Festival near Charleston.

Several years ago, Larry gave a fascinating seminar to University of Alabama at Birmingham biology students and faculty about
solving the mystery of the pollination of the Cahaba lily. Knowing
what type of insect, bird, or bat pollinates the flowers of a plant is an
essential element of its life history and can be critical information to

a wildlife biologist scripting a strategic conservation plan. Larry explained that at the time he initiated his study nobody had a clue what pollinated the flowers. Far from being an expert on vectors of pollination, Larry studied the pollination literature and then carefully examined the color, smell, and architecture of the lily to see what clues might be revealed about its pollinator. Larry discerned that the lilies opened widest in the evening and had the odor of sweet nectar. The clues suggested a nocturnal pollinator. While the flower was large and the nectar buried deep in the funneled crown, the flower petals would not support the weight of a bird or bat. Accordingly, Larry spent night after night watching the flowers of the Cahaba lily. The tedious search turned up nothing. But as serendipity would have it, Randy Haddock, now the chief biologist for the Cahaba River Society and an avid admirer of the Cahaba lily, had heard Larry lecture on the flower and the elusive pollinator. Randy volunteered to assist Larry in his search.

Each night, Randy launched a canoe with a friend and paddled to a sandy bank where the blooms of the lily could be seen in the distance on a central shoal of the river. On the third night at about two in the morning, the two men sighted an object moving between flowers. A brief glimpse with the help of a flashlight revealed a brownish blur with red eye-shine. Randy paddled like crazy for the shoal, but the mystery pollinator had disappeared by the time he neared the lilies. Randy realized that to have any chance of identifying the pollinator he needed to wade into the rushing river waters and wait quietly, flashlight and net ready in hand, next to the lilies. With the determination of a seasoned field biologist, Randy tied off his canoe the next night and waded blindly through waist-deep rapids to the lilied shoal midriver. Here, under a near full moon, he crouched among the lilies and silently waited. At about midnight, a large brown moth with a two-inch wingspan flew abruptly past Randy and hovered over a lily flower. With one well-aimed swipe of his net, Randy, assisted by Larry's key groundwork, had captured the pollinator: a sphinx moth with the scientific name *Paratraea plebeja*. Larry ended his story by making a case for protecting the sphinx moth, for if it were to disappear, so might the Cahaba lily.

Outside of a small cohort of avid fishermen and wildlife biologists, a cornucopia of scaled, shelled, and furred vertebrates shares an interest in catching the fish that populate the Cahaba River. One autumn morning, I paddled my canoe around a bend and came across a pair of North American river otters playing in the shallow river. The steep head-high riverbank adjacent to the otters was studded with emergent tree roots and looked like a good spot to dig tunnels for a den. Or, given the otters' ability to roam twenty miles or more over a day, the pair may just as well have been passing through the area. The two otters acted unconcerned about me at first, perhaps because river otters are severely nearsighted, an adaptation for seeing underwater. Yet soon, their keen sense of smell and pin-drop hearing must have tipped them off that I had back-paddled for a better view. Apparently, I did not pose a threat despite the long history of otters being hunted by humans. River otters have fur that features a remarkable 375,000 hairs per square inch, an adaptation to keep the fur of a twenty-five-pound mammal water resistant. For comparison, the number of hairs on the human head is about one thousand hairs per square inch. The flip side of this design marvel is that the silky smooth, dark-brown pelts are highly prized on global fur markets. Watching the two otters play reminded me that they are the most social of all the members in the weasel family, which comprises minks, badgers, martens, ferrets, and wolverines. Female river otters form families, some raising their young with the help of an unrelated adult female, yearling, or juvenile as a nanny. Male otters form their own social groups with other mature males, in some instances with as many as fifteen individuals in an all-male club. Otters communicate by scent marking, hissing, growling, whistling, and by making explosive snorts to warn of danger. I didn't hear any snorts during our encounter, further evidence that I didn't pose a danger.

Short powerful legs, webbed toes, and long muscular tapered tails transform otters into streamlined missiles capable of ambushing and chasing down fish. Animal behaviorists have discovered that river otters work in teams to round up fish. Couple these factors with the capacity of river otters to hold their breath underwater for up to four minutes and a set of razor-sharp canines, and one can see that evolution has shaped a mean, lean fishing machine. In some instances, the success of river otters in catching fish comes with a price, especially when otters hunt endangered fish species or hatchery fish. In such instances, otters have been shot or trapped and moved to another area. Populations of river otters are under increasing pressure from loss of riverine habitat due to development. While not listed as officially endangered, river otters have vanished from some regions of their natural range. Perhaps habitat loss helps explains why, in the twenty-five years I have been canoeing the Cahaba River, I have only had one encounter with river otters.

River otters, turtles, raccoons, kingfishers, herons, egrets, and other predators of fish in the Cahaba River would be unwise to tackle a full grown gar. My fishing buddy Adam Vines told me that as a boy growing up in Alabama he and his friends would fish in the Cahaba River for big spotted gar. Gar school at the water's surface, making lip-smacking noises as they lift their mouths to the waterline and gulp air on hot days. Adam and his boyhood friends tied twelve-inch red ribbons and small weights to the end of heavy fishing line and cast into schools of spotted gar. The boys would reel their red ribbons past the gar as fast as they could. When hungry, the three- to four-foot fish would take chase and their rows of tiny sharp teeth would get tangled in the fine mesh of the ribbons. The ensuing battles were legendary, for gar fight as aggressively as big pike. Other Alabama fishers have told me they cut pantyhose into long strips and hook a strip to a jig head to snag gar.

It is nearly impossible to catch a gar on a hook. The problem stems from gar having a hard, bony palate that doesn't lend itself to being penetrated, even by a razor-sharp hook. Nonetheless, one day while canoeing the Cahaba with Ken, I discovered hooking a gar is not entirely impossible. I'd cast my worm a little deeper and a bit farther off the riverbank than usual. Suddenly, I had a hard strike and I followed up by forcefully setting the hook. The water was too dark and deep to get a glimpse of the fish, but one thing was certain: it was big. My first thought was a big drum or catfish, but I knew that would be unlikely in the fast-moving waters of the upper Cahaba. Deep pulls bore hard on my eight-pound test, and I was fortunate the drag on my spinning reel was set loose enough to keep the line from snapping. Unlike the Alabama spotted bass we had been catching all morning, this fish stayed deep. By the time I had coaxed the big fish to the surface, my heart was galloping, and my first view of the spectacular three-and-a-half-foot longnose gar didn't do anything to calm my heartbeat count. Ken must have sensed my excitement and my intent to complete the "catch" by boating the fish. "Don't put it in the canoe!" he hollered again and again.

I was unaware that Ken had once shared a canoe with a gar. Apparently, the big fish had turned into a battering ram, smashing and whipping about, slashing fishing gear, whacking Ken's fishing buddy's ankles, flipping over bags of food and bottles of water. It was like having a barracuda or shark in the boat. In retrospect, Ken told me, it was a miracle the gar hadn't knocked the fishing poles into the water. In deference to Ken, I agreed to let him beach the canoe so I could climb out and muscle my big fish up onto the bank. I stood back and took in the splendor of the gar sprawled on the wet sand, the gray-green torso lined with dime-sized black spots that continued across the forehead and down the length of the long, narrow snout. Broad, dark stripes ran down each side of the fish, and dorsal, ventral, and tail fins were similarly striped. The evolutionary lineage of this fish was remarkable. Here, laid out in front of me, gulping air, was a species of fish known to date back over a hundred million years. I had landed a living fossil.

Longnose gar range well beyond the confines of the rocky outcrops, submerged trees, and aquatic vegetation of the Cahaba River; indeed, the species is found throughout much of North and Central America.[11] Big gar live a long time, three to four decades, and forage after dark on crayfish and a variety of fish, including each other.

Females spawn at about six years of age, and despite the huge number of eggs they release, they hedge their bets by provisioning each egg with a chemical defense. The distasteful chemicals may be particularly advantageous because the eggs get stuck to rocks, vegetation, and woody debris in shallow, clear water where visual predators can readily detect them. In contrast to the eggs, the flesh of longnose gar is excellent to eat, and the species has a long history of providing sustenance to Native Americans. Today, most fishers prefer to fish gar for their fight rather than their flesh. Gar have essentially become fish that are caught and released, joining a growing number of fish species known as "trophy fish."

Back on the riverbank, I'd finished admiring my trophy. I crouched down and gently dug my hands into the wet sand just below the fish. Standing, I lifted the gar waist high, waded into the shallows, and slid the longnose back into the river.

On a sunny morning in July 2014, I headed south from Birmingham on Interstate 65. Half an hour later, I exited onto Highway 119 and drove toward the small college town of Montevallo. As I drove through the downtown, I followed signs to Highway 25, a picturesque country road that winds through rolling green hills sprinkled with pastures and pines and rural communities with names like Wilsonville and Harpersville to the east and my destination of Sixmile, Alabama to the west. Sixmile is pretty much a crossroads, and I hadn't had any luck locating it on a road map. But I did discover that Sixmile resides in unincorporated Bibb County, an agricultural and former coal-mining region of central Alabama spanning 622 square miles with a population of about twenty-three thousand people. According to the Bibb County government website, 17 percent of these people today live in poverty. After turning onto Highway 25, I pulled onto the shoulder and shut off my engine, which gave me time once again to read over the directions e-mailed to me the previous day by Jim Brown, a longtime friend from Chandeleur fishing trips and professor of history at Samford University. Jim teaches mainly Russian history courses but also offers a popular course in folklore. While his knowledge of folklore extends across many regions of the world, Jim has become a leading expert on Alabama folklore.[12] Jim's e-mail read, "He lives at Sixmile (a little unincorporated community in central Alabama). Take Hwy 25 heading west from Montevallo; just after entering Bibb Co. you'll cross Sixmile Creek, then it'll be the second paved road on the left, and first driveway on the right." And so it was, thirty minutes later, after getting lost twice, I found myself idling at the mouth of a dirt driveway leading to a single-level red-brick farm home hidden in the pines. Not having a street address, I punched in Jim's number on my cell phone to make sure I had the correct place. "Yup," answered Jim, after I had described the house. "That's the one; tell me how it goes." And he hung up.

"Hello, I'm Jim McClintock, the biologist and author from UAB," I said to the tall, broad-shouldered, graying gentleman in his mid-sixties who opened the door. An awkward silence followed. Nervous that I might not have found the right house, I continued, "Jim Brown told me he called you yesterday to let you know I would be coming out today." Yet again, awkward silence. "Never heard of any Jim Brown," the man standing at the door proclaimed with a straight face. Then, satisfied he'd got one over on me, Tommy Campbell chuckled, introduced himself, and with a welcoming grin invited me inside the home he had built. "Want something to drink?" Tommy asked as I settled into one of two chairs in the corner of the family room. "Thanks, water will do," I said. Tommy headed into the kitchen and returned with two glasses of water, handed one to me, and nestled himself into his easy chair. The time had come for me to learn about a family's legacy of noosing Cahaba River redhorse suckers.

"The story begins in the 1890s with my grandfather on my mother's side, Morgan Lovejoy," said Tommy. Grandpa Lovejoy met an elderly man who taught him about snaring redhorse suckers, which gathered each spring to spawn near Bulldog Bend on the Little Cahaba River, not far from where the Little Cahaba joins the main

Cahaba River. "It's just down the road from where we sit right now," explained Tommy. Grandpa Lovejoy learned how to cut an eighteen-foot bamboo cane pole and wrap string the length of the pole to give it extra strength. Then he'd bend twenty-two-gauge wire into the shape of an apple, big enough to slip over the head of a redhorse. To weight the snare, he'd pour hot molten lead into thimble-sized sand molds and insert eyelets in the cooling lead to fashion weights to hang at the bottom of the wire loop. "You sit right here," Tommy said suddenly. "They're back in the shop." And with that, Tommy got up and disappeared down a hall. When he returned to the family room, he laid an old wire snare, some weights, and a few eyelets next to me on the carpet. "I don't pour hot lead to make my weights anymore. I learned that I could buy fishing bullet weights, cut them in half with a saw, and hammer in eyelets." Tommy picked up the hand-fashioned wire snare off the carpet and handed it to me so I could see how to hang a weight at the bottom of the loop. "The weight keeps the snare tight against the river bottom," he said. Then he showed me how the snare attached to the tip of the pole with a five-foot length of string and how the snare slides tight when slipped over the head of a sucker.

Redhorse suckers (*Moxostoma carinatum*) are impressive fish—both to admire and, I suspect, to snare.[13] They are also considered the finest of live baits by fishers who fish for big striped bass. The genus, *Moxostoma*, means "mouth to suck," a tribute to the fish's buccal peculiarities. The downturned, heavy-lipped mouth reflects its life as a bottom-feeder eating mussels, clams, snails, crayfish, and aquatic insect larvae. The redhorse are brownish with beautiful, sparkling olive or bronze-tinted scales on their dorsum that become white as the scales cascade to the fish's belly. The fish earn the "red" in "redhorse" by sporting bright orange-red tails and fins. Native to the eastern United States and southeastern Canada, redhorse occur in large creeks and rivers with generous flow where they grow to ten pounds. The redhorse favor creek and river habitats with plenty of cobble, gravel, or sand. Little is known of their behavior, but Tommy Campbell has learned a good bit from long hours spent watching the fish. He explained to me that the "horses" redden up and develop "horns" (sharp pointed bumps) on their nose that help in digging spawning beds during the breeding season. The horses wait on either side of a spawning bed, sometimes for days at a time. When a "mare" arrives, the horses drop off either side of the bed and move in tight against her. Pretty soon the mare will start trembling and kicking up silt as she releases yellowish-pink eggs. Then the horses go to work, squirting sperm over the eggs. Both the horses and the mare leave; they don't guard their eggs like some fish. Tommy said he'd watched the fertilized eggs get stuck on shallow rocks and hatch about three or four days later.

"Like my parents and grandparents, I was born in Piper, Alabama, not far from Sixmile," explained Tommy. "Today Piper is nothing more than three or four old houses." Back in 1949, the year that Tommy was born, the Campbell family ate the redhorse suckers caught that spring, just as their parents had during the Great Depression. Tommy remembered that times were really tough when Grandpa Campbell worked at a coal mine near Piper. "Grandpa used to come in after dark each night covered in coal dust," explained Tommy. One night, Tommy recalled, Grandpa came home from a day's work in the mine and told his wife Essie that he'd gotten "covered up," meaning he'd been buried in a mine collapse. Essie had filled a metal wash bucket with warm soapy water and cleaned coal dust from the deep wounds in Tommy's grandpa's back. On Tommy's grandpa's meager mining salary, redhorse suckers and home-grown vegetables were essential to family meals. The suckers were too bony to eat straight away, so the Campbell and Lovejoy families learned to pressure-cook the fish. The tiny bones turned soft and edible under the pressure, and the cooked fish was put up in glass fruit jars. "It was delicious," Tommy remembered. Today, Tommy oversees the family's annual spring redhorse noosing tradition, but he and his extended family don't need to eat the fish anymore. Rather, each spring's catch is donated to an elderly friend who lives nearby in the county. The elderly friend doesn't pressure-cook the suckers like

Tommy's forebearers, but rather slices the redhorse horizontally into wafer-thin slices and fries them until they are crispy. This way, the hot grease dissolves the bones.

Back in the 1930s and 1940s, the family's spring catch of redhorse suckers would be carried from the Little Cahaba River to Piper on stringers dangling from a pole carried between two men. Tommy remembers a time his uncle William Lovejoy was on one end of a pole of fish when the stringer broke, dumping the entire stringer of redhorse suckers into the river. Uncle William fell to his knees and pushed the dead fish to shore, gathered them in his jacket, and carried them home.

The spring spawn snaring typically took place over a week that fell between April 10 and May 10, and most everyone in the extended family, young and old, male and female, participated. If the spawn happened to fall on a Sunday, everyone had to be patient. Grandpa Lovejoy insisted that no fishing was allowed on Sundays from 12 a.m. to 12 p.m. Redhorse noosing days were special. In the morning, everyone gathered at Grandpa Lovejoy's house in Piper to string their poles, rig their wire snares, and prepare dishes for the supper later that evening. Around noon, the Campbell and Lovejoy families headed to Bulldog Bend. Once at the river, there was laughter and good spirits.

Snaring tactics haven't changed much over three family generations. Once the "tame" suckers (the fish become docile when in spawning condition) had been spotted in the river, hovering near the beds, the basic idea was to wade into the river downstream from the fish, drop the snare into the current above a fish holding position, and then finesse the cane pole such that the weighted snare was positioned just above and perpendicular to the fish's head. With practice, one then slid the snare over the fish's head and quickly lifted the pole, tightening the snare around the fish like a hangman's noose. A successful catch often required a number of repeated rakes of the snare. Nonetheless, some members of the family got so good at snaring redhorses that they could snare a fish by feel in the dark of night. On occasion, snaring a fish could turn dangerous. Tommy recalled the time he snared a big redhorse in swift, deep water, slipped, and found himself suddenly being pulled downriver by the fish, while desperately trying to regain his footing and keep his head out of the water. He recollected, proudly, that he landed that fish.

Grandpa Lovejoy was well ahead of his time when it came to conservation. "He was a naturalist," said Tommy. Everyone respected his gentle sermon about leaving a place the way you found it and not killing what you can't use. In a similar vein, Grandpa Lovejoy was a pioneer of sustainable fish management, insisting, said Tommy, that all the redhorse mares be protected. "Leave the mares and let them reproduce," he would tell folks. "The family practice of protecting the mares is still followed to this day," Tommy noted proudly. Yet despite Grandpa Lovejoy and Tommy's commendable conservation efforts, the future of the redhorse sucker is far from certain. Redhorse are uniquely vulnerable because of their specific habitat and bedding requirements. The fish are at the mercy of the impact of siltation that turns the river cloudy and coats the river bottom with layer upon layer of fine sediment, which buries critical redhorse feeding and spawning habitats. The evidence of siltation is as clear as just-cleaned glass. Drive, bike, or walk across a bridge that spans the Cahaba River after a heavy rain storm and you will see chocolate-brown, sediment-choked water. Despite the river clearing over the coming days, the damage has been done.

Hopefully, the redhorse sucker will not go the way of the Alabama sturgeon. This primitive-looking, yellowish-orange armored fish with its long flat nose was finally given species status in 1991. Studies in the lower Cahaba River revealed that the sturgeon grew to thirty inches and had a life span of about twenty years. Just nine years after becoming a species, the Alabama sturgeon was listed as an endangered species. Factors contributing to the fish's rapid demise included water-quality degradation, overfishing, and loss of habitat due to dredging navigation channels and constructing dams. In May 2008, the status of the fish had grown precarious, and the U.S. Fish and Wildlife Service proposed designating the lower eighty-one miles of the Cahaba River as critical habitat for the Alabama sturgeon. However, industries along the lower Cahaba River feared shipping restrictions and fought the designation. Ultimately, the Fish and Wildlife Service dropped its proposal. In July 2009, fish biologists in the lower Cahaba River may have caught the last Alabama sturgeon.[14] The sturgeon was fitted with a radio tracking device in a desperate attempt to locate a few more individuals of the species. Sadly, the radio signal was lost, and six years hence, not another Alabama sturgeon has been reported.

Despite a body length that is fifteen times shorter than the Alabama sturgeon, the federally endangered Cahaba shiner (*Notropis cahabae*), first described in 1989, has become the iconic symbol of the fragility of the Cahaba River and its environs.[15] The silver, delicate-boned, two-and-a-half-inch fish has a distinctive peach-colored lateral stripe running parallel to and above a darker stripe. The fish prefers cool, well-oxygenated water and lives over clean sand substrates in large, shallow shoals in the main channel of the river. Adults spawn in the late spring and early summer, and the fertilized eggs develop in jellylike masses among aquatic vegetation. Tiny crustaceans, aquatic insect larvae, and algae provide sustenance. The Cahaba shiner qualified for its endangered status by exhibiting a distribution that is currently limited to five or fewer areas that measure collectively no more than 370 square miles. The remaining fish are limited to a fifteen-mile stretch of the seventy-six-mile length of river the shiner had formerly occupied between Centreville and Helena, Alabama.

Loss of habitat quality is largely responsible for the diminishment of the Cahaba shiner: siltation, pollutants from storm-generated run-off and wastewater treatment facilities, and exposure to heavy metals from strip-mining activities. When flow rates in the Cahaba River are seasonally low, nutrient-enriched waters challenge the respiratory needs of what the U.S. Environmental Protection Agency has now labeled a pollutant-intolerant fish. While populations of the Cahaba shiner continue to gradually decline, hope remains for the diminutive fish should further environmental safeguards be brought to fruition in the Cahaba River Basin. Why should a tiny fish matter? The shiner matters because its existence reflects the general health of the Cahaba River. Where the Cahaba shiner swims, aquatic insects burst from pupae, mussels filter plankton, snails reproduce, crayfish forage on decaying vegetation, a canoe startles a great blue heron from its perch, and there are plenty of redeye bass, spotted bass, and largemouth bass to catch on a summer afternoon.

According to the Cahaba River Society,[16] an organization made up of a broad spectrum of stakeholders from environmental scientists to corporate CEOs, the two most significant problems facing the three species of bass that live in the Cahaba River are siltation and excessive nutrients.[17] Of less concern, but still potentially stressful, are water-quality problems associated with strip mining in the region and the resultant acid-mine drainage caused by leaching of toxic metals such as iron, mercury, lead, and copper into feeder streams of the Cahaba River Basin. Concentrations of iron in some feeder streams are so high that iron oxides form a yellow crust called yellowboy on the streambed rocks. Toxic metals leached from mines in sufficient concentration can short-wire key metabolic functions, killing bass; at lower concentrations, the metals can insidiously compromise growth and development in larval and juvenile bass.

While the fine silt coloring the river water passes across the gills of bass, it is not life threatening, as it may be in some filter-feeding aquatic invertebrates. Rather, the effect of siltation on bass in the Cahaba River is indirect. The silt settles to the riverbed and, similar to the effect on the redhorse sucker, destroys bass spawning beds and reduces the amount of structure for bass cover. Bass living in heavily silted areas may fail to reproduce or may move elsewhere. Siltation in the Cahaba River is the result of erosion from timber clear cuts, coal mining, and construction sites with improperly maintained siltation fences. The fine sediments washed into the river may also transport pollutants.

Bass are also indirectly challenged by excess nutrients that leach into the Cahaba River from animal waste; crop, lawn, and garden

fertilizers; inadequate septic systems; and wastewater treatment facilities. Currently, over one hundred industries are permitted by the
Alabama Department of Environmental Management to release
treated wastewater into the Cahaba River. As the climate warms and
heavier rain events have become more common, storm waters are increasingly flushing litter and oil from parking lots and roadways into
the Cahaba River. With development encroaching on the amount of
forested land in the river basin that remains to absorb storm waters,
the Cahaba River is increasingly flooding beyond its normal carrying capacity, causing bank erosion. Trees washed free from the banks
become battering rams that scour the rock shoals of Cahaba lilies.
The effect of elevated nutrients such as nitrogen and phosphorus, especially in the slower-moving sections of the lower Cahaba River, has
fueled water-fouling outbreaks of the threadlike green alga *Cladophora*.
The alga uses up the oxygen in the river during the night and blocks
sunlight from penetrating the river during the day, thus challenging
all walks of aquatic life, including the largemouth bass that thrive in
the lower section of the river. On a hot day in a stagnant section of
the river, high nutrients, low oxygen, and alga-steeped water become
a toxic cocktail for a largemouth bass.

4

GULF OF MEXICO

Yellowfin Tuna

I f you fish, don't underestimate the potential rewards of striking up a conversation with whomever is sitting next to you on an airline flight. John Franklin, or Johnny as he preferred to be called, liked to joke and tell stories and seemed an old friend by the time our plane set down on the tarmac. Johnny had that air of Southern hospitality that I have come to appreciate from living in the southern United States. At the time we met, Johnny was in his mid-fifties and vice president of a small construction firm, traveling throughout the country to oversee various large-scale building projects. Johnny was intrigued to learn I was a marine biologist by trade and, to his way of thinking, crazy enough to put on scuba tanks and dive through a hole in the ice in Antarctica. We didn't need to get much deeper into our conversation before we discovered we both enjoyed fishing.

Johnny handed me his business card as we parted at the airport gate and told me to get in touch to plan a visit to his property about twenty miles northwest of Birmingham to fish his private lake. A few weeks later, I e-mailed Johnny and arranged for Ken Marion and me to drive out to Johnny's place. Johnny was the perfect host, providing us access to the twelve-foot aluminum johnboat he kept flipped over on the weedy lake bank, along with advice about the best crank baits and plastic lizards to try in his lake. Pretty soon, Ken and I were making regular forays out to "Johnny's Lake" to fish on weekends. The lake covered about eight acres and was unusual in the sense that it was a former coal-mining operation dammed up on the lower end and fed by a small stream. The lake water was clear, a sign of low nutrients, and between the clear water and likelihood of toxic metals leaching from the fine jet-black coal mine tailings that formed the lake bed, we were surprised to find that the lake sustained a population of largemouth bass.

Ken and I fished Johnny's lake at least a dozen times over the next few years, but one of those fishing trips really stands out in my inventory of bass-fishing adventures. I suspect that Ken's memory of that day is less vivid. As was the custom, first thing in the morning, Ken picked me up in his old 1998 sky-blue four-wheel-drive Jeep Cherokee. While Ken kept the Jeep idling—the engine did not always respond to the ignition switch—I loaded my fishing gear and lunch cooler into the back of the Jeep alongside Ken's electric trolling motor and trolling battery. To load up the back of Ken's old Jeep, one had to be ambidextrous. The hydraulic cylinder on the back rear compartment door was broken. The door slammed shut with tremendous force at the slightest provocation, so I had to be prepared to grab the door with one hand. I had learned about the broken door the hard way, having severed the tip of one of my favorite fishing poles. Once seated in the front passenger seat, the next order of business was to roll my window down for fresh air, a routine reflex triggered by the faint but persistent odor of putrid flesh that permeated Ken's Jeep. The flesh and its subsequent decay were the result of Ken's encounter a year earlier with a snake.

As a herpetologist of some notoriety, Ken was known in Birmingham and the surrounding region as an expert one could contact for help in ridding oneself of a poisonous snake. Ken sometimes kept the captured snake, adding it to the menagerie of snakes he maintained in an animal facility at the university for teaching purposes, or he would drive the snake to a remote area and release it. Ken was participating in an Audubon workshop at a boy's camp an hour's drive north of Birmingham when he was called to remove a venomous copperhead that had slid under a cabin bed. Ken quickly captured the copperhead with the golf-club-sized snake tongs he carried in his Jeep for just such occasions. He put the two-and-a-half-foot snake into a pillow case tied securely with a knot at the top, tossed it into his Jeep where his other show-and-tell snakes were caged, and went off to give the evening's keynote address.

Before driving back to Birmingham later that evening, Ken checked on the copperhead. To his great surprise, the snake had escaped through a small hole in the bottom corner of the pillow case. Ken began searching the Jeep. "I tried to act real casual," Ken told me. "As people at the workshop walked by, I would jump up from peering under a seat and act like nothing was up. I didn't want anyone to think the snake man had lost a snake." Try as he might, Ken couldn't locate the copperhead. Having to get back to Birmingham to lead a canoe trip for the Cahaba River Society early the next morning, Ken drove home in the dark with the copperhead coiled up somewhere in his Jeep.

What was going through Ken's mind as he raced down the freeway one can only imagine, but suffice it to say that controlling the Jeep would have gotten real interesting real fast had the big copperhead slithered across Ken's foot on the gas pedal or slid into his lap. "Every now and then, I turned on the Jeep's ceiling light to peer around," Ken told me. The next morning, Ken still couldn't find the copperhead, which must have slid up inside a seat or behind the instrument dashboard. Ken decided the only course of action was to kill the venomous snake should it not have escaped through a hole in the Jeep's chassis. Accordingly, he parked his Jeep in a parking lot and left the vehicle to roast in the late May Alabama sun. Sure enough, two days later, the odor of decaying snake engulfed the interior of the Jeep Cherokee. The smell was so bad that Ken had to drive the next week with his head stuck partially out of the Jeep's side window. Ken's wife, Vicki, refused to ride in the Jeep for months, and she claims that even today, eight years later, she can still smell that mummified snake.

Ken and I arrived at Johnny's house and stopped to put his Jeep into four-wheel drive before easing down a steep, deeply rutted dirt road that descended a couple hundred feet to the grassy bank of the lake. Ken parked the Jeep, and we got out and rolled the johnboat over and slid it halfway out into the shallow water. While I unpacked fishing gear, life jackets, and lunches from the Jeep, Ken mounted the electric trolling motor to the boat's transom and hooked up the trolling battery. Soon, we were set to fish. Since Johnny's lake wasn't very big, we generally fished the entire shoreline once or twice and then moved off into deeper water before returning once again to fish the banks.

Ken is far and away the better fisher of the two of us. Ken grew up in Missouri, and when he wasn't playing baseball or basketball, he was fishing for trout, bass, or brim. Soon after arriving in Birmingham in 1971, he bought a bass boat and competed regularly in local bass tournaments. Ken has a room full of fishing trophies and at least ten bass mounted on his office wall. On average, Ken catches more fish, and bigger fish, than I catch. Whenever we fish together, Ken likes to be in control of the boat. I don't believe his being at the helm so much has to do with any concern about my ability to handle a boat, but rather that Ken feels he has a better sense of where the fish are and how fast we should or should not fish a given stretch of water. But being in control can exact a price, for the fisher in the front of the boat, whether a canoe, johnboat, flats boat, or two-person kayak, has an unimpeded view and a first-cast advantage. On that particular morning, I believe my advantage paid dividends.

Ken and I had probably been fishing Johnny's lake about an hour and were on our second loop of the shoreline when I hooked into my first good-sized bass, a five-pound largemouth that nailed my plastic finesse worm. Now, for me, a five-pound bass is a good fish, and at the time I was quite content with a bass of that size under my belt. *Heck,* I had thought, *the bass would likely be the fish of the day.* Since my worm had produced, I continued to fish my spinning outfit with a slip weight and six-inch plastic worm on eight-pound test. No more than thirty minutes had gone by before another big fish grabbed my worm and headed for shore. I set the hook and boated a second largemouth that Ken estimated to weigh about six pounds, definitely bigger than the bass I had caught earlier.

By now, Ken must have been silently fielding that age-old question that haunts fishers: *What is this guy doing that I'm not doing?* These frustrating experiences have no basis in science. I have watched two fishers use the same type of bait, the same color bait, the same fishing line, and the same casting and retrieving techniques, and one will catch fish and the other won't. If there had been the slightest chance that Ken had not yet considered this question, he certainly did when twenty minutes later I landed an even bigger largemouth on what I was now calling my "magic worm." Although we didn't have a scale, Ken estimated my third big bass weighed a good seven pounds. "If it had been full of eggs or fattened up on crayfish, a fish that long would have weighed even more," said Ken about the fish I was now holding proudly by the lower lip. I handed Ken my camera to take a picture of me and the bass, my personal record, and I made a few notes on the fish's dimensions so I could have a wall mount for my office crafted solely from the fish's photo and measurements. As I released the fish, I couldn't help but smile. I had just caught back-to-back five-, six-, and seven-pound bass in front of a guy who out-fishes everyone I know. Sweetness.

Johnny was a man of great generosity. When Ken and I ordered a box of Omaha Steaks as a way of thanking Johnny for letting us fish his private lake, he seemed genuinely taken aback when we presented the marbled ribeyes to him on his doorstep. He preferred giving to getting. Accordingly, Ken and I probably shouldn't have been surprised when Johnny invited us to drive down from Birmingham to the coast of Louisiana to spend a few days at his fish camp. Johnny's fish camp was a double-wide mobile home with a screened-in deck co-owned with some of his buddies in the construction trades. The fish camp was on a dirt road about one hundred yards off Highway 23 near Venice, Louisiana, some seventy-eight miles southeast of New Orleans. Johnny told us a couple of his friends would be at the camp with their boats, and we would fish the canals and salt marshes for speckled trout and redfish. And if this were not enough, Johnny e-mailed us a week out and told us he had also booked us on an offshore tuna-fishing trip in the Gulf of Mexico that departed from the Venice Marina. "We'd planned to fish three days," Johnny said. "Now, we'll spend one of these days fishing the Gulf." I'd never fished for yellowfin tuna, but I'd caught a couple of five- to ten-pound blackfin tuna while deep-sea fishing offshore in the Gulf of Mexico and marlin fishing in the Caribbean. I'd been impressed with their fight. So Johnny's message just before we left for the coast got my attention. "Hey Guys, look over the email below from Captain Hunter; it will let you know what you will need for the tuna run. I spoke to him about 10 minutes ago, and they are still loading the boat!! 60 to 120 lbs. Some are getting close to 200 lbs. Limit is 3 per person; if you are *Man Enough,* you are pretty much guaranteed your limit."

The alarm in the bunk room of Johnny's mobile home went off at 4:30 a.m. Ken and I climbed out of our bunks, got dressed, drank a cup of coffee, and spooned down a bowl of cereal in the small kitchen before climbing into Ken's Jeep to drive over to the Venice Marina. The good news was we didn't need to bring any fishing gear as the crew of the tuna boat provided everyone with heavy fishing rods with open-face saltwater reels and tackle. All we had to remember was our lunch, extra clothing, hat, sunglasses, sunscreen, and, for those who needed it, Dramamine. Johnny and one of his fishing buddies followed us in a pickup truck as Ken turned out of the fish camp and headed south on Highway 23. As we drove along in the early morning light, the Mississippi River rolled by on our left, and we passed a host of fish-centric businesses, including the Lighthouse Fishing Lodge, Fin and Feather Cabins, and Reel Tite Fishing Guide Service. Rounding a final bend of Highway 23, we drove another mile and a half on Tide Water Road before turning off to the Venice Marina. Captain Hunter Caballero of Paradise Outfitters met the four of us with a smile and welcomed two other guests joining our chartered tuna trip at the fuel dock in front of the store. Opposite the dock stood an open-air wooden fish-cleaning building sporting a big sign that read "Venice Marina—Fishing Capital of the World." Captain Hunter asked if we had all brought along our Louisiana fishing licenses and briefed us on boat safety. *Tail Whipped* was tied up along the fuel dock and ready to go. The Twin Vee hull design and two Yamaha three-hundred-horsepower, four-stroke outboard engines were designed to propel the thirty-two-foot fishing boat at speeds of sixty to seventy miles per hour. Speed is a big advantage when fishing for tuna in the Gulf of Mexico because schools of tuna run fifty to a hundred miles offshore in deeper water. With a center console, the boat's deck had 360 degrees of uninterrupted fishing space, a feature we would find useful later in the day.

Having never been on a sport tuna-fishing boat, I was curious about the tactics Captain Hunter was planning to use to fish for tuna. In the end, the tactic we employed, "chunking," wasn't even on my radar. Two hours out of the Venice Marina, we found ourselves about fifty miles off the coast under cloudless skies on a glassy, lightly rolling Gulf of Mexico, with nothing on the horizon except the occasional oil or natural gas platform. Despite a November sun, the subtropical air was warming quickly. Captain Hunter slowed the boat and lifted a pair of binoculars off the instrument console, methodically scanned the southern horizon, set the glasses back down, and reaccelerated the boat's engines. This search pattern was repeated until a final re-direction of *Tail Whipped* revealed our quarry: a shrimp trawler under full steam with its nets deployed.

Captain Hunter approached the stern of the shrimper with alarming speed and certitude. If I'd been the captain of the shrimp boat, I would have been concerned. Later, I learned a cooperative symbiosis exists between sport tuna boats and shrimp trawlers in the Gulf. Twenty feet off the back of the shrimper's stern, Captain Hunter cut our two big outboard engines, leaving us with the fading rumble of the shrimper's diesel engine, the cries of laughing gulls, and the slap of wash. The captain and mate quickly lifted two medium-weight

fishing rods with spinning reels from pole holders on the center console. Already strung with silver two-and-a-half-inch spoons, the two
men cast the rods rapidly and repeatedly into the chop left behind by
the shrimp trawler. Initially, I had no idea what was up. Was this how
we were going to fish for tuna? Suddenly, a fish slammed the captain's
spoon, and before he had boated the fish, a second followed on the
mate's spoon. Fifteen minutes later, seven lively five- to ten-pound
bonito lay pounding tail fins against the sides of a large white cooler.
Bonito are muscular, hard-fighting, midwater schooling fish. Like
other members of the Scombridae fish family, which include tuna
and mackerel, their impressive capacity for rapid acceleration, called
"burst swimming," is fueled by myriad capillaries supplying "high
octane" blood to oxygen-demanding tissues. While the oily meat of
bonito is too fishy for most people to eat, their smelly flesh makes
excellent bait. Captain Hunter and the mate slid the bonito-laden
cooler to the back of the deck and, using a pair of sharp fillet knives,
filleted the fresh bonito and sliced the fillets up into one-inch cubes.
The mate slid the bonito chunks off the cutting boards and into large
ziplock bags and stowed the plastic bags in the rinsed cooler. So far,
nobody had asked the captain for an explanation.

"Sit down and hold tight," Captain Hunter reminded us as he
once again fired up the two outboard engines. Soon, we were under
way—full throttle—wind whistling by, baseball caps turned backward or gripped tight in hand. Within twenty minutes, the captain
had spotted another trawler pulling nets after the shrimp known as
"whites" and "browns" by gulf locals. Captain Hunter maneuvered
Tail Whipped in tight to the shrimp trawler's stern and cut the engines. As the wake from the shrimper subsided, the captain seated
himself on the back starboard rail, opened the cooler his mate had
pulled alongside, unzipped a bag of bonito chunks, and tossed a
handful off the side into the clear, dark-blue water. I leaned over the
rail and watched the chunks of fish slowly sink, the morning sunlight
illuminating the water to a depth of about fifty feet. The thought
hadn't dawned on me that Captain Hunter was chumming for tuna.

Moments later, I caught a glimpse of several dark shadows circling upward from the depths, and I realized what was up. By the time the shadows reached a depth of ten feet, they had transformed into a small school of two- to two-and-a-half-foot blackfin tuna.

We watched silver flashes of circling blackfin as Captain Hunter lifted one of the Seeker rods fitted with Penn International 50W salt-water reels from the central console. The big pole was strung with seven hundred yards of one-hundred-pound test. Sitting back down on the rail, the captain pulled a silver-dollar-sized circular fish hook free from the rod eyelet, leaned the rod against the boat rail, and inserted the hook so it was well hidden in a chunk of bonito. Holding the baited line in his right hand, the captain used his free hand to toss another handful of bonito chunks into the water and then slowly hand-lowered the fishing line attached to the chunk of bait. The tuna responded to the smell of fresh bonito and darted in to snap up the chunks. Using his thumb and forefinger to gauge the tautness of the line, the captain waited for a tuna to suck the hooked chunk well into its mouth before releasing his hand line. Quickly picking up the rod and reeling in slack, the captain jerked the rod to set the hook. The stout rod tip bent hard, and the drag, loose enough to allow the tuna to run, squealed. "Who wants it?" said Captain Hunter, peering at the six of us standing aft. We'd previously discussed the question and already set up the fishing order. Ken had first fish.

The blackfin tuna (*Thunnus atlanticus*) that circled below *Tail Whipped* occur in warm waters throughout the Gulf of Mexico and western Atlantic.[1] The common name *blackfin* is a bit of a misnomer because while the silver, oval-shaped fish have a black upper back, the fins are silvery with a tinge of yellow. The tuna spawn offshore in the summer and are remarkable for their rapid growth, becoming sexually mature in just two years and reaching up to three and a half feet and forty pounds over their five-year life span. Having watched blackfin dart about grabbing chunks of bonito, it's easy to picture them as aggressive hunters, using their stout muscular tails to generate speeds necessary to capture shrimp, squid, and small fish in surface to midocean depths. Because of their rapid growth and high fecundity, populations of blackfin tuna remain healthy despite a sport and commercial fishery.

Captain Hunter beckoned Ken to the boat's rail and told him to strap on a fishing belt the mate had dug out of a boat box. Once Ken was belted, the captain lifted the base of the fishing rod into a two-inch-diameter cup on the belt's front center. Ken gripped the lively rod and worked the blackfin, reeling between deep runs and, as necessary, following the fish around the center console. Ten minutes later, Ken teased the tuna out of the depths and reeled the fish back from a last dash toward the prop of one of the twin engines. The blackfin largely spent, Ken lifted his rod and muscled the fish in close enough to *Tail Whipped* to give the mate a clear shot at setting the gaff. "Heads up!" the mate yelled before slinging Ken's flopping tuna onto the back deck. Pulling free the gaff, the mate pithed the tuna and quickly made a deep cut behind its pectoral fins, bleeding the twenty-pound fish before lifting it into an iced cooler. Bleeding the tuna preserves the quality of the flesh. Tuna have a natural body temperature that is higher than most fish and that further heats during strenuous activity. The enzymes that cause decomposition can be slowed by immediately removing the warm blood from the fish. With Captain Hunter chunking over the next few hours, all six of us each boated at least three blackfin tuna. Despite the seemingly endless bounty of blackfin, we were momentarily fished out, and we didn't object when the shortwave radio erupted with a call from a fellow tuna captain to come join him. Soon we were again flying across the Gulf.

Half an hour later, Captain Hunter slowed *Tail Whipped* and positioned the boat about a hundred feet up-current from a group of fishers on another sport tuna boat. "They're catching yellowfin!" proclaimed Captain Hunter. The news ignited a bolt of excitement. These were big tuna, the same fish that Johnny had gotten so excited about when he had spoken on the phone with Captain Hunter a few days earlier, and the same fish Johnny had challenged us to be "man enough" to bag our limit. Captain Hunter used the same technique as he had to catch the blackfin, chumming first with several handfuls of bonito chunks and waiting for the tuna to make an appearance. He didn't have to wait long. Attracted to the bonito, the yellowfin schooled in slightly deeper water than had the blackfin tuna. From my angle, I could barely make out the dark shapes and the occasional flicker of silver. The captain hooked two fish back to back, and Johnny and one of the other fishers each battled a yellowfin at the same time. I was up next. Thirty minutes later, Johnny reeled in a yellowfin that the captain estimated at sixty pounds.

Tropical and subtropical seas favor the global migratory yellowfin tuna (*Thunnus albacares*).[2] Unlike its cousin the blackfin, the torpedo-shaped yellowfin is true to its common name, sporting spectacular yellow fins, especially the tall, curved dorsal fin whose bright yellow coloration is set off against the metallic dark blue of the back and upper sides of the fish's torso. A soft-yellow stripe highlights the lower edge of the dark-blue back and demarcates the transition to a silver belly. Similar to the blackfin, the life history of the yellowfin is distinguished by rapid growth, early reproductive maturity, and a relatively short life span of six to seven years. As young as two years of age, yellowfin in the Gulf of Mexico begin a pattern of summer spawns that are characterized by the repeated release of eggs and sperm every few days. A single female can spawn an impressive four million eggs over a summer.

The record for a yellowfin tuna stood for thirty-three years before the International Game Fish Association (IGFA) All Tackle World Record was broken on September 28, 2012 for the second time in two years off the Pacific coast of Baja California. Guy Yocom and Captain Greg DiStefano landed the 427-pound yellowfin by chunking in a school of tuna about one hundred miles off Cabo San Lucas, Mexico.[3] Taking turns, Yocom was fortunate enough to be the lucky guy with the rod when the record fish took his chunk of bait. Truly top predators, yellowfin can swim up to fifty miles per hour, giving them the rare option to chase down schools of mackerel and flying fish as well as prey on squid, anchovies, and shrimp. Schooling yellowfin often swim with groups of dolphins, porpoises, whales, and even whale sharks and are also attracted to floating objects like logs. And as Captain Hunter and his mate so expertly demonstrated, schools of yellowfin in the Gulf of Mexico follow shrimp boats.

"This is a big fish!" exclaimed Captain Hunter, still peering down into the depths where the chunk of bonito he'd been dangling from the fishing line in his right hand had just been snapped up by one of the circling shadows. Grabbing the rod, he set the hook. "I can't tell if it is a shark or a yellowfin," he said over the whine of drag from the saltwater reel. "Who wants it?"

"My turn!" I yelled, scrambling to put on a fishing belt.

"Keep your thumb lightly against the line as it spins off the reel. You won't slow that fish, but you should keep the line from tangling," said Captain Hunter. "We're going to follow your fish once we get this other one boated," he added, glancing anxiously toward a guest who was working an eighty-pound yellowfin up to the side of the boat. The warm friction of fishing line spinning against my right thumb reminded me that, despite the seven hundred yards of line on my reel, it was possible this big fish was going to spool me and break off. I was relieved when I peered over my shoulder and saw the mate had gaffed the yellowfin and was pulling it over the rail and onto the back deck. Five minutes later, the decked fish was in a cooler. "OK," said the captain as he fired up the two outboard engines. "What I want you to do is keep your rod pointed toward the fish and reel as I move the boat, and keep up, 'cuz if you let slack into your line you'll lose the fish." With that, we were under way, moving slowly toward the fish. Fifteen minutes on the rod, and now, close to a half a mile in front of the boat, the fish had yet to slow. Little did I know that it would be almost an hour and a half before I got my first glimpse of the fish.

"We're going to chase again," said Captain Hunter, watching my reel spool-out line. I'd now been fighting the tuna for an hour, and in the subtropical heat of a sun-drenched afternoon, I was dripping in sweat. We'd been moving *Tail Whipped* off and on to keep the fish's runs under control. Each time we'd stopped, I'd gained a little more than what we had gained following the fish in the boat, although my small gains involved increasingly painful arm lifts of the rod and wrist-wrenching bouts of reeling. Each time I thought I was beginning to make progress, the fish responded with another deep run. A few minutes earlier, Captain Hunter had asked me if I wanted to turn the rod over to someone else. "Nope!" I'd barked back. "I'm going to catch this fish." As far as I was concerned, there was no turning back. The captain nodded reassurance and gave me a wry smile that said "go for it." Like the captain, Ken sensed my growing fatigue and lifted a plastic water jug up and poured the cool water over my head and sweat-soaked neck and shoulders. "Reel!" said the captain, as once again the boat followed the fish.

"It's a 'death spiral,'" Captain Hunter murmured into my ear an hour and a half into the fight. "Big tuna turn onto their sides and spiral upward foot by foot the last several hundred feet to the surface," he explained. I wasn't sure if the "death" in "death spiral" referred to the fish or to me. My fingers, wrists, elbows, and arms coursed with lactic acid, and my lower back ached from the combined stress of standing for so long and repeatedly employing my lower back muscles to leverage the rod against the fish. At least, I reassured myself, the fish's resistance over the last few hundred feet favored a tuna over a big shark. "OK, what you have to do to counter the tension from the fish's spiral is to lift the rod up and reel down," explained Captain Hunter. Figuring that I gained about two feet with each rod lift, the prospect of lifting and reeling a hundred more times to coax the fish to the surface was daunting. Ken poured more cool water over my head, and I lifted the rod and reeled down again and then again. In a comical gesture that revealed just how spent my arms were, Captain Hunter reached over and lifted my rod up with his little finger.

"I see the fish!" I yelled. Peering forty feet down into the clear Gulf water, I could just make out the outline of a dark, torpedo-like shape. "It's a big yellowfin," reassured Captain Hunter, also peering down. The fish was turned on its side, performing its death spiral to perfection, just as Captain Hunter had forewarned. *Please don't come off,* I thought to myself. Yet despite my worries, slowly, surely, with each painful lift of my rod, reel of my reel, drip of my sweat, the six-foot yellowfin surfaced.

I knew I had landed an impressive fish when Captain Hunter and his mate crowded in on either side of me for a photograph of the three of us on the back rail of *Tail Whipped,* holding my yellowfin tuna across our laps. The image would be posted on the Paradise Outfitters web page to beckon future fishers. The big yellowfin was beautiful freshly caught, with its yellow and deep blue a case study in color contrasts. And once the colors faded, the fish would be beautiful again, filleted and divided up among those on board to be served to friends and family as sashimi or grilled tuna steaks. With the big tuna laid out on ice for the trip back to the marina and an official weighing, the time had come for me to give my adrenaline and lactic acid a break.

None of us aboard Tail Whipped *that day* had any inkling that eighteen months later, on Friday, April 20, 2010, forty-one miles off the coast of Louisiana and just a couple of miles from the very spot we had caught tuna, the BP *Deepwater Horizon* drilling rig would experience a wellhead blowout and explode into flames and sink, killing eleven men.[4] The result would be the largest accidental oil spill in human history. The volume of crude oil that gushed from the wellhead five thousand feet below where we had fished remains the subject of some controversy, but the U.S. government estimated that over the next eighty-seven days the leak released sixty-eight thousand barrels of oil a day. Accordingly, a total of twenty-one million gallons of crude oil spewed into the Gulf of Mexico. The oil spread far and wide, coating approximately sixty-eight thousand square miles, an area similar in size to the state of Florida or the nation of Greece. The oil mixed with the seafloor sediments and washed up along the coastal wetlands of Louisiana,[5] as well as the salt marshes and sandy beaches of Mississippi, Alabama, and the Florida Panhandle. Fish as far away as Tampa, Florida were reported with lesions thought to be related to the spill.[6] Despite the wide use of a chemical dispersant (Corexit)—known to contain toxins and endocrine-disrupting compounds—to break up the oil into small droplets to facilitate bacterial breakdown, and in lieu of a massive BP-financed oil clean-up effort, a significant portion of the oil remains unaccounted for to the present day. There is also some question as to the fate of the dispersant, which has been shown to dissipate in warm temperatures but whose degradation is much slower in deep, cold water such as in the region of the wellhead blowout. Moreover, in addition to the more obvious immediate impacts of the spill on marine life, less is known about more insidious, longer-term impacts. Five years after the spill, tar balls with the chemical fingerprints of *Deepwater Horizon* oil and recently discovered traces of the dispersant used during the spill continue to regularly wash up on Gulf beaches.[7]

The eight-hundred-pound Atlantic bluefin released her first stream of ripe eggs just after dark in the warm surface waters of the Gulf of Mexico. It was May, the peak month for bluefin spawning in the Gulf of Mexico, and she had just returned here, her natal spawning grounds. The big female didn't detect the oil slick above her from the gushing wellhead deep below. Neither did the two massive male bluefin that swam alongside her releasing their sperm to fertilize the millions of tiny eggs that now poured from her gonoduct. Her fertilized eggs drifted just below the gulf surface, their porous membranes exposed to concentrations of *Deepwater Horizon* oil known to be toxic to bluefin embryos in laboratory studies carried out several years later by scientists from the National Oceanic and Atmospheric Administration and Stanford University.[8] As her myriad embryos developed over the next three days, each one passed through a critical series of genetically choreographed ontogenetic stages. Tragically, bathed in oiled seawater, the tissues around their tiny hearts swelled, causing heart defects[9] and abnormalities of the spine, fins, jaws, and eyes. In all likelihood, most of her larvae would die outright or develop into juveniles with life-threatening embryonic defects.

While heart defects and embryonic abnormalities were also detected in yellowfin exposed to *Deepwater Horizon* oil, the sensitivity of bluefin tuna to the oil was of greater concern because, unlike blackfin and yellowfin tuna, bluefin tuna such as the Atlantic bluefin species *Thunnus thynnus*[10] are endangered and their numbers have dwindled in the Gulf of Mexico, the western and eastern Atlantic, and the Mediterranean Sea.[11] The species is extinct in the Black Sea. The sad demise of this uniquely warm-blooded, spectacular, dark-blue to silver fish is due to a combination of slower growth rate and longer life span (up to fifty years) coupled with high demand. In Japan, where Atlantic bluefin and its close relatives are prized for sashimi and sushi, an absurd market value may be the fish's ultimate undoing. In 2013, Kiyoshi Kimura, a Japanese restaurateur, paid $1.76 million for a single 489-pound Atlantic bluefin.[12]

Bluefin tuna can grow to enormous size. The current IGFA record Atlantic bluefin was hooked by Ken Fraser on October 26, 1979 off Nova Scotia, Canada. The fish measured twelve feet and weighed 1,496 pounds. The province of Nova Scotia also holds the world record for the longest period of time spent landing a tuna. The famous catch involved six fishermen, one fishing pole, and an Atlantic bluefin that weighed 769 pounds.[13] The epic battle lasted sixty-two hours with the six fishermen taking turns on the rod. With Atlantic bluefin a target of sportfishing and a commercial fishing industry bent on exploiting an arsenal of helicopters, harpoons, rods and reels, long lines, and purse seines to harvest the prized fish, populations have plummeted worldwide. Concern for the Atlantic bluefin and related bluefin species has resulted in a number of nations initiating catch quotas. Even Japan is beginning to show signs of concern; the government recently entertained a proposal sponsored by the Western and Central Pacific Fisheries Commission to reduce by half the allowable catch of juvenile Pacific bluefin.[14]

All of us aboard Tail Whipped *were whipped*. We'd been on
the water for nine straight hours, and the sun, having doled out its
daily allotment of skin damage, was sinking toward the western Gulf
horizon. Between rising at the crack of dawn, catching tuna, and
having to constantly readjust our balance on the gently rolling sea,
we were exhausted. But it was a good sort of tired, a kind of keep-
to-yourself end-of-day tired made all the more introspective because
we couldn't have talked over the outboard engines if we'd wanted.
Instead, we watched the waters of the Gulf of Mexico recede and the
mouth of East Bay appear at the southernmost reach of Plaquemine
Parish. Lining the bay were vast expanses of salt marsh. No white
sand beaches crawling with tourists, no high-rises and casinos, no
wave-washed rocky intertidal littered with tide pools. Just endless salt
marsh, the noblest of biomes serving up its buffet of ecoservices: filtering sediments and pollutants, recycling essential nutrients, providing
nurseries for myriad invertebrates and sport and commercial fish,
and establishing much-needed fortification against future hurricanes
in an age of sea-level rise.

The vibrant-green seaward edge of the salt marsh would soon be
dulled by *Deepwater Horizon* oil pushed ashore by wind, wave, and current. Once oil-coated, the blades of the cordgrass (*Spartina alterniflora*)
and its marsh-grass relatives would be occluded from sunlight and
no longer viable. Without a source of life-sustaining energy, the roots
of the grasses infiltrating the sediments would decay and the plants
would die. Devoid of sediment-stabilizing roots, the marsh sediments
would become unstable and wash away, more than doubling the rate
of erosion that's plagued Louisiana's salt marshes since the Army
Corps of Engineers dammed the Mississippi River in the 1930s and
oil companies cut their boat channels. Dr. Brian Silliman, a biologist
and lead author of a publication in the *Proceedings of the National Academy of Sciences* on the impacts of *Deepwater Horizon* oil on salt marsh
ecosystems, noted that the combination of the oil spill and the abate-
ment of Mississippi River–borne sediments is a poignant example of
how human stressors can have additive effects.[15] Fortunately, after

about a year and a half of oil-induced accelerated erosion, the grasses would grow back and the rate of coastal wetland loss would slow to its pre-oiled level. Whether returning to a pace of erosion that encompasses the loss of a football field of Louisiana salt marsh every hour is reason to celebrate is debatable.

Captain Hunter slowed *Tail Whipped* to thirty miles an hour to better negotiate the narrower bays, bayous, and inlets. Now cruising close to shore, I could make out grapefruit-sized, yellow and white floats that marked the locations of commercial steel-mesh blue crab pots baited with chicken necks or the heads and entrails of menhaden, shad, or catfish. When *Deepwater Horizon* oil coated hundreds of miles of the outer fifteen to thirty feet of the seaward edge of Louisiana's salt marshes, young adult and adult blue crabs probably used their swimmerets to propel themselves deeper into the marsh and out of harm's way. Less mobile were countless tiny juvenile crabs that had recently settled at the outer edge of the marsh. Oil would have coated their sky-blue exoskeletons, clogged their delicate gills, and occluded their tiny stalked eyes and chemical-sensing antennae. Death would have been swift. At equal risk would have been the swimming larval stages of blue crabs: first the zoea and then later the megalopa. At the time of the *Deepwater Horizon* spill, Harriet Perry, a lifelong blue crab researcher at the Mississippi Gulf Coast Marine Research Laboratory in Biloxi, Mississippi discovered specks of oil inside blue crab larvae collected along the Gulf coast.[16] This couldn't have been good news for the larvae. It is impossible to say for sure that reductions in the annual harvests of blue crabs since the oil spill are attributable to *Deepwater Horizon* oil. The decline over the past five years in blue crabs, and for that matter gulf shrimp and oysters, could be similarly tied to changes in salinity due to alterations in freshwater input or coastal water pollutants like fertilizers. But the coincidental timing with the oil spill is good reason to continue to ponder the potential relationship and conduct further research.

Making our way farther north, *Tail Whipped* carried us past shallow bays where abundant oyster reefs have long contributed to a bountiful Louisiana oyster fishery. In 2009, the year following our tuna-fishing trip, oyster reefs along the Louisiana coast produced fourteen million pounds of oysters. The year after the oil spill, oyster production was halved to a little less than seven million pounds. Since then, the Louisiana Department of Wildlife and Fisheries has reported that the state's oyster fisheries continue to have low settlement of oyster spat and poor fishery production.[17] As with the blue crab, it's difficult to know the extent of the role of *Deepwater Horizon* oil in the demise of Louisiana oysters, as well as oyster fisheries in Mississippi, Alabama, and Florida. When the oil spill occurred, Louisiana officials released large amounts of freshwater from diversion structures along the Mississippi River to back-flush the oil slick moving up into sensitive shoreline and salt marsh habitats. Due to the duration and the volume of freshwater that flooded Louisiana's coastal marshes, oyster beds, which cannot survive prolonged exposure to freshwater, suffered considerable mortality. Sperm, eggs, and larvae of oysters exposed to oil and chemical dispersants were also killed off. The decline of Louisiana's oyster reefs has ramifications that extend well beyond the loss of oysters on the half shell and jobs for oyster fishers. A single oyster filters up to fifty gallons of water a day. Imagine the capacity of an entire oyster reef to filter and clean seawater, not to mention provide critical habitat for blue crabs, shrimp, and fish, and protect an increasingly vulnerable shoreline.

Captain Hunter slowed *Tail Whipped* to a wakeless pace as he rounded the final bend into the Venice Marina. The late afternoon light illuminated a marina brimming with sportfishing boats, commercial shrimp trawlers, and smaller boats designed for blue crab and oyster fishing. These boats with their captains and crews would be idled when the *Deepwater Horizon* rig exploded in flames. With vast areas of the coast closed off from harvesting oyster, blue crab, shrimp, and finned fish, the seafood industry would soon be a shell of its former $2.5 billion-a-year enterprise. Seafood processing plants would be shuttered; employees would go on unemployment (if they were U.S. citizens). All in all, the twenty-seven thousand Louisianans whose jobs revolved around coastal fisheries were in for a rough ride. Eventually, BP came around to hire many of the fishing boats and their captains and crews to help clean up the massive oil spill, handing some boat owners cashier's checks for $5,000 as a down payment toward damages to their businesses. In a May 1, 2010 article in the *New York Times,* Robbie Brown wrote that a thousand anxious and angry fishers met at the Venice elementary school to learn how to lay the white-and-orange booms that help keep oil spills in check.[18] The fishers crowding the school auditorium had high hopes that BP would hire them on; with the passing of each lost fishing day, they were losing their shirts. Poignantly, the Venice seafood company Sharkco sold off its last fifty pounds of shrimp for a bargain $3 a pound that same day, the last shrimp the company marketed for months.

Captain Hunter and the crew of *Tail Whipped,* like all the other sportfishing companies at the Venice Marina, had to close down their operations during the *Deepwater Horizon* spill. When I telephoned Captain Hunter at Paradise Outfitters to ask him about the impacts of the oil spill, he told me that Paradise Outfitters had been forced to shut down for six months, from the time of the spill in April until the end of October 2010. Eventually, he was hired by BP to use *Tail Whipped* not to lay boom but as a taxi to run crews back and forth to the brown pelican rookeries on the Chandeleur Islands, a nature reserve and the location of the oil spill's first landfall. Crews hired by BP had already been deployed with clean-up materials and absorbent booms; the crews monitored the pelicans and, as necessary, captured them and returned them to the bird rescue center in Venice to have oil cleaned from their feathers and to be rehabilitated.[19] The brown pelican was of particular concern, having suffered near extinction at the hands of DDT in the early 1970s.

A half a year passed with no sport tuna fishers gracing the Venice Marina docks. Once sport tuna operations resumed, business was slow as sport fishers had been put off by the idea of fishing in an oil-soaked Gulf. But eventually the sport tuna fishing picked back up. Commercial Gulf tuna fishers were similarly challenged by the

oil spill for a much longer period of time. The nation's perception that seafood harvested from the Gulf of Mexico was sullied hurt their market. It didn't matter to the public that no oil was detected in shellfish or fish by the U.S. Food and Drug Administration. Seafood prices plummeted, and posh restaurants in New York City and other cities throughout the northeastern United States sported signs in their windows reading "No Gulf Seafood Served."

A gentle shudder reverberated through *Tail Whipped* as the captain nudged the thirty-two-foot boat up against the wooden dock. The mate leapt off, secured bow and aft lines to the dock's cleats, and, before the captain had even shut down the engines, headed off to retrieve a fish cart that looked like a heavy-duty wheelbarrow from a shed near the marina store. One by one, we climbed gingerly out of the boat, stretching aching muscles and wrestling with varying degrees of dock rock. The mate returned with the fish cart, hoisted up the first of two big blackfin tuna–filled coolers that Captain Hunter had slid onto the dock, then wheeled the cooler to the fish-cleaning facility adjacent the dock. He then followed suit with the second cooler. Both coolers now temporarily stored on a counter where the tuna would soon be cleaned, sliced, and divided up among us, the mate returned to *Tail Whipped* with his fish cart and loaded up the smaller two of the three yellowfin. Ken, Johnny, and I followed the mate as he wheeled the two fish into a warehouse connected to the marina store that housed a certified digital fish scale. "Sixty-two pounds," he called out for the first fish. "Eighty pounds," he called for the second. With the two yellowfin reloaded into the fish cart, the mate disappeared out the warehouse door. Ten minutes later, he was back with my fish and Captain Hunter. The yellowfin, whose likeness would be meticulously rendered by a Florida fiberglass fish replica company from a photograph and measurements and would soon grace the upper wall of my Alabama kitchen, was so big its tail spilled off the front end of the fish cart. Wrapping both arms around the tuna, the mate planted his feet, squatted, and dead-lifted the yellowfin. My heart skipped a beat as he slowly lowered the big fish onto the scale. "One hundred and sixty-seven pounds!" he called.

5

ANTARCTICA

Toothfish

A*ntarctic fish shouldn't be there to catch. With the* exception of the Antarctic Peninsula, this vast continent is surrounded by an ocean that holds a steady temperature of about minus 1.8 degrees centigrade. That's 28.7 degrees Fahrenheit, well below freezing. The only reason seawater at such a low temperature does not freeze is that the salt in the water lowers the freezing point. If you dropped a fish from the Pacific coast of California, the Atlantic coast of New England, or the Mediterranean coast of France into coastal Antarctic seawater, blood would crystallize in its arteries and veins, its tissues would swell, and the myriad chemical reactions that sustain the fish's cells would grind to a halt. Within a minute or two, life would cease, the fish essentially flash frozen.

"I'm going fishing tomorrow!" I told John Heine in the galley at dinner. John was the lead science diver I had recruited to assist my research program in marine invertebrate chemical ecology in the austral fall and early summer of 1989 at the U.S. McMurdo Station on Ross Island, Antarctica. With the support of the Division of Polar Programs at the U.S. National Science Foundation, John and I, along with graduate students Marc Slattery and Jim Weston, were in Antarctica to study the chemical defenses of sponges, soft corals, tunicates, and other slow-moving spineless marine creatures lacking protective shells. The word *fishing*—when uttered by any of the approximately one thousand scientists, cooks, kitchen aides, carpenters, pilots, physicians, computer technicians, or other assorted field assistants at McMurdo Station—meant only one thing: going out on the sea ice to help Art DeVries and his team fish for giant Antarctic toothfish.

Art DeVries is among an elite group of biologists who pioneered marine biological studies along the shores of Antarctica in the mid-twentieth century. This group includes legends like John Pearse, my postdoctoral mentor, who initiated studies of marine invertebrate reproduction and larval biology; John Dearborn, who studied the feeding habits of sea stars and other echinoderms; Paul Dayton, who dove extensively below the sea ice to establish early models of sea-floor community ecology; and Gerald Kooyman and David Ainley, who studied penguins. Fish biologist Art DeVries began coming to McMurdo Station in 1961 and has returned just about every year since. In the late 1960s, Art discovered that Antarctic toothfish, belonging to the taxonomic family Nototheniidae, produce antifreeze[1] that helped the fish to diversify and dominate a fish fauna that was devastated when Antarctica separated from South America and was plunged into a deep freeze. Today, notothenioid fish with the anti-freeze make up a whole two-thirds of the two hundred or so species of fish that live in these icy waters. Antarctic fish that lack antifreeze live very deep, where a slight depression in the freezing point exists and antifreeze is not necessary. The antifreeze molecule doesn't lower the freezing point of the body fluids of fish, but, rather, it binds to microscopic crystals of ice in the supercooled blood, keeping the tiny crystals from contacting one another. Antifreeze molecules are like a referee at a boxing match who jumps between the fighters to separate them from one another. If the crystals cannot touch one another, they can't explode into the latticework that is ice. Art and his wife Chris Cheng leveraged his discovery in basic biology to explore avenues of applied biology. For example, the genes that produce the fish anti-freeze might lead to transgenic mechanisms to increase freeze toler-ance in fruits like tomatoes, lemons, and oranges. The fish antifreeze could help provide clues to extending human organ survival, treating hypothermia, and facilitating long-term space travel.

I departed the next morning for Art's fish hut in a Spryte, a tracked vehicle powered by a smelly diesel engine and designed to provide the necessary traction to travel across snow and ice. One of Art's fishing assistants drove, pulling back first on one handle and then a second to steer the vehicle as we negotiated the dirt road-ways of "Mactown" to reach the sea ice transition. Here, the dirt road met the sea ice that enveloped McMurdo Sound, and the metal plates laid out to strengthen and smooth the transition zone clanked loudly against our Spryte's tracks. The ice road led us toward the ice runway where U.S. Navy C-130 cargo planes arrived from and departed for Christchurch, New Zealand, some 2,400 miles to the north. We followed a series of red flags on bamboo poles planted along the sea ice at one-hundred-yard intervals. Several miles out of Mactown, we veered off the road and continued west across Mc-Murdo Sound, toward the distant Transantarctic Mountains studded with harbors, bays, and immense dry valleys sweeping to the sound. On that day, and off and on over the next eight years, I would gaze across McMurdo Sound and admire these snow-covered peaks and the illusory cliffs at their base. These spectacular cliffs are Fata Morganas, named for King Arthur's half-sister, Morgan le Fay, who was rumored to change her shape. These mirages appear below objects as light is bent when it passes through layers of air of varying temperature above the ice. With our road now nothing but faint traces of windblown snow tracks, we peered ahead, looking for the next wind-tattered flag to guide us.

The bright orange fish hut first appeared as a tiny speck on the horizon. We were now traveling across ten-foot-thick sea ice suspended over a seafloor lying fifteen hundred feet below. Here, about three miles from McMurdo Station in deep water, was where the giant Antarctic toothfish lived that Art sought for studies of fish antifreezes, or, more commonly, that he and his fishing technicians caught and released in a long-term study of population biology.[2] As we pulled up to the fish hut, the driver whipped the Spryte around 180 degrees so that the supplies in the back could be easily unloaded and carried into the hut. I pushed down my door handle, popped open the door, and slid my feet out onto snow-dusted sea ice. The immense landscape before us was breathtaking. I zipped open my day pack and pulled out my 35 mm SLR Minolta loaded with a fresh roll of Kodachrome 64. Adjusting the wide-angle lens, I snapped several photographs of 12,500-foot Mount Erebus, with its perennial smoke plume, poised majestically behind the cluster of orange and green buildings that was my temporary home away from home. Art's fish hut, like all huts fabricated at McMurdo Station, was a simple rectangular affair that measured about ten by fourteen feet and was constructed of two-by-fours and plywood. Inside, a Preway heater was plumbed to a barrel of diesel fuel hung on the adjacent outside wall of the hut. In the center of the plywood floor, a square opening framed a three-foot diameter hole in the sea ice bored by a tractor-like ice-drilling rig. A gas-powered hydro-winch equipped with a spool of 3/32-inch stainless steel line was attached to the hut floor and its spool positioned over the ice hole. The engine that powered the winch was situated outside, and the winch's driveshaft passed through a small hole cut in the wall of the hut.

Art met us at the door of the hut. "Come in," he said, pulling the door shut after we'd stepped inside. He slid the door latch into a heavy-duty socket aligned on the adjacent wall. Clearly, the reinforced door was designed to withstand high winds. In the center of the hut, the steel winch line on a near-empty spool disappeared through the ice hole and into the deep. Art explained to me that he came out to the fish hut the previous morning to bait four-inch stainless steel hooks with chunks of New Zealand yellow-eyed mullet. Then he lowered the line (weighted at the bottom with a fifty-five-pound lead weight) and baited the next hook. When all fifteen hooks were baited, Art dropped the fishing line down to a depth of about 1,500 feet, leaving the baited hook closest to the bottom thirty feet above the seafloor. He discovered that if he put the baited line too close to the seafloor, the bait was quickly eaten by hordes of voracious amphipod crustaceans. He also found that a twenty-four-hour set was long enough to catch fish but a short enough time period to avoid stressing the fish that he tagged and released for his population study. One of Art's fishing technicians slipped out of the hut and fired up the gasoline engine. Art flipped a switch and the winch's spool began to slowly rotate, reeling in the steel line dangling through the hole in the sea ice. "This is going to take a while," yelled Art over the engine noise, giving me one of his wry signature

grins. I sat down on a wooden bench along the wall of the hut and waited to see what, if anything, we caught.

The Antarctic toothfish has long been mistakenly called the giant Antarctic cod, though the fish is not in the cod family.[3] The cod moniker is a misnomer, probably derived from the fish's flesh tasting like cod. Other Antarctic fish, including the common rock cod, are similarly misnamed. The Antarctic toothfish (*Dissostichus mawsoni*), while decidedly not a cod, is, quite correctly, giant. Adults are capable of growing to six feet and top out at 485 pounds. The common name *toothfish* refers to the presence of two parallel rows of teeth in the upper jaw, a pattern called biserial dentition that is seen in some sharks. Antarctic toothfish are by far the largest fish that live in the Southern Ocean. As such, they are important top predators. Moreover, the species belongs to a small group of notothenioid fish, which, despite lacking swim bladders, have a light cartilaginous skeleton that renders the adult neutrally buoyant.[4] This is a wonderful adaptation that frees the toothfish from expending valuable energy swimming to hold position while opening up a vast foraging domain spanning both seafloor and midwater. In contrast, the vast majority of smaller Antarctic fish spend their entire lives on the seafloor. I observed their resting habits while scuba diving in McMurdo Sound in the 1980s and 1990s. Swimming along the seafloor, I often came across a lethargic foot-long fish. Most were so sluggish that I could pick them up with my hand then return them to the seafloor.

Given the frigid temperature, Antarctic toothfish grow quickly during the first five years of life, attaining a third of their adult body size while foraging on crustaceans, octopi, squid, and small fish. After reaching five years of age, their growth slows considerably, and sexual maturity doesn't occur until the fish are thirteen to seventeen years old. Almost nothing is known of the seasonality of spawning or the numbers of eggs produced. As adults, the big fish move off the shallower shelf and into deeper waters over the Antarctic slope where skates and various fish, including the particularly abundant silverfish, serve as prey. The big toothfish fall prey to some of Antarctica's most conspicuous predators: sperm whales, killer whales, and even the occasional giant squid. Weddell seals, known to grow to eleven feet and to reach 1,300 pounds, have been filmed blowing air into cracks in the sea ice to scare out small fish, but they much prefer preying upon big Antarctic toothfish.

John Pearse recounted a wonderful story about an encounter he had in 1961 with a Weddell seal that surfaced, in a fish hut off McMurdo Station, with a large Antarctic toothfish in its jaws. John had gone out to the hut with two colleagues to retrieve a baited fish trap he had deployed to capture marine invertebrates. "The seal came to the surface utterly exhausted, released the fish as it caught its breath, and I reached down and grabbed the fish," John explained to me. "The seal was perturbed about me stealing the fish," he continued. John and his colleagues brought the big toothfish back to the laboratory at McMurdo Station, where they took a group photo of all three of them standing out front on the snow, holding the fish. Judging by the photograph John shared with me, the toothfish looked to be about three and a half feet long and must have weighed forty or fifty pounds. The seal would have had to expend considerable energy to catch and subdue a fish that size, not to mention surfacing hundreds of feet with the big fish in its grasp. No wonder the seal was perturbed. John realized that his catch was likely the first-ever intact adult specimen of an Antarctic toothfish. In 1961, the Antarctic toothfish specimen that scientists referred to as the "type specimen" was a juvenile collected during the Discovery Expedition led by Sir Douglas Mawson in the early 1930s. Members of Robert Scott's British 1910–13 Antarctic Expedition had failed to collect an intact adult Antarctic toothfish, finding only a large adult floating, in an ice hole, without its head. Scott's team decided that since the big fish had been decapitated by a predator, the specimen had little scientific value, so rather than preserve the fish for science, they ate it.

Scott's men surely enjoyed the Antarctic toothfish. The fresh fish would have been a wonderful respite from more conventional British rations supplemented with seal or penguin. Art DeVries periodically hosted an invitation-only sashimi party in his McMurdo laboratory where the delicious cheek meat of a toothfish that had donated its organs for science was sliced thin and served with wasabi, fresh ginger, and soy sauce. The balance of Art's toothfish was donated to the station's galley, where it was baked and served as a popular entree for all those at the station. While I was at McMurdo in the 1980s and 1990s, Art regularly made a Thanksgiving donation of a big toothfish to the galley cooks, and the fish would appear on the buffet line, stuffed and festively garnished like a holiday turkey. John Pearse gave the intact toothfish that he and the Weddell seal had collected to his colleague, fish physiologist Donald Wohlschlag, who presumably found a permanent home for the fish in the collections of the Smithsonian National Museum of Natural History in Washington, D.C.

"Shouldn't be much longer," said Art, awakening me from the trance-inducing sounds of the winch reeling line. I stood and edged up to the ice hole. The seawater in McMurdo Sound is astoundingly clear, and my fishing expedition with Art occurred well before the plankton bloom that temporarily clouds the water for several weeks in the late austral summer. Looking down through the ice hole, I could see well over a hundred feet into the dark-blue water. "There," said one of the fishing technicians. The first hook appeared below us, this one empty of bait. Several baited hooks followed. "Fish on!" called the technician, and as Art slowed the winch, we crowded in to take a look. The torpedo shape of a giant Antarctic toothfish that had to be close to a hundred pounds appeared out of the depths. As the big head of the mottled gray fish broke the water's surface, it peered up at us with large circular brown eyes and a prehistoric toothy grin.

Art stopped the winch, and with the fish still mostly submerged, the two fishing techs managed to hold the creature and gently work the hook free from the large protruding lower jaw. Grasping each side of the head by the gill covers, they hoisted the big fish out of the water and slid it into a V-trough kept cold on the uninsulated fish-hut floor. One of the technicians leaned into the ice hole and soaked a cloth with cold seawater and then laid the cloth over the fish's eyes. "If we were keeping this fish for antifreeze work, we'd load it into a wooden 'fish coffin' and take it back to a fish tank in the aquarium building," explained one of Art's technicians. Instead, Art and the two fishing technicians weighed the big fish on a scale, measured its length and girth, and then attached a Floy dart identification tag to the second dorsal fin, which was then backed up with a second tail-locking tag. Lastly, the toothfish was injected with a solution of tetracycline that deposited a fluorescent ring in the fish's otolith, a flat circular bone in the fish's inner ear. Fish otoliths produce annual growth rings, much like rings on a tree trunk, that can be used to age an individual. I've used tetracycline in my own research to mark the growth rings of skeletons of sea urchins in California and Antarctica. If a fish is later recaptured, the scientists can count the number of annual rings deposited in the otolith since the fluorescent tetracycline injection, which makes it possible to estimate growth over a known period of time. No longer than five minutes after being hoisted up through the ice hole, the work on the Antarctic toothfish was complete, and the two fishing technicians gently lifted the fish up by its gill covers and slid it back into the icy sea. By the end of the morning, I had watched Art and his team repeat the tag-and-release process with three more big toothfish that surfaced on the line.

Art's beloved Antarctic toothfish, the fish whose antifreeze brought him international fame and whose population biology has been the focus of countless days, weeks, months, years, and decades of study, has essentially disappeared from McMurdo Sound. Art's population study began in 1971, and over the next thirty-three years, he and his team caught, tagged, and released more than four thousand Antarctic toothfish. During that time, seventeen of the tagged fish were recaught, a small number but sufficient to indicate a resident population or at least returning migrants moving back through the sound. For the first twenty-five years of the study, the numbers of toothfish Art's team caught were plentiful, each year ranging from two hundred to five hundred fish with many large adults. But something happened in the mid-1990s. Despite Art's team fishing just as long and hard as ever, the numbers of caught fish began to decline. Suspiciously, the drop in the numbers of fish Art's team hoisted each day coincided with the initiation of a commercial Antarctic toothfish fishery approved by the Commission for the Conservation of Antarctic Marine Living Resources (CCAMLR). These commercial fishing operations in the Ross Sea and McMurdo Sound, mostly carried out by fishers based in New Zealand, continue to this day. By the austral summer of 2003, Art and his team were catching very few fish, and in the years that followed, not a single adult was caught. With the Antarctic toothfish virtually gone, Art aborted his tag-and-release program in McMurdo Sound.

Antarctic fish biologists, including the world's authority, Joseph Eastman, a professor at Ohio University, suspect that the initiation of the commercial fishery for Antarctic toothfish in the Ross Sea and McMurdo Sound is responsible for the disappearance of Art's fish. This fact is not particularly surprising when the life history of Antarctic toothfish is considered by fisheries experts. Sustainable fisheries require target species that grow rapidly to reproductive maturity and produce large numbers of viable offspring. Fish biologists have long known that Antarctic toothfish take a very long time to become reproductive and that almost nothing is known about how many offspring they produce or their rates of larval and juvenile survival. Accordingly, most fisheries biologists would consider Antarctic toothfish too big a risk for a fishery. In a 2008 publication directed at CCAMLR, Art DeVries and fellow Antarctic biologists David Ainley and Grant Ballard posited that the total allowable catch of Antarctic toothfish should be greatly reduced and that the fishery in the Ross Sea should cease entirely until the population in McMurdo Sound recovers.[5] The three biologists also recommended a long-term program to monitor the effects of the Antarctic toothfish fishery on the marine ecosystem. Their own observations suggested that as numbers of Antarctic toothfish plummeted in McMurdo Sound so did the numbers of one of the fish's key predators, killer whales. At the same time, the prevalence of silverfish, one of the Antarctic toothfish's favorite prey, had greatly increased in the diets of Adélie penguins. Ecologists call such dramatic shifts in who-eats-whom following the removal of an important predator *trophic cascades*. Such cascades can dramatically alter marine ecosystems. If the depletion of Antarctic toothfish can rewrite aspects of the marine ecology of McMurdo Sound, then similar consideration should be given to the ecosystem-level impacts of the fisheries that have decimated populations of the related Patagonia toothfish.

Sometimes names matter. The Antarctic toothfish's closest cousin, the Patagonia toothfish (*Dissostichus eleginoides*), is found in deep waters of the southern Atlantic, Pacific, and Indian Oceans, as well as in the Southern Ocean. It exploded on seafood markets in 1977 after its trade name was ingeniously changed by fish wholesaler Lee Lantz.[6] Lee took the distasteful sounding "Patagonia toothfish" and turned it into the savory "Chilean sea bass." Chefs loved the flaky white fillets. In 2001, Chilean sea bass was named *Bon Appétit* magazine's Dish of the Year. This was unfortunate. Much like its cousin the Antarctic toothfish, the Patagonia toothfish has the attributes of a species vulnerable to overfishing: late reproductive maturity (ten to twenty years) and long life (up to fifty years). Moreover, glaring gaps in knowledge of the fish's early life history remain. In a news report in a 2011 issue of *Nature*, Stanford professor Stephen Palumbi remarked that harvesting Patagonia toothfish "is not like fishing for fish—it's almost like logging for trees."[7] Palumbi's point was that the fish's slow growth makes it similar to trees in a cultivated forest, much like the managed longleaf pine forests where I live in Alabama, which require upward of thirty-five years to mature.

By the mid-1990s, increased market demand for Patagonia toothfish drove up prices so high that illegal, unregulated fisheries sprung up around the globe. Remote regions in the southern Indian Ocean were particularly attractive to poachers. In 2002, the National Environmental Trust in Washington, D.C. reported that for every ton of Chilean sea bass caught legally, there were five or six more tons caught illegally. At the same time, toothfish catches declined.

Heeding the warnings that a major fishery was on the brink of collapse, many restaurants removed Chilean sea bass from menus, and some fish wholesalers stopped selling Chilean sea bass or marketed only toothfish caught in geographic regions deemed sustainable by the Marine Stewardship Council (MSC), an international nonprofit organization that promotes sustainable fishing. How representatives of the MSC estimate sustainable populations of Patagonia toothfish in the absence of knowledge of their early life history, while keenly aware of their slow reproduction and growth, is open to debate.

A secondary consequence of the growth of the Antarctic and Patagonia toothfish fishing industry was the transition of a fishery that had historically relied on trawl nets to a fishery primarily employing longline fishing tactics. This change occurred because trawls generally netted smaller sizes of toothfish, while toothfish hooked by longlines were, on average, bigger. Longlines, as their name implies, can be very long, some measuring up to sixty-two miles. An individual line may be provisioned with as many as thirty thousand hooks. Unfortunately, baited longlines, unlike nets, also catch seabirds. Over the past eight years, I have helped lead a philanthropic climate change–themed expedition cruise to the Antarctic Peninsula for the travel company Abercrombie & Kent. Two fellow expedition biologists, ornithologists Patricia Silva and Marco Favero, give a compelling presentation about the toll that longline fishing imparts on threatened albatross. These seabirds, some with wingspans of ten feet, soar for days over the oceans in search of food for their young. Sadly, albatross and other seabirds chase the longline baits, and if hooked or tangled, they drown as the weighted lines sink.[8] Companies that longline fish for Antarctic and Patagonia toothfish are required to follow international guidelines to reduce the impacts on seabirds. These guidelines include limiting line deployments to the austral winter when seabirds are less apt to be feeding, deploying lines at night, attaching heavier weights to sink the lines rapidly, and employing various visual and sound devices on the lines and fishing vessels to scare away the birds. Unfortunately for the industry, these regulations reduce the catch of toothfish and are difficult to enforce. Marco and Patricia, now married, continue to raise both public awareness and funds to help reduce the use of longlines, enforce current regulations, and develop new longline technologies to better protect seabirds. Ultimately, with fewer longlines deployed in the Southern Ocean, a time may come when a fish biologist will again hoist a giant Antarctic toothfish from the waters of McMurdo Sound.

The 250-foot R.V. Laurence M. Gould, the U.S. National Science Foundation's (NSF's) "big orange taxi," rounded the southwestern end of Anvers Island, having successfully transited the Drake Passage between South America and the Antarctic Peninsula, passed through the South Shetland Islands, and sailed south to the Palmer Archipelago via the protected waters of the Gerlache Strait. After three and a half days at sea, I was eager to get my first glimpse of the U.S. Palmer Station.[9] After all, seasoned field technicians and scientists I had met at McMurdo Station called the environs of Palmer Station the "French Riviera" of Antarctica. As we rounded Bonaparte Point and its welcoming three-foot-high plastic flamingo, I leaned against the ship's railing, inhaled the fresh ice-cold air, and watched a tiny cluster of navy-blue buildings, nestled snugly below the Marr Glacier, appear in the distance. The landscape was stunning. Above the glacier, the Marr Ice Piedmont swept northwest, blanketing the entire thirty-eight-mile length of Anvers Island, topped with 9,055-foot, pyramid-shaped Mount Français. Off to the southeast, the spine of the same mountain range that is the Andes, the famous mountain chain reemerging from the Drake Passage to span the entire 832-mile length of the Antarctic Peninsula, dominated the landscape. I didn't know it in the austral fall of 2000, but this station and its support personnel were to provide the infrastructure, technical know-how, and community goodwill to support my collaborative research program to the present day with colleagues Chuck Amsler and Bill Baker.

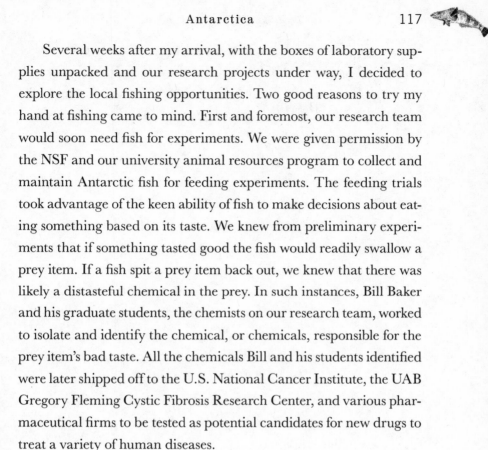

Several weeks after my arrival, with the boxes of laboratory supplies unpacked and our research projects under way, I decided to
explore the local fishing opportunities. Two good reasons to try my
hand at fishing came to mind. First and foremost, our research team
would soon need fish for experiments. We were given permission by
the NSF and our university animal resources program to collect and
maintain Antarctic fish for feeding experiments. The feeding trials
took advantage of the keen ability of fish to make decisions about eating something based on its taste. We knew from preliminary experiments that if something tasted good the fish would readily swallow a
prey item. If a fish spit a prey item back out, we knew that there was
likely a distasteful chemical in the prey. In such instances, Bill Baker
and his graduate students, the chemists on our research team, worked
to isolate and identify the chemical, or chemicals, responsible for the
prey item's bad taste. All the chemicals Bill and his students identified
were later shipped off to the U.S. National Cancer Institute, the UAB
Gregory Fleming Cystic Fibrosis Research Center, and various phar-
maceutical firms to be tested as potential candidates for new drugs to
treat a variety of human diseases.

The other reason I wanted to go fishing was because I love to fish.
Outside of helping Art use a gas winch to haul up four giant Antarctic
toothfish in McMurdo Sound, I'd yet to catch a fish in Antarctica on
a rod and reel. Time to check out the fishing gear I'd seen stacked in
a corner of the aquarium building: two six-foot poles and two much
shorter poles, each no more than a puzzling two and a half feet in
length. The fishing poles and their casting reels turned out to be in
various states of disrepair. The tackle was similarly worn out, the line
on the reels old and frayed, and the single pole with tackle sported a
rusty nickel-sized fishing hook and a lead weight tied crudely a foot
above the hook. Oddly, someone had tied a piece of faded red yarn
just above the crusty hook, an inch and a half of yarn dangling off
either side. I poked around looking for more tackle and came across
a few odds and ends in a nearby cabinet drawer—not much to speak

of except a few hooks, a couple of fishing weights, an ancient spool of ten-pound test line, and bits and pieces of colored yarn.

"Yep, people either fish in the housing of the seawater intake or off the pier where the ship docks," said Rob Edwards, the Palmer Station lab manager.

"What do they use for bait?" I asked.

"Colored yarn," Rob answered. The fish bite on yarn? "Yep," he said again, smiling. I headed back to the aquarium building and picked out one of the short, stubby rods. Rod in hand, I selected a piece of red yarn from the drawer, snipped off a three-inch section, and cinched the yarn in the middle just above the hook. With my miniature fishing pole rigged, I retrieved a five-gallon plastic bucket stored in the aquarium building. Leaving the fishing gear and bucket in the aquarium building, I headed to the biolab mudroom where a long line of orange hooded jackets hung. Sliding the jackets apart, I found one that fit and bounded up the stairs to my small second-floor dorm-style room where I tucked a pair of gloves, a beanie, and sunglasses in the pockets of the jacket and pulled on rubber knee-high work boots.

Stepping out the door of the aquarium building, I headed across the deck and down a set of metal stairs to a boulder-strewn path that led to the station's seawater intake on the edge of Arthur Harbor. The seawater intake pipe dropped through the housing to the seafloor before extending 140 feet offshore. The pipe provided running seawater for the tanks in the aquarium building and, following desalination, all of the station's drinking water. Unfortunately, the intake pipe was prone to being crushed by car-sized icebergs, or growlers, that calved off the Marr Glacier and were carried by currents along the shoreline like bowling balls in a bowling alley. Accordingly, a stout wooden housing extended offshore, encasing the pipe. Near the point where the pipe entered the housing, a hatch door opened to a ladder descending down to a wooden platform that rested just above the high-tide mark. The platform provided space for a person to sit and, off the shore side of the platform, a place to drop a line.

I climbed down the ladder and set the bucket and rod on the corner of the platform and flicked on the bare lightbulb. Like marbles in a tin can, the grating sound of ice moving back and forth over the rocky shore was amplified inside my makeshift fish hut. Lying on the platform, I peered into the shallow water. There were no signs of fish, just drift algae and a few grazing limpets, quarter-sized flattened snails with shells shaped like Asian fishing hats. Sitting up, I picked up the short fishing pole, a perfect length for such cramped quarters, and pulled the yarned hook free from its eyelet. Holding the rod tip above the water, I popped the release on the casting reel and hand-fed line until the hook reached the seafloor. Jigging the rod up and down about eight inches, I watched red yarn wiggle. Suddenly, the yarn disappeared and a sharp tug was followed by tail wags. The vigor of the initial fight surprised me, given the frigid water, but as suddenly as it started, it ended, the fish spent. I lifted the line from the water and admired the fish's coloration, a striking transition from brownish-green back to yellow underbelly, and I gently removed the hook from its lower lip. The fourteen-inch yellow rock-cod, my first Antarctic catch, found its way into a bucket of freshly dipped seawater.

The common names yellow rock-cod, yellowbelly rock-cod, and black rock-cod are being phased out, not because the fish is imperiled but because its common names are passé. As with the giant Antarctic cod, the term *cod* was misappropriated. Bill Detrich, a leading Antarctic fish biologist and an expert on *Notothenia coriiceps*,[10] is promoting a new common name for the fish, the "bullhead notothen," a bit of a mouthful, but accurate. *Bullhead*, because if asked to describe the fish, most would first mention its bull-shaped head, and *notothen* because this is an easy abbreviation of Nototheniidae, the taxonomic family that encompasses the vast majority of Antarctic fish and to which this species belongs. Bullhead notothen live mostly on shallow Antarctic seafloors but are also found down to depths of about six hundred feet. The fish frequent the dense forests of macroalgae near Palmer Station, and Bill and Chuck and other divers on our Palmer team periodically hand-collect them when diving. The bullhead no-tothen perch next to rocks and among holdfasts of macroalgae, their dark mottled colors making them difficult to spot as they blend with their background. A bull-shaped head comes in handy as the big skull supports an immense jaw used to consume just about anything. In addition to amphipods, isopods, polychaete worms, krill, and other assorted invertebrates and small fish, like sea cows, the fish also graze on those macroalgae that are not chemically defended. One of our postdoctoral fellows, Katrin Iken, now a professor in the Marine Sciences Institute at the University of Alaska Fairbanks, used bullhead notothen in her feeding experiments at Palmer Station. Katrin maintained about ten fish at a time in individual tanks. She soon had each fish named, something best left to experimental animals like Katrin's fish, which will eventually be released back into the wild. One of her favorite fish acted like a puppy, surfacing enthusiastically with its mouth open at feeding time and ready to eat anything. Katrin named that one after one of our graduate students who was always hungry.

At various times over the past fourteen years, our Palmer research team needed fairly large numbers of bullhead notothen to carry out taste tests. When fish were in demand, Maggie Amsler, Chuck's wife and a marine biologist whose extensive research career in Antarctica makes her particularly accomplished among women polar scientists, sprang into action and organized a Palmer Station Fishing Derby. The derby Maggie organized in May 2004 took place over a weekend, with the winner promised not only the satisfaction of supporting science but also a fine bottle of wine. Just about everyone on station tried their luck with hook and line, and a variety of artificial and natural baits were employed by the fishers. Some used brightly colored yarns as jigs; others searched the rocky shore at low tide for limpets. The fresh meat scooped from the shell held firmly to the hook, and its scent attracted fish. In the end, Marge, our station chef, won the fishing derby by landing a record nine keepers off the station pier. In addition to winning the prized bottle of wine, Marge proudly took home a certificate naming her the Palmer Station Fisherwoman of the 2004 Austral Winter. Our research group was delighted that Marge was so pleased to be recognized at the fishing derby. Next to the power generator operator, the chef is probably the most important person to keep happy at a remote Antarctic field station.

As I discussed in my recent book *Lost Antarctica: Adventures in a Disappearing Land,*[11] the Antarctic Peninsula is arguably the most rapidly warming region of our planet. Measurements made at Vernadsky, the Ukrainian research station twenty miles south of Palmer Station, indicate that over the past sixty years, average midwinter air temperatures along the western Antarctic Peninsula have risen ten degrees Fahrenheit. Sea temperatures are also rising, causing a depletion of annual sea ice. Marine life whose ecology is intimately associated with the disappearing sea ice—including Adélie penguins, Weddell and leopard seals, and krill—are at particular risk. Furthermore, Antarctic fish, including the bullhead notothen used in our research, are also susceptible to the impacts of warming temperatures. Fish that live in polar seas are considered stenothermal, a term that describes a capacity to tolerate only a small range of temperatures. In contrast, eurythermal fish can handle wide fluctuations in temperature. Antarctic fish biologists such as expert Joe Eastman are unsure what the final outcome will be for Antarctic fish when it comes to climate warming, although Joe believes there is reason for concern. According to Joe, when it comes to Antarctica, "it's one of the big scientific questions of the day."

So far, experiments that have exposed Antarctic fish to gradually warming temperatures have been equivocal. Joe suspects that Antarctic fish that developed antifreezes are in part what they are today because of our Earth's long history of climate change. "Over the last ten million years, the ice sheets periodically bulldozed the Antarctic shelf, and there was [also] periodic warming of ice shelves and sea ice," Joe explained. "Disruption promotes ecological opportunity and evolution," he continued. Yet Joe is concerned that Antarctic fish may simply have become too good, too specialized, at living in ice-cold water, to survive warming. "Antarctic fish have lost their heat-shock proteins (proteins, induced by heat, that protect other proteins from being damaged), and their enzyme systems have been slimmed down under constantly cold conditions," Joe told me in an e-mail. Along the same lines, some Antarctic fish known as icefishes (family Channichthyidae) have lost the oxygen-carrying pigment hemoglobin from their blood. Joe is particularly concerned for the future of this group of Antarctic fish: "I see the icefishes as more vulnerable than the red-blooded species to the decreased oxygen content of warming waters." As a polar marine biologist, I too worry that the reacquisition of such essential biochemical elements as heat-shock proteins, robust enzyme systems, and oxygen-carrying pigments will require much longer periods of time than are available given the current rate of anthropogenic-driven climate warming. For the first time in our Earth's history, polar environments are warming on a time scale measured in decades rather than millennia.

Ocean acidification, the direct result of the world's oceans having absorbed a third of the atmospheric carbon dioxide released from the combustion of fossil fuels, will similarly challenge Antarctic fish.[12] Since the onset of the Industrial Revolution, our oceans have on average become 30 percent more acidic. The chemical process of ocean acidification is quite simple. When carbon dioxide dissolves in seawater, it forms carbonic acid that contributes to the growing acidity of the sea and reduces the availability of carbonate ions, robbing marine organisms of the calcite and aragonite building blocks they use to sustain, produce, and repair their shells and skeletons. Antarctica is the canary in the coal mine when it comes to ocean acidification because the temperature of the Southern Ocean is colder than elsewhere[13] and the colder the water, the easier it is for carbon dioxide to dissolve in seawater. Moreover, Antarctic marine organisms are uniquely at risk because their shells are thin and weakly calcified, making them more prone to ocean acidification. The preponderance of thin shells may be the result of the energetic cost of producing a shell, a cost that is a little higher in cold water than in temperate or tropical waters. But more likely, the thin shells are the result of Antarctic marine organisms living in an environment where predators capable of crushing shells don't occur.[14] No sharks and few skates exist in Antarctic waters, and fish that have adapted to Antarctic waters lack the powerful crushing jaws boasted by those in temperate and tropical seas. You won't hear parrotfish crunching a meal of hard coral as you do when snorkeling over a reef in the Bahamas. Also, no predators with claws can be found, not a single lobster or crab. With no crushing predators, clams and snails and other Antarctic marine invertebrates haven't evolved the thick, heavy, ornamented shells that litter the beaches of Florida, California, France, or New Zealand. Ironically, this has left them vulnerable to ocean acidification.

Studies on the impacts of ocean acidification on fish in warmer climes reveal startling news. In a particularly poignant study, juvenile clown fish, the bright-orange, white-banded fish that live in association with sea anemones on tropical coral reefs and were made famous in Disney's *Finding Nemo,* lose their sense of smell and become disoriented when exposed to near-future conditions of ocean acidification.[15] This is serious because the larvae of clown fish develop at sea, and juveniles must employ their keen sense of smell to locate a home reef. In a related study, scientists found that clown fish exposed to ocean acidification lose their ability to respond to the sounds of predators. In this ingenious study, the sounds of reef fish and shrimp that prey on small clown fish were recorded. Juvenile clown fish were placed in a tube and given a choice of swimming toward or away from the predator sounds emanating from one end of the tube. Most of the fish in seawater with current levels of ocean acidification swam away from the sounds of predators. But when clown fish were exposed to seawater with levels of ocean acidification expected to occur by the end of the century, the fish lost their ability to avoid predators, moving indiscriminately in either direction within the tube. Scientists are concerned. On September 2, 2014, the U.S. National Marine Fisheries Service announced that the clown fish may warrant protection under the U.S. Endangered Species Act because of growing threats, including the stress of ocean acidification. In yet another coral reef fish, the spiny damselfish, scientists found that near-future levels of ocean acidification altered a key brain neurotransmitter known as gamma-aminobutyric acid, which is involved in a number of neurological processes, including the visual system.[16] With exposure to elevated ocean acidification, the visual acuity of the damselfish was reduced, rendering fish less capable of reacting to rapid visual events such as a predator attack. Damselfish can only hope that predatory fish prove similarly impaired by ocean acidification.

Antarctic fish have yet to be tested to see if ocean acidification impedes their sense of smell, hearing, or sight. The few studies of ocean acidification carried out to date on Antarctic fish have focused on the cellular level and combined possible interactive effects of warming and ocean acidification. These studies suggest that Antarctic fish do have a limited cellular ability to acclimate to warming and ocean acidification but that some species of fish will fare better than others. What may prove more challenging to Antarctic fish are the impacts of ocean acidification on their prey. Krill, the shrimplike invertebrates that can be important to fish diets and that are key components of the diets of penguins, seals, and whales, are threatened by ocean acidification. A 2011 study led by So Kawaguchi, a krill biologist at the Australian Antarctic Division in Kingston, Tasmania, found that levels of ocean acidification that are projected to occur in deep Antarctic seas by the year 2100 caused serious abnormalities and prevented hatching in 90 percent of the krill embryos tested.[17] And in a 2013 paper, which appeared in the prestigious journal *Nature Climate Change*,[18] Kawaguchi and his colleagues predicted that unless carbon dioxide emissions are mitigated, levels of ocean acidification in the Southern Ocean will collapse krill populations with "dire consequences for the entire ecosystem." Another prey of Antarctic fish, and also Arctic fish, are pteropods, or "sea butterflies." Sea butterflies are tiny swimming planktonic snails and are so numerous they play an important role in the cycling of carbon in the world's oceans.

They exist in two styles, shelled and naked. Our chemical ecology research team found that naked Antarctic sea butterflies contain distasteful chemicals that protect them from fish predators. But shelled sea butterflies, whose shells are made from the mineral aragonite, lack chemical defenses and can be important components of polar fish diets. For example, shelled sea butterflies were found to be key to growth and survival of juvenile humpback salmon in Prince William Sound, Alaska. In Antarctic seas, the early life stages of many notothenioid fish include shelled sea butterflies in their diets. And like krill, shelled sea butterflies are at risk from the growing impacts of ocean acidification. In 2012, an article published in the top-tier journal *Nature Geoscience*[19] by a team of European and American scientists reported for the first time that populations of Antarctic sea butterflies from various regions of the upper six hundred feet of the Southern Ocean have severely pitted shells, a sure sign that these animals are, both literally and figuratively, dissolving away. The authors of the article predict that as carbon dioxide absorption by surface waters increases as a result of human activities, "the upper ocean regions where aragonite-shelled organisms are affected by dissolution are likely to expand." How will the loss of shelled sea butterflies influence the success of juvenile fish that rely on them for food? Time will tell.

6

NEW ZEALAND

Rainbow Trout

L uke, *my fourteen-year-old son, held out his beet-red* hands so I could massage warmth back into them. "They hurt!" he proclaimed, still anxious to once again lower his baited hand line despite the ice-cold waters of Halfmoon Bay. We were on Stewart Island, or Rakiura ("glowing skies") in the Maori language, for a weekend getaway from the carriage house we'd rented adjacent to a bed and breakfast in Dunedin, a picturesque city perched on the southeastern coast of the South Island of New Zealand. It was austral spring in 2007, and our family was living in New Zealand while I was on a three-month research sabbatical at the Portobello Marine Laboratory. I was studying the effects of different foods on growth in the edible sea urchin, *Evichinus chloroticus*. The project was part of a government-funded aquaculture program led by my New Zealand colleague Mike Barker. My research involved coming up with fortified diets to make sea urchins produce lots of tasty "caviar."

Our family's voyage to Stewart Island had been more challenging than we had anticipated. We drove our leased sedan down from Dunedin to the port town of Bluff, where we spent the night at Land's End, a well-manicured hotel with a stunning view of Oyster Cove. Next to the hotel, the Motupohue Scenic Reserve sat with a coastal hiking trail that wound along a rocky intertidal sprinkled with algae-laden tide pools. I didn't know much about our ferry ride to Stewart Island the next morning. Our Rakiura National Park brochure simply read, "Experience Foveaux Strait in comfort and style on board our express catamarans." Arriving at the Bluff Visitor Terminal forty-five minutes before our scheduled departure, we leaned into a blustery, cold wind as we made our way to the dock to pick up our reserved ferry tickets. Rounding the terminal, I first glimpsed the "express catamaran." This was no ordinary ferry, and as we were soon to learn, this was no ordinary body of water.

The Foveaux Strait was discovered in 1804 by Captain Owen Smith, an American sealer. Smith shared the news of his discovery with an aide to the governor of New South Wales, a Major Joseph Foveaux, who somehow managed to supersede the governor in the naming of the strait. The water is shallow, ten to fifteen fathoms on average, and a strong persistent current flows eastward at three or more knots. The winds, in contrast, blow westerly, and in a storm-prone region accentuated by its proximity to Antarctica, winds are often gale force (defined by the U.S. National Weather Service as 39 to 54 mph). The combination of shallow water and a strong directional current with an opposing wind adds up to a seaborne roller coaster. In 1823, French naval officer Jules de Blosseville wrote, "Whirlpools are frequently to be met and the position is one of great peril when the directions of the waves are in contrary to that of the wind." Over a fourteen-year span (1998 to 2012), twenty-three sailors lost their lives to the Foveaux Strait, including six muttonbirders (hunters of sooty shearwaters, a dark-chocolate-brown medium-to-large seabird) who collectively drowned when their trawler sank in 2006. The list of ships that sank in the strait in the latter half of the nineteenth century is impressive: *Jack Frost* (1886), *Laughing Water* (1870), *Halcyon* (1877), *Helen and Jane* (1879), *Arrow* (1881), *Little Denham* (1883), *Marie Ange* (1884), *Champion* (1885), *Nellie* (1888), *Camille* (1892), *Philadelphia* (1898), and *Aparima* (1899). The historical records of these ill-fated barques, schooners, steamers, cutters, ketches, and brigantines share a dire terminology. Phrases like "dragged her anchors," "carried out to sea," "washed overboard," "threw her on to the reef," "heavy seas breaking on board," "completely broken up," "all hands bailed and pumped to no avail," and "never seen or heard of again" litter the reports.

Had I known about the nautical history and oceanography of the Foveaux Strait, I wouldn't have been quite so surprised by the design of the thirty-foot catamaran: rows of individual seats with seat belts, an abundance of seasickness bags, and an engine and navigational console with enough gauges, levers, switches, and handles to outfit

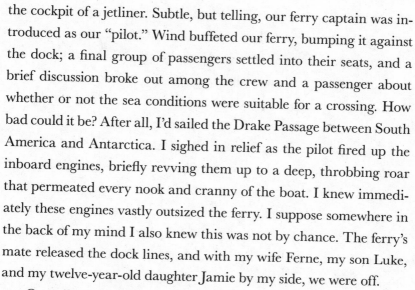

the cockpit of a jetliner. Subtle, but telling, our ferry captain was introduced as our "pilot." Wind buffeted our ferry, bumping it against the dock; a final group of passengers settled into their seats, and a brief discussion broke out among the crew and a passenger about whether or not the sea conditions were suitable for a crossing. How bad could it be? After all, I'd sailed the Drake Passage between South America and Antarctica. I sighed in relief as the pilot fired up the inboard engines, briefly revving them up to a deep, throbbing roar that permeated every nook and cranny of the boat. I knew immediately these engines vastly outsized the ferry. I suppose somewhere in the back of my mind I also knew this was not by chance. The ferry's mate released the dock lines, and with my wife Ferne, my son Luke, and my twelve-year-old daughter Jamie by my side, we were off.

Our pilot had no intention of sitting on his swivel stool. He remained upright in front of the instrument console with legs slightly spread, feet planted, body braced so as to best lean into the sea, reminiscent of a seasoned naval officer. Leaving Bluff behind, the initial two- to three-foot cross-swell allowed the pilot to combine the power of big engines with the sheer weight of the boat to set a course and speed that pushed us through, rather than over, the waves. This tactic moderated the motion in the passenger cabin, yet we hadn't been under way for more than ten minutes before the first passenger heaved loudly into a seasickness bag. The response of the stewards was swift and practiced, moving to the sick passenger to offer comfort and assistance. But no amount of goodwill and care can forestall the inevitable. As every deep-sea fisher knows well, once someone lets it go, the chain reaction is as predictable as rain falling on Seattle. By the time the second passenger heaved, the winds had strengthened and the cross-swells had increased to four to five feet. As the swell increased, the time lag, or "period," between the waves decreased. This was unlike any swell I had encountered boating or surfing. Wave followed wave, so immediate in time and space that there wasn't a measurable period. The pilot shifted to gunning the big inboard engines to power the catamaran up the face of a swell at a speed and angle that balanced safety with keeping us on course. Once we reached each wave's crest, the pilot backed off the big engines, guided the catamaran in a controlled slide down the back side and across the split-second trough, then gunned the boat back up the face of the next wave. He was as absorbed in controlling his vessel as an astronaut landing a manned spacecraft on the moon.

Ferne and Jamie didn't have the inherent resilience to motion sickness that Luke and I enjoyed. By now, both were feeling sick and fearful, and the gyroscopic view of big waves outside the panoramic windows wasn't helping matters. Ferne put her arm around Jamie, hugging her close. Luke, on the other hand, was having the time of his life. "This is better than a roller coaster," he said, beaming at me, blissfully ignorant of my increasing anxiety. By the time we were halfway across the Foveaux Strait, the swells had peaked at about ten feet, and a full third of the twenty-five passengers had found their seasickness bags. Later, perusing travel blogs written by tourists who had taken the express catamaran to Stewart Island, I came across a half-serious commentary about crossing the strait that read, "Apparently there have been times when the passengers have been lashed to the bulkheads for their own safety."

The brochure in the tourist office in the port village of Oban on Stewart Island advertised offshore boating trips featuring "traditional hand-line" fishing. I was intrigued. I'd been out on any number of half- or full-day "party boats," some with as many as a hundred people on board. The trips had all been rod-centric; customers were each provided stout five- or six-foot fishing rods with twenty- or thirty-pound line strung on durable bait-casting reels. The crews on these party boats, after briefing passengers about life jackets, what not to flush down the sea toilets, and how best to throw up over the railing, spent most of their time untangling fishing lines wrapped on rod eyelets and rod tips, negotiating "fish-on" rod and line crossings and associated ill tempers, and unraveling countless rat's nests from reel spools. Hand lining might offer a welcome reprieve from party boats. In typical friendly Kiwi (New Zealander) fashion, the young

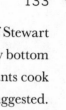

man in the tourist office explained that hand-line fishing off Stewart Island meant catching lots of blue cod, an abundant and tasty bottom fish. We might even consider having one of the local restaurants cook up our fresh fillets for dinner, the tourist office employee suggested. I couldn't resist the temptation to try something novel yet rooted in tradition. With Ferne and Jamie still recovering from the ferry crossing, I reserved a spot for Luke and me on the next morning's half-day hand-line fishing trip.

Luke and I arrived at the boat dock in waterproof hooded jackets, jeans, sunglasses, and, considering New Zealand's proximity to the hole in the ozone, plenty of sunscreen. A light wind checkered the bay's surface waters. The captain and first mate welcomed us and four others and briefed us on boat safety. The thirty-foot fishing boat, painted blue and white, was outfitted for both recreational and commercial fishing. The open back deck was enclosed by a waist-high safety railing, and a sturdy, centrally located work table provided plenty of surface area for a stack of yellow Anton's Ltd plastic bins, each bin containing coils of tightly woven, light-blue, eighth-of-an-inch-diameter fishing rope that served as our hand lines. An avocado-green cooler propped against the back rail seemed a likely repository for fish. Aft, the pilot's cabin adjoined a room with seats for passengers, and a door opened out to the back fishing deck. Invited by the captain to board, Luke and I stowed our day packs, laden with cameras and snacks, in the cabin and settled in for the short thirty-minute cruise to our first fishing site at the mouth of Halfmoon Bay.

Offshore, bracing sea air filled our lungs, and one-foot swells gently rocked our boat and hinted at a splendid, fishable morning. Arriving at the first of what would turn out to be a host of different fishing sites, the captain prompted his first mate to drop anchor in about a hundred feet of water. Luke and I, along with our other four fishing guests, gathered on the open back deck to hear a briefing by the captain on the art and science of hand lining. The fishing setups were relatively simple in design. A nickel-sized hook with a two-inch shank was tied off to a sturdy metal ring the circumference of a quarter. Next, an eight-inch section of bright-yellow, quarter-inch braided nylon rope was tied off to the metal ring and to a hole drilled in the end of a rectangular, six-inch-long, eighth-inch-thick metal bar that served as a generous fishing weight. A foot-and-a-half-long yellow nylon rope was attached to the other end of the metal bar and tied off to the light-blue fishing line.

Hand-line fishing consisted of baiting the hook with a chunk of cut bait (raw squid), strategically positioning the coils of fishing line at one's feet (with the line's end secured to the boat), and, holding the fishing line in one hand, allowing the baited line to sink to the bottom in a hand-controlled release. When the line went slack, the bait was on the bottom. After we retrieved a foot of line, the bait dangled just above the seafloor. More so than when using a rod, the feel of a blue cod biting the bait was obvious. A quick upward jerk of the hand line set the hook. Cod were then retrieved in a hand-over-hand motion, making sure the line coiled loosely, and tangle-free, on the deck. The captain or mate was responsible for removing our fish from the hooks and quickly rebaiting lines. We were ready, but before we dropped lines, the captain and his mate demonstrated the hand-line technique by deploying their own hand lines, which was impressive. Their hand and arm motions were practiced, rapid, and smooth, and in less than two minutes, the captain and mate had each tossed a flopping sixteen-inch blue cod in the bottom of a plastic bin, ready to be cleaned, filleted, and packed into ziplock bags for storage in the iced cooler. "Drop lines," said the captain, standing at the back railing against a sky full of eager seagulls.

My hand line slid between thumb and forefinger and, before I could have recited the alphabet, went slack. I lifted my bait a foot off the seafloor and cinched the line tight between my fingers. Bites were instantaneous: *tappity-tap, tap, tug, tap, tap, tug.* In that timeless reflex of fishers, I yanked line and felt *bumpity-bump, bump*—hooked. I glanced over at Luke. He was into his first cod, lifting right arm over left arm. "Watch your line," I said, enjoying the paternal satisfaction of a father-son catch. "Coil the line behind your feet so it doesn't tangle when you're on to your next fish." We hand-pulled struggling, shiny blue cod over the rail and lowered the fish to the deck, where the mate removed the hooks and rebaited our lines then back our hand lines went, into the deep. This was definitely not "sit and wait" fishing.

Two scenarios could have prompted the captain to hoist anchor: first, if upon arrival at a new fishing spot the captain or mate failed to land a cod within a minute's time; second, if the frenetic pace of fish hoisted from the sea began to slow. This fast-paced fishing was heaven for an impatient fourteen-year-old. Luke couldn't have been happier, hauling up fish after fish, despite freezing hands. I've had fishing buddies who, like Luke, had to be catching fish. They pulled their bass boats up to a lake bank, and if their crank bait or plastic worm didn't produce within five minutes, they were on the move; if a speckled trout hadn't graced their skiff after ten casts, time to go; if a dry fly didn't yield an immediate swirl, time to tie on a wet fly. Others I have fished with have extreme patience, reworking the same section of a riverbank inch by inch, letting cut-bait rest on the seafloor an hour, retrieving a plastic worm at the pace a mushroom erupts from a rain-drenched lawn. After a lifetime of fishing with both types of fishers, I can't say which of the two styles results in more fish caught. For me, the patient approach best allows the opportunity to enjoy the graceful beauty of a bend in the river, the reflections on a lake, or the vibrant greens of marsh grass lining a saltwater flat.

New Zealand blue cod are cod-like[1] but are not members of the family Gadidae that houses the common groups of true cod: the Pacific cod, Atlantic cod, and Greenland cod. Blue cod, however, do share similarities with cod: they are groundfish, living and swimming near the seafloor, and they occur in huge schools that sustain themselves on seafloor crabs, molluscs, sea urchins, and small lobsters and fish. Because of strict catch limits and the required use of hand lines rather than trawls, the New Zealand blue cod fishery is sustainable. This has not been the case with Northern Hemisphere groundfish such as the Atlantic cod that have been the backbone of a major commodity with complex networks of trade for over a millennium. What makes cod so attractive is both the ease with which large numbers of individuals can be harvested (in the early twentieth century they were reported in almost biblical abundance on shallow offshore shoals) and their mild, white, moist fillets.

The most poignant example of a fishery that has historically suffered from exploitation is the Atlantic cod fishery in the northwestern Atlantic Ocean.[2] These gray-green to brown-colored fish are harvested at an average size of ten to twenty-five pounds. Atlantic cod reach reproductive maturity in as few as two to three years, making the fish, if managed properly, a strong candidate for a sustainable fishery. Nonetheless, a combination of the use of various-sized factory trawlers, poor catch management strategies, and greed has contributed to dwindling cod populations along the northeastern coast of Canada and the United States, which ultimately collapsed in the early 1990s. *Collapse* is a vernacular term in the fishing industry that is not used lightly. In fact, this word is reserved for instances when a given stock of a select species of fish or shellfish declines to a level 95 percent below its average historic catch. A collapsed stock can be serious business because, contrary to expectation, the fishery may not rebound even in the complete absence of fishing pressure.

The degree to which various factors contributed to the demise of the northwestern Atlantic cod fishery can be debated, but advancements in fishing technologies were certainly in the mix. As with most resources exploited by humankind, adaptive technology focuses on increasing yield per unit effort while reducing costs, although not necessarily the cost of a product to the consumer. In the first half of the twentieth century, the fishing technology at hand limited the catch, facilitated regional fishing, and targeted specific genders and species of groundfish. In the early 1960s, however, technological advances in fishing tactics set the stage for an ecological disaster. Powerful steel bottom-trawlers came online, equipped with sophisticated fish-finding sonar, along with the capacity to pull fishing trawls deeper and scour larger tracts of the seafloor. Moreover, the larger trawlers—essentially floating factories—had the capacity to process and freeze fish aboard ship and therefore remain in operation at sea for longer periods of time. As a result of these advances in technology, the catch of Atlantic cod along the coast of Canada and the north Atlantic states of the United States skyrocketed, reaching new heights and peaking in the early 1970s. Over the next two decades, the catch of cod per unit effort steadily declined as the numbers of surviving fish became insufficient to replenish the population. What was playing out on the seafloor was a classic example of what Professor Garrett Hardin, my boyhood neighbor in Santa Barbara, California, famously coined "the tragedy of the commons."[3] In this example, the interests of individual cod fishers, each utilizing a common resource for their own personal betterment, contributed to a tragic, irreversible collapse of an entire fishery by way of exploitation of the commons. By 1992, the depleted Atlantic cod fishery reached such dire straits that the Canadian government was forced to place a moratorium on the entire fishery. The coastal communities of Newfoundland were particularly hard hit as twenty-two thousand people intimately tied to the cod-fishing trades were displaced, and a way of life that had existed for half a millennium came to an abrupt halt.

Seafloor ecosystem impacts from a long history of intensive trawling such as that off Newfoundland can be profound, depleting Atlantic cod and countless other species of groundfish and invertebrates. Noncommercial species caught in trawls are lumped together into what is loosely termed by the fishery as "incidental by-catch." Yet as my own studies with Chuck Amsler and Bill Baker, and those of Paul Dayton at Scripps Institute of Oceanography, have revealed in the Southern Ocean, and as marine ecologists have found elsewhere, nearshore ecosystems are complex, interwoven systems. Species that compose by-catch may in fact serve as glue that sustains the dynamics of a seafloor community, much as in the tower-crashing block game of *Jenga*. At first, players removing individual blocks do little to alter the arrangement of the block tower. Eventually, however, a tipping point is breached when the removal of a key block results in the tower's collapse. With cod largely eliminated from the seafloor, the community assumed an "alternate stable state," featuring a new cast of predator and prey. Twenty years after cod collapsed, despite a sustained moratorium on Atlantic cod fishing off the Canadian coast, the cod fishery shows few signs of a rebound.

The two-decade-long Canadian moratorium on fishing Atlantic cod is not the last word on attempts to protect a devastated fishery. In November 2014, federal regulators with the U.S. National Oceanic and Atmospheric Administration (NOAA) placed an emergency six-month restriction on recreational and commercial Atlantic cod fishing in several regions of the Gulf of Maine.[4] Fishing vessels were limited to taking a paltry two hundred pounds of cod per trip, a reduction in catch representing a loss of several millions of dollars and a significant financial burden on fishers. The tough new restrictions followed on the heels of decades of poor returns on cod and an annual catch that yielded the lowest catch since scientists at NOAA began monitoring the cod fishery four decades earlier. Also taken into account by NOAA experts were cod-spawning levels that had fallen to 3 to 4 percent of the desired level targeted to sustain the fishery. Fishery biologists cited overfishing as a contributing factor but also turned to the potential negative impact of a rapidly warming sea. The Gulf of Maine resides in the top 1 percent of the world's oceans when it comes to oceanic warming due to anthropogenic climate change. Increased seawater temperatures can displace Atlantic cod, which require cold, oxygen-rich waters. The draconian regulations placed on cod fishing were the result of a growing concern among NOAA fishery experts that, barring intervention, Atlantic cod in the Gulf of Maine were poised for imminent collapse.

The 2014 restrictions on harvesting cod in the Gulf of Maine should never have become necessary. A decade earlier, a suite of tough government fishing regulations were enacted that required lower catch quotas, assignment of cod fishers to regional sectors of the Gulf, and on-ship cod fishery observers. The ambitious goal was to rebuild stocks in the Gulf of Maine over a ten-year period. Fishers closely adhered to the new regulations, and by 2008, the cod fishery had begun to rebound. Catch quotas were relaxed, and some fishers even went out and bought new boats, optimistic for the first time in years that they could turn a profit. But the fishers' hopes were dashed when a reassessment of the cod fishery in 2011 indicated that the rebound had steeply fallen off. In September 2012, the U.S. Department of Commerce declared the entire groundfish fishery off the northeastern United States a disaster, providing Congress an opportunity to approve emergency funds for the financial relief of severely impacted cod fishers. Sadly, to date, despite the long history of Congress subsidizing agriculture, they have yet to act, and as time passes, so does a way of life.

Luke and I, sporting sore, red hands, leaned contentedly against the starboard railing as the captain skillfully docked our vessel and the mate tied off bow and stern lines. With the boat secured and gangplank in place, the mate hoisted the heavy cooler off the back deck and, with an audible grunt, slid the day's cleaned catch onto the weathered dock planks. Tired and satisfied, our four fellow fishers clambered one by one off the vessel, tipped the captain and mate, and gratefully accepted two-quart ziplock baggies stuffed with blue cod fillets. Luke and I followed suit, and carrying our ziplocks of fillets in our day packs, headed off on foot across the Oban village beachfront, up a steep, winding road, and to our rental cottage with a distant view of Halfmoon Bay. Ferne and Jamie met us at the door, eager to hear about hand-line fishing and equally excited about several South Island kākā, a greenish-brown subspecies of large New Zealand parrots, that had perched on our cottage window sill looking for handouts. That evening, we dined at the quaint Church Hill Restaurant and Bar where the chef prepared fillets from our hand-line catch. Mild and moist, the delicious blue cod fillets were batter-dipped, fried, and served with fresh-cut wedges of lemon, french fries, and a mixed salad adorned with a scarlet wildflower.

My research sabbatical in Dunedin also provided an opportunity to pursue a long-standing dream—to fish for New Zealand rainbows. My love of rainbow trout fishing is deeply rooted.[5] For this I credit my father, who began taking me into the high California Sierras at the age of five to fish, hike, and camp. Later, when I was a Boy Scout, he helped lead summer backpacking and fishing trips in the Sierras that later led to family backpacking that continued through my John Muir–tinged college years. I have vivid memories of my dad and me spending white-knuckle stormy nights tucked into plastic tube-tents; being lifted by Dad from my sleeping bag, early morning, to be dipped in icy streams; and day hikes climbing from base camp to tree line to fish virgin, trout-crowded lakes with inexpensive Zebco rod and reels. We tied dry flies to four-foot leaders and attached clear, sausage-shaped plastic floats that made the line easy to cast. Retrieving our flies, we celebrated surface strikes of hungry fish. We filled stringers with small, native rainbows that we cleaned and rolled in crushed graham cracker then fried, head and skin on, in butter.

Rainbow trout similarly highlighted my youth in the mountains behind Santa Barbara. While high school classmates were pursuing more traditional teenage activities, I spent my spring and fall weekends backpacking with a close-knit group of buddies in the adjacent Santa Ynez wilderness. Our favorite haunt, Santa Cruz Creek, was reached via a hefty fifteen-mile hike along a trail that climbed and descended 4,000-foot Little Pine Mountain. At the time, the California condor was yet to become the target of a captive breeding program, and I had an unforgettable experience watching a condor glide past me as I descended the steep trail to Santa Cruz Creek. Overnighting at primitive campsites, we slept in small tents or outside and day-hiked packless, bounding upstream, across creek-smoothed boulders, fishing rods in hand, with spinner baits and jars of salmon eggs stuffed into jeans pockets. Beside the creek, we enjoyed the smell of sun-warmed sagebrush. For school projects, we photographed Indian paintbrush, lupine, California poppies, oaks and sycamores, dragon flies, swallowtail butterflies, scrub jays, and blue belly lizards. But

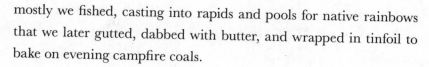
mostly we fished, casting into rapids and pools for native rainbows that we later gutted, dabbed with butter, and wrapped in tinfoil to bake on evening campfire coals.

I hadn't been in New Zealand for more than a day or two before I searched the Internet for a fishing tackle store. The white lettering across the front of the two-story sea-green warehouse read, "Allan Millar's Hunting & Fishing, New Zealand." A former furniture outlet, the large sporting goods store on George Street in Dunedin was home to an impressive array of hunting rifles and supplies, along with spinning, bait-casting, and fly rods; reels; and fishing tackle. Anticipating fishing for New Zealand trout, I'd brought from home my collapsible two-piece spinning rod and a Shimano spinning reel. Mike Barker, my host at the Portobello Marine Laboratory, had kindly lent me one of his fly outfits, an eight-and-a-half-foot Martens fly rod with a Leeda reel, for the duration of my three-month visit. Accordingly, I parked my rental car in the gravel lot behind the sporting goods store with two objectives: first, to talk to someone about what spinners and flies to use to catch New Zealand rainbows and, second, to see if anyone could suggest local spots near Dunedin to fish for rainbows in the late afternoon.

"Woolly Bugger," said Grant Ashton in a Kiwi accent that made the name of the fly sound comical. Grant was the go-to guy in the store when it came to fly-fishing, and he sounded like he knew his stuff. While I'm not an expert fly-fisher by any stretch, I knew enough to know a Woolly Bugger was a wet fly, or streamer, which is about as common a fly as they come. Grant explained that in New Zealand the Woolly Bugger catches trout in just about any lake, creek, stream, or river. Maybe it's the fly's generic nature, resembling a host of aquatic insects, that makes it potent, or perhaps it's because the fly closely resembles the larval nymph of the common dobsonfly—an early life history stage also called a hellgrammite—that trout have a hard time resisting. Either way, Grant's enthusiasm for the Woolly

Bugger resulted in me sliding half a dozen of the inch-long, black bushy flies into a small ziplock bag. "For your spinning rod, I'd use this for rainbows," offered Grant, dangling between his thumb and forefinger a spinner bait that had a narrow one-and-a-half-inch body, a single gold spinning blade, and a small red tube at the base of the lure that wrapped the shank of the treble hook. I bought three.

"There are some small reservoirs around Dunedin to fish rainbows," replied Grant to my query about local spots to fish trout. "The one I'd recommend is not far from here; some of the others are a bit dodgy," he continued, grabbing a pencil from the counter to sketch directions on a piece of scrap paper. "The rainbows are stocked," said Grant, "but then in a way, so are all the trout in New Zealand—yup mate, no native trout here." Back in my rental car, I decided to visit the nearby reservoir that Grant had recommended and take a look. The drive took me up hills past the Otago Golf Club; the road seamlessly transitioned to Leith Valley Road, which narrowed to a series of tight switchbacks that climbed through foothills sprinkled with pastures dotted with yellow-flowered gorse, beech forests, and views of the city of Dunedin. A small, empty, dirt parking area along the right side of the road was marked with a sign that read "Sullivan's Dam." I climbed out of my car and followed a well-trodden trail that ran about two hundred feet to the southern end of the oblong reservoir. The end of the reservoir where I had parked ran to the southeast and was composed of an earthen dam that extended about five hundred feet, reinforced with several layers of basketball-sized rocks. Surrounded by a pine and spruce forest, the narrow, half-mile-long reservoir sported trails along its grassy banks that disappeared into the woods at the reservoir's northern end, presumably completing a circuit around the entire lake. As I walked the length of the dam, the steep bank descended below the clear water to a depth sufficient to obscure the reservoir's bottom. Strolling up the left bank of the reservoir, I could see that the depth dropped off more gradually, perhaps reaching ten to fifteen feet over the distance of a long cast. I could make out lots of submerged logs

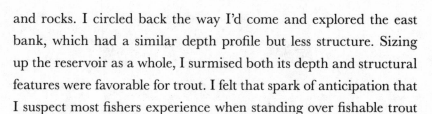

and rocks. I circled back the way I'd come and explored the east bank, which had a similar depth profile but less structure. Sizing up the reservoir as a whole, I surmised both its depth and structural features were favorable for trout. I felt that spark of anticipation that I suspect most fishers experience when standing over fishable trout waters. I'd be back the next day.

I didn't get a bite the first two times I fished the reservoir; however, on my third visit, persistence paid off. I fly-fished the east bank, a spot where plenty of open space allowed me to coil my line at my feet and to keep overhead casts from snagging bushes and trees. Stripping line with successive casts, I used the weight of the line to carry my fly a good forty feet. With practice, I got better at stopping the forward motion of the rod at the end of the final cast, settling the tippet and Woolly Bugger gently onto the water's surface. Then, with tiny line tugs, I danced the fly across the surface a second or two before it broke the air-water interface. After the fly sank passively for about five seconds, I combined lifts of the rod with my right hand and line retrieval with my left, working the fly back to shore a foot at a time. Without so much as a nibble during my past two outings, the strike caught me by surprise. Hooked, the trout made a rod-bending dash for deeper water. The fish quickly ran off the ten feet of line coiled at my feet, with the zipping sound of drag signaling the trout's transition to the reel. Exploiting both the flexibility of the rod and a lightly set drag, I played the trout, cranking line between runs. Halfway to shore, the trout leapt, and the rainbow along its sides caught the late afternoon light. My "Yes!" echoed across the deserted reservoir. Pulling the rainbow up on the grassy bank, I removed the hook, threaded the sixteen-inch fish on a rope stringer, slid the fish back into the water, and tied the loose end of the stringer around a semisubmerged boulder. By dusk, three rainbows graced my stringer. It was time to head home, time to clean trout for dinner.

I fished Ross Creek Reservoir several times a week over the balance of my three-month stay. In addition to the day I landed my first New Zealand rainbow, one other day stood out. The experience wouldn't have been as memorable had I not shared the misty, rain-soaked afternoon with one other fisher, a young Kiwi probably in his twenties, who also happened to be at the reservoir. In the hallowed tradition of two fishers worried about spooking fish, or too keen on fishing to share a nod, we silently gravitated to opposite banks of the reservoir. The young Kiwi caught the first fish, and even across the quarter-mile width of the reservoir, I could make it out to be a big rainbow. Ten minutes later, he landed a second trout about the same size, and I decided to try something different, retreating from my fly rod to my spinning rod. The rainbow hit my gold spinner like a ton of bricks, twice the impact of the two- to three-pound trout I'd been catching on the reservoir. The fish took off, parallel to the bank, toward the dam. Sensing I needed to wear down a fish this size, I let the big trout pull drag while I followed along the bank. The timing of my decision to attempt to slow the run was dictated by the proximity of the fish to the rocks at the base of the dam, a sure opportunity for the fish to tangle line and break free. Bending my rod into the fish, I cranked five feet of line and then stopped to let the fish run a similar amount of drag. Repeating the pattern, I engaged the fish in a zero-sum game, where progress was measured in the trout's build-up of lactic acid rather than its distance from shore. In small increments, I began to reel in a little more line than I gave back to the fish. Slowly, the math worked. Fifteen minutes after the strike, I beached a spec-tacular rainbow. The deep red tint of the fat, twenty-six-inch, seven-pound trout pointed to a mature female, its tattered tail testament to sweeping spawning beds. As daylight faded, the young Kiwi fisher strolled over to admire my trout. I congratulated him on an equally impressive pair of rainbows. We bemoaned the foul weather, said our good-byes, but neither of us mentioned the afternoon's amazing fishing. I suspect, like me, he was considering the possibility that the reservoir had been stocked that morning with big, dumb hatchery trout.

Mike Barker, my New Zealand host, had promised me a weekend trout-fishing trip to Lake Wanaka before my sabbatical wrapped up.

The twenty-six-mile-long, deep glacial lake was situated 170 miles west of Dunedin, poised between the Crown Mountains and the Southern Alps. Mike grew up fly and spinner fishing the streams, rivers, and lakes in the Lake Wanaka region of the lower South Island. We finally managed to sync our schedules to go fishing on the last Saturday of November. In the Southern Hemisphere, late November is late spring, and as Mike and I drove west from Dunedin along a winding two-lane road through rolling hills carpeted in gray scrub and vines of native jasmine and clematis, he mentioned that given the late winter that year we might be a little early in the season to catch rainbow and brown trout. If the lake hadn't warmed, the trout might still be lying low, waiting on early summer plankton, insect nymphs, and baitfish. And in late spring, the Clutha River emptying Lake Wanaka was likely to be too swift for trout fishing, yet Mike's tone of voice insinuated the river was worth a look. Fish or no fish, I was eager to spend the day with Mike, surrounded by some of the most stunning scenery anywhere.

Mike's forewarning turned out to be true. We donned chest-high waders and stood for several hours in frigid lake waters, cheating an offshore breeze to double the distance of our fly casts. Nary a tap or swirl. I tried a spinner, nothing. We moved down the shore and tried again—same story. The lake was as quiet as an Alabama bass lake in January. Eventually, we packed up our fishing rods and drove over to look at the Clutha River. Pulling off the road along the river, we parked and followed a well-worn footpath through the bushes to the water's edge. The swollen river roared by us like a locomotive, a sixty-foot-wide collage of swirls, boils, and white water cascading into and over partially submerged rocks, far too lively for me to toss a fly or spinner. Mike smiled and pointed out a faint trail that descended a steep, rocky hillside on the opposite side of the river. As a teenager he'd hiked down the trail regularly in the summer to fish his favorite spots. When it came to the numbers and sizes of trout caught, Mike's eyes said it all. He'd landed more than his share of rainbows and, he reminisced, browns too.

Rainbow trout, similar to their brown trout counterparts, start out life in a graveled tributary where their parents spawn eggs and sperm.[6] Should the natal tributary feed into a stream or river that readily empties into a lake, the larval or juvenile fish may be destined to grow up as lake trout. Unlike brown trout, none of the New Zealand rainbows have developed a lifestyle that interfaces with the sea, a somewhat surprising outcome for a trout whose ancestral stock is rooted in fertilized eggs collected from steelhead, a type of trout that migrates as an adult to the sea and returns to freshwater to spawn (fish that migrate from sea to freshwater are called anadromous). New Zealand rainbows feed mainly on small prey such as insects and their aquatic larvae, aquatic invertebrates, and small fish. In some lakes, rainbows will target baitfish such as smelt and the abundant larvae (whitebait) of koaro, a species of fish called a climbing galaxias in Australia because of its ability to "rock climb" straight up the faces of waterfalls and concrete sluices of dams using unique downward-projecting fins. This climbing tactic allows the koaro to penetrate farther up streams and to inhabit upland waters with fewer fish competitors.

Brown trout are even more aggressive feeders than rainbows. In a remarkable example, brown trout living in the New Zealand backcountry have learned to exploit the unique reproductive cycles of beech trees that grow along the headwaters of streams. Every three to five years, the beech trees produce a bumper crop of flowers and seeds, a phenomenon called masting.[7] As the abundant seeds and flowers fall to the forest floor, they attract huge numbers of predators, including insects and mice. Much to the delight of brown trout, the droves of nocturnal mice attracted to the abundant food cross headwaters in the dark, providing easy fodder for trout feeding frenzies. Brown trout have been found with as many as twenty adult mice in their stomachs, and in a "mouse year," a seven-pound brown trout can explode in a few months into a ten-pound trophy. Such aggressive feeding behavior has led fisheries biologists to suspect that brown trout are more common than rainbow trout in most New Zealand waters because they out-compete rainbows for food. Other fishery biologists attribute the success of brown trout to their greater ability to adapt to changing environmental conditions.

"Didymo?" I asked Mike. The large block letters at the top of the wooden sign posted along the Clutha River read, "Didymo—Invasive Alga." Below these three words, the text read, "All rods, reels, fishing lines, tackle boxes, nets, clothing, and other equipment should be thoroughly soaked in a decontamination solution. Felt soled waders prohibited." Mike explained that the sign was a warning to fishers about a messy invasive alga that was introduced to the South Island of New Zealand in 2004. Despite intensive mitigation efforts, the alga had spread rapidly across the island. The locals call the alga "rock snot" because the green-brown organism coats rocks along streams and rivers with thick, slimy mats. *Didymosphenia geminata* is an organism belonging to a group of single-celled algae called diatoms that encase each cell in a geometric, silicon glass case called a frustule.[8] Didymo grows rapidly in cold, low-nutrient waters, and while not a direct hazard to humans, the cells produce stalks that form long stringy chains. These stalks form mats that reduce the availability of food for fish and turn a lovely stream or riverbank unsightly. To reduce the infestation of this invasive alga in New Zealand, fisheries managers encourage fishers to remove obvious clumps of didymo from their clothing or gear after fishing and, after they get home, to scrub and soak their clothing and fishing gear in either scalding hot water or a 2 percent solution of bleach. Studies have shown that these treatments, followed by a forty-eight-hour drying period, will prevent spread of the alga when clothing and equipment come in contact with another waterway. The stuff is a mess, and the rapid spread of the mats of algae brings home the considerable damage that invasive aquatic and marine species can bring to bear on ecosystems and their inhabitants, including sport fish such as trout. Infestations are not restricted to New Zealand. A recent study in eastern Canada reported that rock snot infestations were proliferating in freshwater habitats. However, the authors of the Canadian study believe that the infestations are not the result of a human introduction such as occurred in

New Zealand but rather are a likely consequence of climate warming: seasonal spring ice melt is increasingly spread over longer and longer periods of time and is therefore less disruptive to the excessive growth of rock snot.

New Zealand rainbow trout are themselves invasive and are not immune from imparting significant impacts on freshwater ecosystems. Unlike algal rock snot, however, both rainbow and brown trout were intentionally introduced to New Zealand streams, rivers, and lakes in the late nineteenth and early twentieth centuries to seed the sport of trout fishing. The rainbow trout (*Oncorhynchus mykiss gairdneri*) that swim today in the waters of New Zealand have their origin in fertilized eggs collected from steelhead in California's Russian River in 1877. The fertilized eggs were subsequently hatched and the adults released in the Auckland region of the North Island. Later, rainbow trout from the Auckland stock were liberated in waters throughout the country. While the economic success of what is today a world-class trout fishery cannot be disputed, the jury is still out on whether the introduction of a highly predatory fish such as the rainbow trout has resulted in harmful community disturbance. The potential negative effects of introductions of salmonid fishes (trout and salmon) in forty-five countries to date include competing with native species for food, preying on native species, altering of the habitat, transmitting diseases, and interbreeding that may produce new hybrid species.

Ample evidence exists that both introduced rainbow and brown trout have displaced a number of native New Zealand fish (members of the Galaxias taxa).[9] In 1994, scientists further examined potential community-wide effects of introduced trout in New Zealand streams. The scientists found that the numbers of insects declined in manipulated stream channels seeded with trout when compared to identical stream channels lacking fish or channels with only native fish. However, the trout in the study had no negative effect on the types of stream insects present in the stream channels. In an important discovery, the investigators found that channels with trout developed more non-invasive algae in them than channels with no fish or with native fish. Trout had altered the very base of the food chain. Whether streams with more algae are damaging to stream communities has yet to be explored. One thing is clear, however: regardless of the possible negative impacts of introduced trout, the prized fish won't be leaving New Zealand any time soon. Trout have become so ubiquitous and so ingrained in New Zealand culture that Kiwi fishers have essentially come to think of trout as native to their country.

When I think back to coming home empty-handed with Mike, I'm reminded of jumping out of my sedan into a chilly, light rain and quickly popping the trunk in front of our carriage house in Dunedin. I was relieved to see the seven-pound rainbow I'd caught at Sullivan's Dam still lay on the floor of the trunk, wrapped in a moist kitchen towel I'd brought along to wipe my hands while fishing. Driving home from the reservoir, I'd imagined the big fish had vanished from the trunk, its existence a figment of my imagination. Ferne, Luke, and Jamie admired my catch, taking my word that the fish far outstripped my record for a New Zealand trout. Ferne snapped one more photograph of me holding the trout in our family room as flames crackled in the potbellied stove, and then I slid the fish into our knee-high kitchen refrigerator.

The next morning, I loaded the trout into my car and drove down to Harbour Fish City, a fish market on the corner of Saint Andrews and Great King Street. The fish merchant behind the counter smiled as I entered the market, and when I undraped the wet dish towel and presented him with the big trout, he congratulated me on a "fine catch." Two days later, I returned to the market where I paid the merchant and received a package wrapped tight in newspaper. Over the next few weeks, after I got home from long days at the Portobello Marine Laboratory, I would crack open cold bottles of Steinlager to chase down slices of my smoked rainbow.

7

BAHAMAS

Bonefish

C ontrary to general perception, fishing can be dangerous, even life-threatening. Fishers are tossed from boats and are swept by powerful waves off rocky intertidal platforms, breakwaters, and piers. Some fall through lake ice or are pulled to sea by strong rip currents. My own encounter with fishing and death occurred when I was in my mid-twenties. At the time, I was a graduate student participating in a research cruise aboard the *Seward Johnson*, a scientific vessel operated by the Harbor Branch Oceanographic Institute. We had departed Melbourne, Florida and were on our way to deploy the *Johnson Sea Link*, a manned submersible we planned to use to collect deep-sea echinoderms (feather stars and sea urchins) off the coast of San Salvador, a remote island halfway down the Bahamian chain that is famous for its wall diving and close proximity to deep water.

As our ship approached Cockburn Town, our captain received an emergency request from island officials to assist in their search for a body. The targeted area was the seafloor along a short stretch of coast a few miles from town. Sadly, the subject of the search was a young, local Bahamian fisher who had gone free diving that morning and never returned. On board our research vessel were two crew members trained in scuba diving. While the ship's marine technicians winched a Zodiac from the ship's deck to the sea, the divers quickly suited up. As soon as the Zodiac was operational, a dive tender loaded up scuba tanks, regulators, and dive belts and then joined the two divers and boat operator on the twelve-foot rubber boat. An hour later, word came that the divers had found the body at a depth of fifty feet. The young man, drowned, was clutching the end of a Hawaiian sling, a hand-held six-foot spear propelled by a thick band of rubber that's stretched and fired much like a slingshot. A large Nassau grouper lay dead on the seafloor next to the fisher's body, the other end of the spear protruding from its torso.

What happened to cause the fisher's death is sheer speculation. Perhaps the tragic outcome was the result of an epic struggle between man and fish. The young man, who apparently spent a great deal of time spearfishing, was in tip-top physical condition and capable of diving repetitively to depths of fifty feet. It seemed unlikely that the fish, despite its large size, had won a wrestling match. More likely the young man had drowned because of shallow-water blackout, a medical condition common enough to have its own acronym: SWB.[1] The condition is caused when repetitive free dives (diving without an air tank) result in expanding, oxygen-starved lungs sucking oxygen out of a diver's blood. The result, too little oxygen delivered to the brain, causes a rapid, totally unexpected blackout, most often as a diver ascends the last fifteen feet of a free dive. Essentially, one second the diver is fine, the next, unconscious. Without a diver buddy, the diver will likely drown. Ironically, experienced divers such as the young Bahamian, are more susceptible to SWB than beginning divers, whose lungs haven't yet adapted to removing oxygen from the bloodstream to supply the lungs. If SWB was, in fact, the culprit, then the free diver probably died near the sea's surface and his body drifted to the seafloor along with his speared grouper.

Saddened by the young man's death, I gazed at the island from the ship's deck. The blue water softened shoreward to shades of turquoise and lime green. At that moment, I had no idea that San Salvador would wind through the course of my life. I'd later learn that the Bahamians on the small island were like a tightly knit family: at the time of the young man's death, a population of about five hundred. "Everyone on this island knows everybody's business," emphasized the staff of San Salvador's Gerace Research Centre[2] to the hundreds of college students whom Ken Marion and I would bring to the island over the next two decades. Among such a close community, a life lost is tragic, especially that of a skilled fisher, who'd chosen to provision his extended island family with the sea's bounty, a son who, unlike so many other sons who left for Nassau, stayed home.

Ken and I warily eyed the aging twin-prop Cessna outside of the Twin Air terminal at the Fort Lauderdale airport. Donald Gerace, the director of the field station, had informed us that if we could get ourselves to Fort Lauderdale, he'd provide us free air transport to San Salvador, put us up at the station, and give us a tour of the island. Ken and I were exploring Caribbean field stations to teach a tropical ecology class for our students at the University of Alabama at Birmingham. The Jamaican field station brochure boasted armed security guards with dogs that patrolled the perimeter of the station at night. We hoped San Salvador offered something off the beaten track, a place where our students would be safe. With our luggage stowed, the pilot motioned us into a fuselage crammed with construction materials, boxes with televisions, small air conditioners, toys, cartons of drugstore goods, and bags brimming with groceries. With Ken and me belted, the pilot quickly pointed out the safety cards, escape door, and fire extinguisher. Twenty minutes later, our small plane climbed through gathering late-morning thunderheads. We settled back into our seats for the hour-and-a-half flight, trying to ignore the rainwater leaking through the ceiling and dripping onto our heads and shoulders.

I breathed a sigh of relief as the Cessna's wheels hit the tarmac. As the plane taxied, I caught sight of the small thatched-roof airport and the adjacent outdoor waiting area with a group of departing college students. As we drew closer, I closely scanned the students: tanned, sunburned, pleasantly worn out, smiling and laughing. Don met us on the tarmac with a mischievous grin. "Welcome!" he yelled. "Toss your luggage in my station wagon, and I'll be back in a minute." And with that, he rushed off to negotiate with a customs official sizing up the boxes, cartons, and bags. Don was a wheeler-dealer and a jack of all trades, an essential attribute when running a remote field station. After showing us to our quarters in the former U.S. naval base-turned-research station, Don offered to give us a whirlwind tour of the island.

Don drove his station wagon like the New Yorker he was, tearing down roads covered in windshield-high grass. Other roads were so tightly bordered by dwarf palmetto, poison wood, and gumbo limbo trees that branches scraped our station wagon. The car approaching speeds of fifty miles an hour, Ken and I prayed that Don knew where the curves and potholes lay. By the time we'd driven the twenty-eight-mile circumference of the island and, later, snorkeled some of the reefs, we were sold. Fringing reefs teemed with tropical fish, brain corals, sea fans, sea urchins, and a variety of sponges and green algae. Further offshore, lush barrier reefs sported barracuda, large schools of blue tangs, and bush- and tree-sized staghorn and elkhorn corals, offering opportunities for our students to experience a small boat trip and deepwater snorkel. Two small neighboring islands were also within boating distance, one island littered with chattering, nesting seabirds, including magnificent frigate birds, boobies, and brown knotties; the other island home to a rare, endangered subspecies of San Salvador rock iguana. A mangrove-lined tidal creek presented an opportunity to snorkel among prop roots and their nurseries of tropical fish and invertebrates. Hiking trails penetrated the island's brushy interior, providing access to numerous freshwater, low- and high-salinity, and sulfidic lakes, each with its own unique suite of bacteria adapted to the extreme conditions, and some with tiny clams, snails, and fish.

The coastal research station offered everything Ken and I needed to teach tropical ecology: open-bed trucks with bench seating for carting around students; a basic two-story dorm building where women enjoyed the privacy of the top floor, men the bottom floor; a cafeteria with simple, ample meals; and a bare-bones laboratory for each class—a place to meet with our students, compile species lists, and store sampling gear for field experiments. Even better, the nearest student watering hole was a full two-mile hike down the road. While passing through Cockburn Town, we'd noted a harbor carved from

limestone that was the size of a football field and a potential fishing spot. Just in front of the station, across a coastal road and a thick cluster of sea grapes, an old concrete boat ramp greeted the bay. Just a fifteen-minute walk from the station was Graham's Harbour, where a weathered concrete pier jutted fifty feet offshore before collapsing into the sea. Ken and I could bring our two-piece fishing rods and fish during the half-day off we planned to give our students during their week-long studies on the island. Over the next twenty years, we brought fifteen classes of UAB students to the island to teach them about tropical ecology. We celebrated immersing Alabama students in a living laboratory, and we celebrated fifteen half-days of fishing.

My earliest memories of fishing on San Salvador take me back to half-days when Ken and I either tossed lines off the station's boat ramp or hiked down the road to fish the end of the Graham's Harbour pier. Both spots produced a few good game fish. I cast a two-inch silver spoon as far offshore as my Shimano spinning reel, wound with eight-pound test, would allow. The strikes, when they came, were powerful. Mostly, I battled one- to three-pound bar jacks (also called carbonero) that fought long and hard. Bar jacks (*Caranx ruber*) are beautiful, silver fish with a distinct dark-blue horizontal stripe running along the top of their backs and tail fin. Just below the dark-blue stripe, a second neon-blue stripe seemed to glow underwater as we released the fish. Snorkeling and scuba diving on San Salvador, I saw countless bar jacks in their natural habitat, usually swimming in tight schools. The jacks rarely swam over the reefs but rather prowled over nearby sand flats and sea grass beds where they are keen predators of small fish, squid, and crustaceans. Bar jacks are supposed to be good eating, but ciguatera illness has been associated with consuming their flesh. The neurotoxins that cause ciguatera are produced by various species of dinoflagellates (single-celled organisms with whip-like tails) that occur in tropical seas as part of the plankton or attached to seaweeds.[3] Toxic planktonic dinoflagellates are consumed when small filter-feeding fish swim with mouths open, using their gills as sieves; toxic forms attached to seaweeds are eaten incidentally by small herbivorous fish. The toxin-tainted fish, are, in turn, eaten by bigger fish, and in this fashion, the ciguatera-causing toxins are concentrated as they move up the food chain in a process called bio-accumulation. Unfortunately, the toxins are not inactivated when the fish is cooked. Symptoms of ciguatera range from nausea, vomiting, and muscle discomfort to numbness and hallucinations. Remarkably, the toxins can be transferred from mother to infant in breast milk or even between partners during sexual intercourse. Recurring symptoms of ciguatera illness can persist for a very long time, in some instances for decades.

Casting a silver spoon off the far end of the hurricane-wrecked pier in Graham's Harbour, I encountered another species of fish that boasted both fight and ciguatera. Fishers recognize the species not by its bite but, more often, lack thereof. "Barracuda have a knack for cutting you clean," Ken lamented, and we learned to tie off spoons to leaders made of wire or twenty-pound test whenever we fished the pier. When hooked, barracuda were exceptional fighters, despite their relatively small size in Graham's Harbour. Snorkeling on offshore barrier reefs, I spotted big silver-green barracuda, some seeming to stretch six feet, magnified by mask and water. Territorial, or curious, the barracuda spooked our snorkeling students, the fish's sinister appearance accentuated by rows of sharp teeth protruding from grinning jaws.

Outside of harboring the toxins that cause ciguatera, barracuda (members of the genus *Sphyraena*) are quite harmless to humans. Contrary to tall tales, barracuda don't attack swimmers, snorkelers, or divers, provided they aren't wearing sparkling jewelry that might be mistaken for a small fish. Barracuda aren't the only fish attracted to the flash of jewelry. I found this out the hard way this past May while snorkeling with my ecology students in San Salvador. We'd been on the island for several days, and one of the most common echinoderms I liked to show off to my students, the donkey dung sea cucumber (*Holothuria mexicana*), was nowhere to be seen. Snorkeling on the morning of our third day, I discovered an individual of the brown, foot-long, worm-shaped animal wedged up against a laundry-basket-sized boulder. Holding my breath, I dove below the water's surface, reached down with my right hand, and grasped the sea cucumber. Surprisingly, the cucumber was wedged so tight against the base of the boulder that I couldn't pull it free. With rekindled determination, I surfaced, drew another deep breath, and returned to the cucumber, this time grabbing one end of the cucumber with my right hand and reaching down to grab the other end with my left hand. As my left hand passed in front of a hole hidden below the boulder, I felt a searing pain shoot the length of my arm. I wrenched my arm back as if I'd touched a red-hot stove top. In retrospect, had I been able to ignore my involuntary (autonomic) nervous system, I might have been able to lift the boulder with my free hand and grab the moray eel that had sunk its teeth into the midsection of my ring finger. As morays generally don't release their prey, I would've had to wade to shore with the eel attached to my finger and get Ken to pry open the eel's jaws or drive me back to the station to cut off the eel's head. Of course, none of this happened because the "fight or flight" component of my involuntary nervous system didn't give me the option. The down side of my reflexive response was that the moray's clenched teeth ripped the length of the distal half of my finger, cutting flesh and fingernail. I lifted my hand to my dive mask to closely examine the damage. My ring finger was a mess.

"You're lucky the moray didn't take your whole finger," commented the young Bahamian physician in the examination room at the San Salvador Medical Clinic. A nurse had my left hand splayed flat on a gauze-covered table and was in the process of administering twelve stitches, six on the top and six on the bottom of the finger. "I'm going to put you on a general antibiotic to be safe," continued the doctor. At the time, neither I nor the doctor was aware that some species of moray eels harbor a nasty array of pathogenic bacteria and toxins. For instance, the green moray (*Gymnothorax funebris*), often displayed in public aquariums, possesses a cocktail of pathogenic bacteria, a hemolytic toxin (kills red blood cells) and a neurotoxin (ciguatoxin). The fact that I didn't suffer any of these ill effects supported my contention that I had been bitten by the more benign spotted moray (*Gymnothorax morninga*), a species known to frequent the waters of San Salvador. "You'll need to stop by the clinic to get your wounds cleaned and checked every other day until you leave the island," the doctor advised as I stood to leave. "And as soon as you get back to Alabama, you need to follow up with a doctor there," she added. When I did get home, the doctor I saw took one look at the severity of my wound and, after sneaking off to her office to Google "moray eel," promptly wrote me a prescription for another course of antibiotics. Fortunately, my finger healed rapidly with no nerve damage. Despite proudly sporting a scar befitting a marine biologist, my wedding ring won't be on my finger on future dives.

Ken and I had admired the extensive sea grass and sand flats we'd seen in regions of Pigeon Creek on the southeastern corner of the island. "My uncle can take you bonefishing," said the Bahamian woman manning the front desk of the Riding Rock Inn, the only place on San Salvador, outside of the Club Med, that hosted guided fishing trips and the occasional marlin tournament. Ken took the phone number she handed him, and we returned to the open-bed truck parked outside brimming with students and snorkeling gear. We'd admired the island's mangrove and sea grass flats for years. It was time to see if we could line up a bonefishing trip for our fast approaching half-day off. Later that evening, Ken called the number. "The guide's going to take us bonefishing off Pigeon Cay and wants us to meet him at his house first thing tomorrow," explained Ken. The next morning, with class dismissed until after lunch, Ken and I loaded our spinning rods, tackle, hats, water, sunscreen, and extra sunglasses into one of the station's rickety old vans. Driving west from the station, we passed Rocky Point and then wound south, passing through Cockburn Town and down the coast to Fernandez Bay with its ten-foot-high white cross marking the spot where Christopher Columbus purportedly first came ashore in the New World on October 12, 1492. A mile or two later, we turned into Sugar Loaf Settlement and parked in front of a semicircle of small houses painted in bold Bahamian colors. The layout suggested an enclave of an extended family. Ken and I knocked on the door and were immediately greeted by a young man in his early twenties. "Sorry, man, my cousin won't be able to take you bonefishing," he said in the unhurried melody of Bahamian English. "But no worry, I'm supposed to take you," he continued, as Ken and I exchanged looks of concern. And with that, our newly established fishing guide loaded a small gas-powered outboard engine, a can of gas, several well-worn rods and reels, a tackle box, and a cooler into his pickup truck and motioned for us to toss our gear in the truck bed and join him in the cab. We were off: Pigeon Creek or bust, but given the clatter of the truck's engine, hopefully not the latter.

Half an hour later, we pulled off the road just past the first in a cluster of long-abandoned, ferociously weathered cottages. At the water's edge lay our twelve-foot fishing skiff, flipped upside down and tied off to the trunk of a coconut palm. Old Place Settlement had once hosted a thriving fishery. Mounds of football-sized conch shells littered Pigeon Cay across the creek from where we stood, providing telltale clues to the demise of the fishing village. San Salvador, like most inhabited Caribbean islands, had once sported a queen conch fishery. The sweet meat of the snail's foot was diced and kneaded into a dough to make conch fritters, and the lustrous pink shell was fashioned into pottery and jewelry. Unfortunately, queen conch (*Strombus gigas*), while easily harvested, grow far too slowly to support a sustainable fishery. Making matters worse, the conchs reproduce late in life, resulting in adults being harvested at about the same time they start laying their coiled egg ribbons. The queen conch fishery in Florida collapsed in the mid-1970s. Faced with a similar predicament, the Bahamian government instituted protections, including a ban on the use of scuba diving for commercial conch fishing and cracking down on the illegal use of air compressors by conch divers during the summer, when conch fishing is prohibited. Today, the conch in the fragrant fritters cooked in huts adjacent to San Salvador's bars comes from conchs collected from outlying, uninhabited islands.

Ken and I and our fishing guide lifted the overturned skiff, sending land crabs scurrying for cover, and gently righted the boat. Our guide fitted the bracket of the outboard engine over the boat's upper transom and slowly tightened down the wing nuts. Poking around in his tackle box, he came across a rusty, sun-hardened boat plug and forced it into the hole at the base of the transom. Meanwhile, eager to fish, Ken and I loaded the gas can, cooler, and fishing gear into the boat. With everything packed, the three of us slid the small skiff knee-high into the waters of Pigeon Creek and climbed aboard. After countless attempted pull starts, and almost as many choke adjustments, the engine, at long last, sprang to life. We were ready to bonefish.

Other than the mouth, Pigeon Creek is really more of a bay, hosting vast expanses of shallow sand flats and sea grass beds framed by red-and-black mangroves. Where we'd launched the boat, the flats were about a half-mile wide and extended several miles in either direction to the north and southeast. Despite seemingly perfect bone-fishing conditions (no wind, clear water, our own private, virgin flats), over the next three hours of fishing we didn't catch or see a bonefish or, for that matter, any fish. Ken and I didn't know whether to attribute the disappointing result to our inexperienced guide, the lack of a flats boat that would have allowed us to fish shallower water, the bits and pieces of dead crab and shrimp the guide had brought along for bait, the tidal conditions, or, paradoxically, no fish to be had. Determined that we catch something, the guide abandoned the flats, motoring quickly out the mouth of Pigeon Creek and into an adjacent coastal bay surrounded by a few small islands. A few minutes later, we anchored over a dark-blue patch of water near Tall Island. Over our last remaining hour of "guided" fishing, Ken and I floated over the coral reef and reeled in small, hungry squirrelfish, goatfish, queen triggerfish, red hinds, and even a Nassau grouper. Nothing we caught, however, was big enough to take back to the station's kitchen staff to share with their Bahamian families.

Coral reefs all over the world, including those in San Salvador, are in trouble.[4] Marine biologists have identified two distinct categories of controls that influence the structure and health of coral reef communities—bottom-up and top-down impacts.[5] Bottom-up impacts include such things as excessive nutrient runoff from agricultural fertilizers that enhance coral-smothering seaweeds or toxic pollutants from industry that kill sensitive corals. Bottom-up impacts on coral communities are not an issue for coral reefs on remote islands such as San Salvador, but they do impact coral reef health in heavily populated coastal environments. The Miami region of Florida is a case in point.

Top-down impacts on coral reef structure and health are exemplified by what Ken and I experienced fishing the coral reef near Tall Island. We didn't catch any big fish, and some types of fish seemed to be rare or missing. Fish that live on coral reefs display a variety of feeding habits: some are herbivores, some carnivores, and others generalists. Among the most important groups of reef fish are those species that intensively graze seaweeds. Parrot fish and surgeonfish are good examples, as they are generally abundant and aggressively mow down seaweeds; they are the sheep of the oceanic pastures. Without these fish, seaweeds soon grow to cover the reef and out-compete the corals for nutrients and space. Corals also compete with seaweeds for sunlight because hard corals possess tiny algal plants called zooxanthellae (symbiotic dinoflagellates) that have a mutualistic relationship with their host coral. In this win-win partnership, the symbiotic algae receive nutrients and a place to live within the coral polyp, and the coral receives the products of algal photosynthesis (sugars) that satisfy up to 90 percent of their energy needs. Ken and I suspect that many of the reefs surrounding San Salvador, like so many coral reefs worldwide, are suffering from overfishing. Without sufficient fish grazing, the reefs become inundated with fleshy seaweeds and the corals lose their algal symbionts. Eventually, the corals die. I've seen coral reefs in the Caribbean, including a reef near the Columbus monument on San Salvador, so overgrown with seaweeds they have essentially become coral graveyards. Without living corals, reef calcification becomes insufficient to keep pace with rising sea level. Ecosystem services are squandered, the reefs no longer serving as nurseries for invertebrates and fish or effective coastal barriers against increasingly powerful tropical storms and hurricanes.

With fewer and fewer bar jacks and barracuda being caught near the station, Ken and I decided it was time to test the fishing in the harbor. We'd passed through Cockburn Town enough times in our truck with our students to know that the harbor typically housed six to eight thirty- to forty-foot offshore sportfishing boats docked in slips and, on occasion, a larger, visiting yacht. The harbor's water was azure, the color of the sky on a summer's day, but deep enough to obscure a view of the bottom. We hadn't any idea what we might catch, and our expectations were low. At the far end of the harbor, adjacent to the boat slips, a gazebo stood with two picnic tables surrounded by coconut palms: a nice spot to enjoy a respite from the searing sun, cool down in the sea breezes, read a book, and leave fishing gear while going for a walk. When it came to finding a place to buy bait to fish the harbor, Ken and I were out of luck. Nobody on the island sold frozen squid, shrimp, or anchovy—not the small grocery store, the pharmacy, or the shack under the almond tree where an elderly woman sold her handwoven straw baskets and dolls. Accordingly, we began slipping leftover hot dogs into ziplock baggies whenever they were served in the station's cafeteria. We wrote our names on the baggies and stored the hot dogs in a community refrigerator in the mosquito-infested faculty lounge.

Hook and line tied off to a dime-sized fishing weight, I cast a chunk of hot dog toward the center of the harbor. After my bait sank to the bottom, I tightened line slack and sat down on the edge of the concrete wall. When I didn't have even a nibble, I thought that fishing the harbor was a nonstarter. By the time the yank came, I'd relaxed to the point that my rod and reel were almost pulled out of my hands. "Fish!" I hollered as I stood up and set the hook in one fluid

motion. Ken waved from across the harbor where he'd been walking the bank and tossing a three-inch plastic grub without success.
Shocked to hear my spinning reel screaming drag, the trajectory of
my line indicated that the fish was making its initial run down the
length of the harbor and away from the docked boats. Tightening my
grip on the rod's handle, I let go with my right hand and used my free
thumb and forefinger to slightly tighten the reel's drag adjustment
knob. With eight-pound test line, I was going to need to balance controlling this fish in the tight confines of the harbor with setting just
enough drag to wear the fish down without it breaking off. I needed
to stay in the saddle.

Bonefish (*Albula vulpes*) are found worldwide and are notorious for
their fight.[6] I consider them, pound for pound, to be the strongest fish
I've ever tackled. The long, thin, tapered body has a bluish-green
tinge when viewed from the top, but both sides are silvery and lined
with horizontal rows of scales that give the fish a striped appearance.
The fins are gray and exaggerated in size, especially the dorsal fin
and the tail fin; the latter contributes to the fish's tremendous fighting
capabilities. Bonefish have a comical, cone-shaped snout, and like
most bottom-feeding fish, the mouth projects downward. Somewhat
unique, the top of the mouth and the tongue's surface harbor dental
plates coated with tiny, granular teeth designed to crush and grind
prey. With the exception of the one in the harbor that had swallowed
my hot dog, bonefish forage in shallow estuaries, bays, and grass
flats, taking advantage of high tides to prowl the shallows in schools.
Their diet consists of small fish and a host of bottom-dwelling marine invertebrates, including polychaete worms, crabs, shrimp, snails,
and clams. Being amphidromous, bonefish can move freely between
offshore saltwater environments and the near-fresh waters that are
found in the upper reaches of tidal creeks, estuaries, and bays. Moreover, like freshwater gar, bonefish have the rare ability to gulp air to
offset the low levels of oxygen that periodically occur in the shallows
of estuaries and bays heated by a tropical sun. The fish mature at
about two years of age and gather in the spring to spawn in deeper,

offshore waters where currents disperse their embryos and larvae. As the larvae develop, they adopt a ribbonlike shape that is retained until they grow to about two inches—at which time, as juveniles, they move into shallower water.

As the fish I would soon know to be a three-pound bonefish continued its run down the length of the harbor, I followed along with a deeply bent rod, taking care between spurts of line drag to keep my footing on the top of the harbor's wall. One misstep and I would be free-falling six feet into the water with no way to crawl back up. Given this fish's strength, the 1971 sixteen-pound world record bonefish caught by Jerry Lavenstein in Bimini must have felt like a Great Dane on the end of a leash, chasing a squirrel. As the fish neared the mouth of the harbor's channel leading to the sea, I tightened down, reeling line between rod lifts. I was able to turn the fish before it reached the boulder-lined channel, but it was now headed back up the harbor toward the docked boats. By now, Ken had walked back around the harbor to see what I'd hooked. "It's acting like a bonefish," he said, looking up between casts. "Long runs and staying down." At the moment, a few other possibilities had crossed my mind. The fish could be a palometa, a species similarly colored to bonefish with spectacularly elongated dorsal and ventral fins and, despite their small size, known to fight almost as vigorously as a bonefish. My catch also might be a cowfish, a rectangular, box-shaped fish with small horns that Ken and I had often seen in sea grass beds while night-snorkeling with our students. I once caught one of these comical-looking fish off the station and was impressed with its ability to fight. As my line approached the boats, I knew it was time to see if I could handle whatever fight remained in the fish on my eight-pound test. With some trepidation, I screwed down the drag adjustment knob one more time and began working the fish away from the boats and toward me and the harbor wall. The tactic worked well at first, and I was briefly lulled into thinking I could bring the fish to the wall in a straight shot. Halfway in, the bonefish had other ideas. Once again the fish turned and ran, this time directly toward the nearest boat slip. There was nothing I could do other than lay into the fish.

Fly-fishing for bonefish has become so glamorous it has spawned a global industry in and of itself. Expensive flats boats capable of floating in as little as six inches of water sport guides on towers who pole and point to tailing bonefish. High-end clients wearing hundred-dollar fishing hats, two-hundred-dollar breathable fishing shirts, and two-thousand-dollar fly outfits try their luck. Bonefish lodges dot tropical islands and mainland coasts across the planet, charging fishers eight hundred dollars a night. In *A Pirate Looks at Fifty*,[7] Jimmy Buffet describes the dreamlike experience of setting his solo-piloted floatplane down off the shores of uncharted Caribbean islands to cast into schools of hungry bonefish that had never seen a fly. Even San Salvador has its occasional bonefish purist. Early one morning, Ken and I arrived to fish the Cockburn Town Harbor and discovered a massive yacht tied off to the harbor wall not far from where we planned to fish. The motor yacht stretched over one hundred feet, too large to fit a boat slip. Later that morning, a stunning twenty-foot flats boat returned to the harbor and tied off to the stern of the yacht. Stepping off the flats boat was a fishing guide with fly poles and a well-dressed gentleman who was almost certainly the owner of the yacht. It was pretty clear that the flats boat was part of the package, towed by the yacht, and that the yacht's owner and his guide had been out bonefishing all morning. Both guide and owner looked frustrated.

As the yacht owner walked past us, he paused to watch Ken hoist a lively, flopping bonefish from the harbor. The timing couldn't have been better. Clearly upset by Ken's catch and sizing up our worn-out jeans, T-shirts, and modest rods and reels, the yachtsman grudgingly inquired, "What'd you catch it on?" "Hot dog," said Ken, after a brief pause for effect. Marching off without as much as a nod in our direction, the yachtsman exclaimed, "Damn! I spend thousands trying to catch a bonefish, and these guys are catching them in the harbor on hot dogs!"

Sport fishers have long contemplated what constitutes a "catch." Does catching a fish necessarily require that the fish is brought to the shore or boated? If so, why don't fishers say, "I landed three big ones" or "I boated ten fish"? In my experience, the term *catch* depends on who's making the call. For some, hooking a fish for an arbitrary period of time before the fish breaks free is a catch. A billfish fisher might consider a fish caught that cuts the leader when leaping. For others, getting a fish up to the side of a riverbank or boat is a catch. Fish that are pulled from the water but then escape back into the water with a sudden thrust of the tail are considered caught by some but not by others. Stricter fishers may deem a fish a catch when it's flopping on the floorboards or well up on the stream bank. My own interpretation of a catch is tempered by the type of fish. An eight-ounce sunfish that is reeled halfway back to the boat before escaping is several notches down my catch spectrum from a five-hundred-pound marlin that runs out a mile of 130-pound line, leaps into the air, and breaks off.

Ken and I had good reason to admire the lineup of sportfishing boats docked next to the gazebo each year we fished the harbor. The boats glistened with promise. Each boat represented an investment of over a million dollars, and each was provisioned with an elegant air-conditioned interior, a spotting deck, and a large, padded fishing chair affixed by heavy hardware to the back deck. It was a chair where, when securely belted, good things happened. The boats were in the harbor for only one reason: blue marlin, long considered the top game fish on the planet. And San Salvador was known for its blue marlin. Fishers flew in from around the world to try their luck. The island delivered and for good reason. Its geology was perfect.

The geology of San Salvador differs from many of the other islands in the Bahamian Archipelago in an important and fundamental respect. Its geographic position relative to the Little Bahama Bank and the Great Bahama Bank, two prominent shallow-water regions of the Florida continental shelf, is great for marlin fishing. The island is not positioned on either bank. Rather, the formerly submerged, carbonate island is isolated and surrounded by the deep sea. The "wall" for which San Salvador is famous closely parallels the west coast of the island and plunges three thousand vertical feet, a height equivalent to the sheer granite face of El Capitan in California's Yosemite Valley. As a graduate student, I descended San Salvador's wall aboard the *Johnson Sea Link* submersible.[8] Tightly squeezed into the lower chamber of the *Johnson Sea Link*, it took me and a former navy diver thirty minutes to reach the base of the wall. Directly above us, the pilot and chief scientist operated the sub from within a five-foot-diameter acrylic sphere. While we rested on the seafloor, the former U.S. Navy diver took sadistic pleasure in telling me the story of the two men who in 1973 died of carbon dioxide poisoning and hypothermia exactly where we lay in our lower chamber. One of the ill-fated men, thirty-one-year-old Edwin Clayton Link, was the son of industrialist Edwin Albert Link (the designer of the *Johnson Sea Link*). Edwin Albert was also famous for inventing the flight simulator and as a pioneer in underwater archeology and ocean engineering. When the *Johnson Sea Link* became entangled in debris from the scuttled destroyer USS *Fred T. Breyer*, the lower chamber had not yet been equipped with sufficient thermal insulation or carbon dioxide scrubbers to remove the deadly gas. When the submersible was finally freed twenty-four hours later and hoisted to the surface, it was too late for the two men in the lower chamber. Following the tragedy, thermal insulation and carbon dioxide scrubbers were added to the lower chamber. Deeply wounded by the loss of his son, Edwin Albert Link dedicated his life to designing an unmanned rescue vehicle called the Cabled Observation and Rescue Device (CORD), capable of freeing trapped submersibles. To this day, CORD operates in seas around the world.

The San Salvador wall provided spectacular views despite the one small circular window on my side of the chamber. Before we started back up the wall, the pilot, following the directions of the chief scientist, used the sub's manipulator arms to collect stalked crinoids.[9] Palm-tree-shaped and about two feet tall, these deepwater echinoderms once formed dense meadows in ancient shallow seas. Now, rarely viewed in their natural habitat by humans, they appeared out my sub window as apparitions from the Paleozoic. As we began our ascent, a deepwater shark swam by the sub, momentarily illuminated in our floodlights. Over the next three hours, we rose up the wall, pausing to collect brittle stars and sea urchins or to take photographs of sponges, soft corals, bryozoans, hydroids, and other wall-encrusting marine invertebrates. Approaching the wall's upper reaches, we began to see more and more fish, the greatest numbers and diversity swimming past us in the final three hundred feet of the ascent. The wall creates ideal oceanic conditions to attract blue marlin and other big game fish, serving as a conveyor belt that brings deep, cold, nutrient-rich water to the ocean's surface. The upwelled nutrients enrich blooms of phytoplankton, which in turn feed zooplankton. The plankton in turn nourish small fish, consumed by larger fish, which ultimately provide for the fish at the top of the food chain: the blue marlin, tuna, sailfish, and wahoo. Combine this abundance of food with easy access to "offshore fishing" no more than a five-minute motor from the harbor to the wall, and you have the perfect ingredients for big game sportfishing.

Off and on, when Ken and I visited the harbor, we stopped to chat with the skippers or crew living aboard the visiting sportfishing boats. Most of the skippers were following orders from an owner to keep the boats harbored, carry out maintenance and minor repairs, and wait for the owner to fly down to San Salvador with a business client. Countless deals have been cut over a day or two of marlin fishing. Every few weeks, a skipper might be directed by the owner to sail to another island or to return to a home port along the coast of Florida. Despite the private nature of the sportfishing boats, Ken kept on the lookout for a skipper who might have the latitude to charter his boat and take us fishing during our half-day off. One year, during a brief stopover at the harbor with students, Ken struck up a conversation with a skipper who was allowed to charter the boat he captained. We jumped at this rare opportunity and made arrangements for a half-day fishing trip the next morning. We'd fish for blue marlin and maybe get into some tuna.

Neither Ken nor I had ever fished for blue marlin. By the time we stepped aboard the forty-foot sportfishing boat the next morning, our anticipation was palpable. Following a few words from the skipper about life jackets and cold drinks, Ken and I climbed the steep steps to the upper deck and bridge. The mate tossed the bow and stern lines, and as the skipper edged our boat out of the slip, I took a minute to size up the two rigged fishing rods that were positioned in the gunnel rod holders below me on the lower deck. Each of the seven-foot rods had a thumb-sized diameter that belied flexibility, and both sported Penn reels the size of buckets, strung with over a mile of 130-pound monofilament line. These rods meant business. While we could have started trolling on the wall just five minutes from the harbor mouth, the skipper told us he preferred to fish for marlin at the south end of the island near Sandy Hook, a sharp point of land with a stunning white sand beach that nudged right up against the wall. Between the throb of the huge inboard engines, the wind whistling past at twenty knots, and views of the coastal limestone cliffs, the ride was exhilarating. Half an hour later, the skipper cut the engines, and as we gently rolled with the mild swell, he and the mate prepared to troll for marlin. First, the skipper set up a "teaser," which is a two-foot-long, brightly colored, hookless lure whose sole purpose was to be pulled behind the boat by a thin rope line to attract big game fish. Meanwhile, the mate prepared two marlin lures, each consisting of a foot-and-a-half lure-like device composed of a big "jig head" attached to a skirt of bright-colored streamers. The mate threaded the end of the fishing line through a hole in the top of the jig head and tied off a huge hook with a gap that measured about two and a half inches between the shank and the hook tip. The mate then strung the hook through the mouth of a sixteen-inch, freshly thawed, elongate baitfish called a ballyhoo, a species that belongs to a group of fish known as halfbeaks (because the lower jaw is much longer than the upper), and finished up by attaching a separate section of line tied off to a second hook that he poked through the ballyhoo's tail. When finished, the tail ends of the ballyhoo hung below the skirts of the two marlin lures.

With the teaser and lures ready to go, the skipper returned to the bridge and got the boat under way. Once we were moving at about five knots, the skipper locked the steering in place and returned briefly to the lower deck to assist the mate. First, the skipper tossed the teaser into the churning white water behind the engines. The coils of thin rope spun off the deck until the end of the rope, tied off to an eye bolt on the center of the transom, grew taught. Peering back behind the boat, Ken and I could see the teaser in the distance, skipping along the water's surface. Next, the skipper and mate each lifted a rod and, standing on opposite sides of the boat, clicked the release buttons on the reels and dropped the marlin baits into the sea, sustaining enough drag to prevent spool snags. When the men had released about four hundred feet of line, they engaged the drag, set the poles in their holders, and clipped the lines into the outriggers (the ten-foot aluminum poles on each side of the boat that keep the two towed lines from tangling). When a fish hits, the clip at the end of the outrigger releases the line back to the fishing reel. The tug of this transfer often helps set the hook. With both lines fishing, the skipper returned to the bridge and accelerated the boat to about eight knots.

As our skipper guided the vessel along the contours of the wall, the mate explained that Ken and I would be taking turns with the belt. The coveted fishing belt was strapped around the waist and secured with a heavy front-locking clip. When battling a fish, the front and center three-inch-diameter cup accepted the rod's base, while connecting fixtures on each side of the belt clipped off to straps attached to each side of the chair. Ken nodded, and I belted up. Fishing was slow, and an hour passed without any action. Then one of the rods jerked, a small jolt triggered by the reel's line popping free of the outrigger. "Fish on," yelled the mate, and the skipper cut the engines and climbed down to retrieve the other line. The mate lifted the rod and jerked it deeply, twice, to ensure a set hook. "You won't need the chair," he said to me, slowing my adrenaline rush. Standing against the back rail, the mate transferred the rod to the cup in my belt and hesitated a second or two to make sure I had full control of the rod before letting go. I could feel the fish struggling against the line, a distant *whump, whump, whump*. As I worked the rod and reel, I could tell the fish was vastly outgunned by my heavy fishing gear: no rod bend, no squeal of drag, an easy crank. Soon, I eyed a fifteen-pound blackfin that had intercepted the marlin lure. The mate gaffed the tuna and hoisted it to the deck. The fish, bleeding and with tail flopping, was destined for an iced cooler and, later in the day, the marine station's kitchen. In a few minutes, we were again under way, this time with Ken belted, ready for action. The next hit came sooner than the first, and Ken stood and reeled in a twelve-pound, iridescent blue-backed, silver-gray wahoo that, with the mate's assistance, joined the blackfin tuna in the cooler. Wahoo are sleek, strong game fish that are considered to be among the best by gourmets. We suspected the fish would be prized by our station's kitchen staff. As our morning of marlin fishing dwindled, I reeled in one more similar-sized blackfin tuna to add to the cooler.

With Ken belted, our thoughts turned to the approaching afternoon and a fringing reef we planned to snorkel with our students. Suddenly, one of the two rods bent fast and hard as its line exploded free of the outrigger. "Could be a marlin!" yelled the skipper, as he shut down the engine and leaped down the steps to reel in the second rod. Ken, wide-eyed, obeyed the mate's urging to sit down so that he could clip Ken's fishing belt into the two straps on the chair. The rod tip was bucking and the reel drag singing as the skipper positioned the base of the rod in Ken's belt cup. Ken peered down at the reel in his lap spinning out line, then, with a look of helplessness, glanced up at me. Later, he told me he'd been afraid to put his hands anywhere near the spinning reel for fear of wrapping a finger. What the skipper later estimated to be a five-hundred-pound blue marlin[10] ran out a good seven hundred feet of line before it leapt. Unlike Ken, I saw the jump clearly from my vantage point. It was a moment I'll never forget. "It's a marlin, all right!" I yelled, awestruck by the big fish's blue-black back and long bill. Once again, Ken glanced at the screaming, bucket-sized reel, yet to engage the fish. The skipper, too, saw the jump and knew Ken was into a big marlin. Darting back up the ladder to the bridge, he ignited the engines and slammed the boat into reverse. By this point, the little line that was left on the reel had Ken worried as the marlin was rapidly spooling. Just as running out of line seemed imminent, the mighty fish leapt again, providing another display of its powerful, fusiform body, followed by a distant splash as it fell back to the sea. Ken's line went limp. "Shoot!" yelled the skipper. "It cut the line, and got the lure, too." Ken, saddened, slowly unclipped his belt from the chair and reluctantly handed the rod and reel to the mate, who set to work reeling in a mile of empty line. "About one out of every ten big marlin cut the line with their tail when they leap," explained the skipper, still stinging from the loss of his hundred-dollar marlin lure.

The two blackfin tuna and the wahoo Ken and I had caught on the sportfishing boat lay on the shiny metal counter next to the industrial sink in the marine station's kitchen. Fresh offshore fish were rare on the island, and we were pleased to present the bounty to our Bahamian cooks. Pleasantries were exchanged, and Ken hinted that the tuna steaks would taste good that night at dinner. Whether it was a dilemma that ensued after we departed about how to distribute the fish to a cafeteria full of students and faculty or whether something was lost in communication, Ken and I never saw the fish again. But knowing they fed the families of our Bahamian friends, that was absolutely fine.

8

COSTA RICA

Tarpon

Ken's face was bright red. Worse, he was soaked from head to toe with sweat, the kind of profuse perspiration brought on by battling a 130-pound tarpon less than eleven degrees north of the equator. Eddie Brown, a famous tarpon guide, had been on his cell phone ever since the tarpon exploded on Ken's jig twenty minutes earlier. Tarpon are renowned for their leaping abilities, and Ken's big fish was no exception, jumping over and over, each head-wagging leap of its six-foot length followed by a deep dive and screams of drag. As Ken grasped the bucking, bent rod, I saw the exhaustion in his eyes, heard it in his grunts, and smelled it in his sweat. Perhaps sensing the trembling in his arms, Ken worked extra hard to reel the big fish to the boat. As each run shortened, Ken leaned harder into his medium-weight rod, well aware of the delicate balance between manhandling a fish this size and having it snap a line with a test-weight five times less than the weight of the fish. At last, Ken got the big tarpon up close, well within range to poke a gaff through the skin of the lower jaw and hoist the fish halfway out of the sea for a quick photo. Captain Eddie Brown, tall and broad shouldered, glanced down at Ken and his tarpon. "He's not ready," he said calmly, pausing only long enough from his conversation on the cell phone to utter the brief proclamation. Ken peered up at Eddie in stunned disbelief. Given a last-minute reprieve, the massive tarpon rolled and dove out of sight.

Ken and I were on the Atlantic coast of Costa Rica, staying at the Tortuga Lodge with fourteen college students enrolled in our tropical rainforest ecology class, a complement to the tropical ecology field class we'd started teaching several years earlier in the Bahamas. Our practice of giving our students a half-day off during the course gave us an opportunity to fish for tarpon. Six days earlier, we'd flown from Birmingham to Miami to San José, the capital city of Costa Rica.

Our Costa Rican naturalist guide and bus driver met our class at the airport, and our bus wound up narrow, pot-holed roads to our hotel in the verdant hills above the city.

The next day, we drove higher into the mountains to the cloud forests of Monte Verde. We spent two days exploring the towering rainforest and lecturing to our students about the ecology of the rainforest's under- and over story, hiking the trails, and negotiating wobbling suspension bridges high in the canopy. We searched for and found the rare resplendent quetzal, considered one of the world's most beautiful and colorful birds, with its iridescent green-and-blue three-foot tail feathers. We visited a small garden abuzz with fifteen or more species of hummingbirds. Feeders with sweetened water dangled from poles, which allowed our students to observe a wide spectrum of the hovering birds sporting short, medium, and long, thin beaks, each uniquely sculpted to fit into a different-shaped flower. Driving east, our bus descended from the cloud forest, and we spent the next night at a hotel at the base of 5,480-foot Mount Arenal, one of six active volcanos in Costa Rica. As we lay in our beds, we watched through our hotel room windows as lava spilled from the caldera. We listened to distant explosions of red-hot, ricocheting boulders rolling down the volcano's slopes.

The next day, we continued to the nearby La Selva Biological Station,[1] a preserve run by the Organization for Tropical Studies, made up of sixty international colleges, universities, and research institutes. Our students ate lunch in the station's cafeteria with a cadre of faculty and graduate students who were studying such things as how tropical insects detect and locate the plants they pollinate and how rainforests influence global climate change. Our tour of west central Costa Rica and its environs ended when we abandoned our bus at the end of a dirt road on the Rio Tortuguero and boarded two eighteen-foot, open-canopied riverboats.

Heading northeast, we roared down the tannin-laden river, passing caiman (small alligators), flocks of pink flamingos, and equally pink spoonbills scooping up small crustaceans from the sediments.

At times, we seemed to have stepped back in time, passing fish camps composed of thatched-roof huts perched atop wooden posts. After a three-hour journey, we docked in front of the Tortuga Lodge, a beautifully landscaped riverfront cluster of hardwood buildings hugging a length of the Rio Tortuguero that parallels the sea-turtled beaches of the Atlantic. We stayed for three days, exploring the rainforests of Tortuguero National Park. Like tracing an artery to a capillary, we navigated river to creek, spotting white-faced capuchin monkeys, three-toed sloths, keel-billed toucans, pygmy kingfishers, and basilisks called "Jesus Christ lizards" because they skittered across the water on webbed toes. We led our students on hikes under towering trees on sloppy trails to see the bright-blue wing flashes of the Blue Morpho butterfly and columns of leaf-cutter ants carrying foliage that was later masticated by tiny worker ants into mulch to grow a fungus that nourished the entire ant colony.

Eddie was right about Ken's tarpon. The big fish dove hard after Ken reeled it tight to the boat, an indication that gaffing the fish would have been premature. Years later, I learned why. In January 2012, Ken and I went on a guided fishing trip in the coastal waters of Florida's Everglades National Park. I hooked a fifty-pound tarpon with a jig tipped with a live shrimp and was wrestling the fish to the side of the boat when our guide, Benny Blanco, reached out with his gaff and popped the hook free from the fish's jaw before it had reached the boat. "Why'd you do that?" I asked, a little surprised that there wouldn't be a photo of me with my fish. "I've started letting 'em go before they get to the boat," explained Benny. "That way, they won't keep slamming against the hull and get themselves all beat up." Benny went on to explain that instead of taking boat-side photos, he switched to using the camera in his cell phone to record tarpon being reeled in by his fishing clients. He then sent the clients the video clips.

Fortunately, the biggest tarpon Ken had ever hooked had but five minutes of play left in it before Eddie gently gaffed its lower jaw. Ken, exhausted, watched as Eddie used both hands to power-lift the fish half out of the water so I could snap a quick photo of Ken and his catch. Eddie lowered the upper torso of the fish back into the sea, slid the gaff free, and, using a pair of needle-nose pliers, carefully removed the jig's hook from the lower lip. For a moment, the tarpon lay quietly next to the boat. Then, with a flick of its tail, Ken's big fish disappeared.

"Silver king" is an apt name for the Atlantic tarpon (*Megalops atlanticus*).[2] The fish's brilliant chrome sides are crowned by a greenish hue that stretches the length of the dorsum. Except for the head with its gold eyes, diamond-shaped scales coat the body. An upturned mouth and accentuated lower jaw render a mischievous grin. Atlantic tarpon can reach a length of eight feet and grow to four hundred pounds. The International Game Fish Association all-tackle world record Atlantic tarpon was caught by Max Domecq on March 20, 2003, off the coast of Guinea-Bissau in West Africa.[3] The fish weighed an impressive 286 pounds. Like many other big game fish, longevity in tarpon can be extensive: thirty years in males and as many as fifty years in females. A female in the Chicago Shedd Aquarium lived for sixty-three years, yet in the wild, most fish probably succumb to factors other than old age. Tarpon are remarkably tough, tolerating huge fluxes in salinity that give the fish the latitude to move freely between saltwater and freshwater. Their swim bladder is packed with spongy alveolar tissue that allows the organ to function in buoyancy and also as a "lung." Combine this with their practice of gulping air, and tarpon are uniquely adapted to chase down prey in oxygen-poor bays and estuaries. Despite their toughness, normally energetic tarpon become sluggish when water temperatures fall to sixty degrees Fahrenheit, and the fish die below fifty degrees.

Tarpon gather offshore in the late spring or early summer to breed. Despite fish biologists having attached satellite tags to follow the seasonal movements of sexually mature fish, knowledge of tarpon-spawning sites remains elusive. Each female releases over ten million eggs, and fertilized embryos pass through several planktonic larval stages before, as juveniles, the fish move into bays, estuaries, and rivers to grow quickly on diets of aquatic insects and small crustaceans. Once adults, some, but not all, tarpon move back to the sea. Those that do return to the sea may join populations that live inshore or offshore, where, as aggressive predators, they feed on crabs, penaeid shrimp, and fish. Juvenile tarpon fall prey to large fish and wading birds, including storks and herons, but as adults, tarpon have few predators other than sharks. Because tarpon are generally considered too bony to be eaten by humans and are largely protected by catch-and-release fishing policies, the primary pressure on tarpon populations comes from the loss of marsh habitat as a result of development, sea-level rise, and increasingly powerful storms.

The schooling and feeding behaviors of tarpon are impressive to see firsthand. I did so at a waterfront restaurant over a bowl of gumbo and a bottle of beer at the Fifteenth Street Fisheries in Fort Lauderdale, Florida. Ken and I were drawn to the restaurant not for its live tarpon, of which we were unaware, but for the seafood and view. The rambling wooden restaurant was perched along the west bank of the Intracoastal Waterway near the Port Everglades inlet to the Atlantic Ocean. Upstairs, a lovely dining room murmured with patrons, the fresh fish of the day sketched on small table-side chalkboards. Downstairs bustled a more informal section of the restaurant, with both indoor and outdoor seating and a bar where bands played on warm evenings. Extending from one end of the restaurant, a wooden walkway led to the waterfront.

To the right, a dock extended fifty feet along the waterway in front of the restaurant, forming a U-shaped harbor about the size of a large swimming pool. Forty to fifty tarpon, ranging from thirty to a hundred pounds, swam below the dock. When Ken first saw the schooling tarpon, he couldn't resist walking next door to the adjoining market and buying a bag of frozen shrimp. Returning to the dock, he handed me a few, and we tossed pieces of shrimp and watched the powerful fish rush in to beat out their competitors (other tarpon and smaller jacks), snatching pieces of shrimp with strikes at the surface, making loud smacking noises.

The locals knew about the tarpon at the popular restaurant, and while dining there one evening, we witnessed a young man in his early twenties who either had a death wish or was trying to impress the young ladies. Rather than toss shrimp into the water, he lay on the edge of the dock and held a shrimp in his hand, allowing one end to dangle in the water. At first, the young man's timing was good; he released the shrimp and whipped his arm back at the very instant a tarpon would strike. But a few minutes later, we noticed the hand he was using to feed the tarpon was bleeding, a sign something had gone wrong between a shrimp release and a hungry tarpon. Despite the wounded hand, the young man decided to one-up himself, clenching one end of the next shrimp with his teeth and lowering his head, face first, to the water's surface. Ken and his wife Vicki and I exchanged knowing glances. Sure enough, a tarpon exploded through the water's surface, and despite the fellow's best intention of pulling off a record-breaking push-up, the tarpon's gaping mouth engulfed both the shrimp and the young man's chin. Face intact but ego bruised, our entertainer retreated to the bar. Had he lost his life to the tarpon strike, I suspect that the former daredevil would have been eligible for a Darwin Award,[4] a sober but humorous distinction for individuals when they remove themselves from the gene pool and, in so doing, improve the odds of our species' long-term survival.

When Ken and I arrived at the Tortuga Lodge with our students, we were unaware the lodge also served as home base for Costa Rican Eddie Brown and his brother, Roberto, both internationally recognized tarpon and snook guides who started fishing when they were fifteen years of age. Captain Eddie Brown was outgoing with a booming voice. He won the National Tarpon Tournament several times, and rumor had it he was the undisputed tarpon king of Costa Rica. Eddie had been featured on television, guiding professional fishers after big tarpon. Given the chances of booking a tarpon guide of his fame on short notice, we were fortunate to schedule a half-day trip. Eddie explained we'd leave the lodge early in the morning and be back for lunch and that he'd provide the fishing gear. We'd look for tarpon schooling along the coast. Meanwhile, Ken and I admired Eddie's nineteen-foot sportfishing boat tied off to the pier in front of the lodge.

Our fishing morning dawned with calm winds and a blue sky. Eddie, having risen early, had the boat ready to go. Rods were strung and lined up in holders, and a cooler was packed with iced bottles of water. We pulled free of the lodge's dock, and Eddie steered the boat north, downriver. We were headed about a mile to the spot where the Rio Tortuguero emptied into the Atlantic Ocean. Eventually, we arrived at a long spit of sandy beach that marked our approach to the river mouth, and we could see ocean waves breaking in the distance. River mouths that enter the sea are notoriously dangerous. Having grown up surfing in Southern California, I knew that surfers target river mouths where shifting sands build shallow sandbars, forming ocean waves that rear up and break hard. Captain Eddie told Ken and me to sit down and hold on tight. Before we knew it, we were headed out of the river mouth, and Eddie was gunning the boat, full bore, up the face of a five-foot wave. We made it over the crest just in time, barely avoiding the wave's breaking lip and powerful white water. Ahead, another wave reared up. Eddie gunned the boat up and over at least five more waves until we escaped, relieved, to the open sea.

Several years after our students first stayed at the Tortuga Lodge, Ken and two of his fishing partners, Bruce Cusic and Ron Thrasher, attended an annual fund-raising dinner hosted by the Cahaba River Society in Birmingham, Alabama. When it came time to auction the big-ticket items at the gala, the three well-lubricated friends decided to jointly bid on an all-inclusive trip for six to a Costa Rican tarpon-fishing lodge not far from the Tortuga Lodge. The package vacation seemed a steal, so all three friends were surprised when they won the trip without any competing bids.

When the three fishers and their wives arrived at the empty fishing lodge, the proprietors were surprised they'd come to fish during December. The Atlantic Ocean was stormy and waves at the river mouth high. Tarpon fishing would be challenging, if not impossible. When Ken, Bruce, and Ron gathered on the dock the first morning, the two tarpon guides split the three fishers into two boats. Ken and Ron went with the guide who piloted the lead boat, and Bruce accompanied the other guide in a second boat. As they neared the entrance to the sea, Ken looked over his shoulder and noticed yet another boat following them. "Why is there a third boat?" Ken asked his guide. "If anyone goes into the water, that's the boat that rescues them," the guide responded. Ken looked up and saw that the waves breaking at the mouth of the river were at least six feet high. The guide accelerated rapidly up the first wave, and the boat broke through the wave's lip just as it crested. The forward momentum was sufficient to launch the boat completely into the air. Ken told me that he thought he had broken his back when the airborne boat hit the water. While the lead boat's guide had timed his approach to punch through the crests of the waves, Bruce's guide had not been as deliberate in maneuvering his boat. A huge wave broke into the vessel, and Bruce found himself buried in a cascade of ice-cold water. For a few seconds, Bruce thought he was going into the sea. Somehow, the guide managed to get the craft moving and eventually joined the lead boat on the outside of the swells. The third boat wasn't needed, this time.

Now safely in the Atlantic Ocean, Eddie headed our boat south toward the village of Tortuguero, paralleling the beach about a quarter mile offshore over a depth of about one hundred feet. Despite gently rolling seas, the surface was glassy. Half an hour later, Eddie saw what he'd been looking for—a distant school of fish churning up the water's surface. Shutting down the engine, Eddie lifted the first of two rods out of its holder and tied on a jig head with a chartreuse skirt. The lure, no bigger than a standard two-and-a-half-inch bass lure, and the medium-size rod and spinning reel, were surprisingly modest for big tarpon. Once Eddie handed Ken and me our rigged

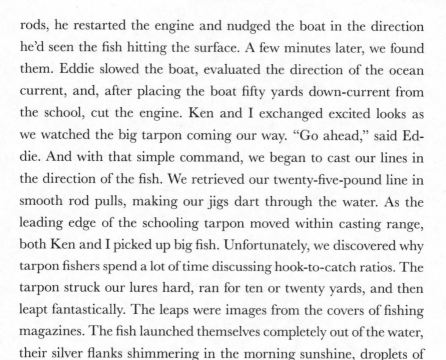

rods, he restarted the engine and nudged the boat in the direction he'd seen the fish hitting the surface. A few minutes later, we found them. Eddie slowed the boat, evaluated the direction of the ocean current, and, after placing the boat fifty yards down-current from the school, cut the engine. Ken and I exchanged excited looks as we watched the big tarpon coming our way. "Go ahead," said Eddie. And with that simple command, we began to cast our lines in the direction of the fish. We retrieved our twenty-five-pound line in smooth rod pulls, making our jigs dart through the water. As the leading edge of the schooling tarpon moved within casting range, both Ken and I picked up big fish. Unfortunately, we discovered why tarpon fishers spend a lot of time discussing hook-to-catch ratios. The tarpon struck our lures hard, ran for ten or twenty yards, and then leapt fantastically. The leaps were images from the covers of fishing magazines. The fish launched themselves completely out of the water, their silver flanks shimmering in the morning sunshine, droplets of seawater sprinkling the sea's surface. As the tarpon leapt, they slung their heads violently back and forth. The combination of head wags and a bony, hook-resistant palate resulted in the fish tossing the lures, if not on the first leap, then on the second, third, or fourth. After hooking six big fish only to watch each toss my lure, I began to wonder if I were going to get one to the boat.

The seventh tarpon hit my jig like a bull redfish, hard and deep. As it burst from the sea, it was abundantly clear the fish was big—really big—as big as the 130-pounder that Ken boated later that morning. *Please don't come off,* I thought to myself as Ken reeled in his line. My hopes rose as the fish remained on the line after the initial series of leaps. The big tarpon ran out drag in thirty-second bursts countered with two- to three-minute bouts of intense reeling. It seemed each time I worked the tarpon within twenty feet of the boat the fish would see the boat, spook, and dive. "You gotta wear him down," said Eddie nonchalantly, as if catching a fish this size was as routine as a short-order cook flipping a fried egg. "Keep your rod tip up," demanded Eddie. "Don't let it go under the engine!" he yelled.

It was clear that Eddie was in charge, and I was sure that he would equally have ordered about the most skilled saltwater fisher. After what seemed about an hour but was in fact twenty minutes, Eddie gaffed the lower lip off my tarpon and lifted it half out of the water. Ken snapped a quick photo of me and my fish. I didn't mind that the rest of the tarpon I hooked that morning threw their lures.

Next to tarpon, snook are the most popular among the fishers who hire Eddie and Roberto at the Tortuga Lodge. Snook are reputed to be tremendous fighters on light to medium tackle. In the mid-1990s, a few years after Ken and I began visiting the Tortuga Lodge with our students, Ken stayed at the lodge with a middle school biology class from Delaware. Ken's friend from Birmingham, Buzz Peavey, a travel agent, fisher, and naturalist, had invited Ken to help teach the class. Ken and Buzz approached Captain Eddie about the possibility of snook fishing, and Eddie agreed to take them on a half-day trip.

The appointed morning arrived, and Ken and Buzz boarded Eddie's boat and found themselves flying full-throttle up a series of rivers, first to the north and then to the northeast. The fishers soon lost their bearings as Captain Eddie dodged down side-canals from river to river, heading to some undisclosed location. After an hour and a half of racing along, enjoying glimpses of monkeys, parrots, hawks, and iguanas, the two fishers and Eddie reached the Rio San Juan. Demarcating much of the border between Costa Rica and Nicaragua, the river has been the focus of numerous territorial disputes and conflicts. Eddie pulled the boat up in front of a tiny primitive shack perched on a cut made in a slope of the riverbank. Positioned next to the shack was a lone flagpole flying the blue and white colors of Nicaragua. The door opened and out of the shack emerged a border patrol agent in his early twenties, dressed in partial military garb—boots, camouflage fatigue pants, and a sleeveless white T-shirt. Eddie tied off the boat to the rickety dock and opened the cooler. The guard accepted the six-pack of Imperial beer, and the two men chatted for a few minutes. Ken didn't notice any paperwork exchanging hands.

Half an hour after making their border stop, Eddie tied off the fishing boat to a dock in the Nicaraguan village of Greytown near the mouth of the Rio San Juan. The local boats, some roped to the dock, others pulled up on the shore, were in various states of disrepair. All sported weathered outboard engines, many without cowlings. "I'm going to see the mayor for a fishing license," announced Eddie, departing with another six-pack under his arm and leaving Ken and Buzz seated, alone, in the docked fishing boat. The two fishers nervously surveyed their surroundings. On the wooden boat dock and the surrounding muddy bank, a group of about ten teenagers sprawled, dressed, much like the border guard, in partial military outfits. A number of the young men gripped rusty AK-47 rifles. Ken and Buzz didn't speak more than a few words of Spanish, and the Nicaraguan soldiers apparently didn't speak any English. An awkward silence enveloped the men, who, on and off, glanced uncomfortably at one other. Ken told me later that the twenty minutes that Eddie was gone seemed more like an hour.

When Eddie returned from his visit with the mayor, it took just fifteen more minutes to motor the fishing boat to a delta where the Rio San Juan broadened into a series of sandbar-littered inlets and channels before entering the sea. Eddie raised the outboard engine and slid the boat up on a sandy beach. Ken, Buzz, and Eddie walked along the shore, wading in ankle-deep water, casting jigs and spoons from medium-weight spinning rods into the surf. Eddie was encouraging, even optimistic, at first, explaining that big snook piled up in these inlets and channels at the mouth of the river. But after two hours of fishing and only a single jack crevalle between the three of them, Eddie suddenly announced they were leaving. Ken and Buzz's big snook trip hadn't produced a snook, but the wildlife glimpsed on the two-hour return run to the Tortuga Lodge was just as good as what they'd seen on the trip out.

I had better luck than Ken and Buzz with catching a big snook on the 2012 fishing trip that Ken and I took to the Florida Everglades. Snook are tropical fish, in the genus *Centropomus*,[5] and are opportunistic ambush predators that hide in wait for crabs, shrimp, and, especially, small to medium-size fish. A study carried out by fisheries biologists of the Florida Fish and Wildlife Research Institute examined the stomach contents of 432 snook collected from Charlotte Harbor, Florida.[6] The scientists reported that fish composed an impressive 70 percent of the prey that was in the snooks' stomachs. The best places for snook to ambush fish is at the mouth of a creek or river or by hiding in structure, especially the entangled systems of prop roots that support red mangrove trees.

"They're starting to come back," remarked our Florida fishing guide Benny Blanco, explaining that two years earlier, in January 2010, an arctic cold front had plunged temperatures in the Everglades as low as the upper twenties. The record freezing-cold air drove coastal water temperatures down below fifty degrees Fahrenheit, and snook, known to be extremely sensitive to low temperature, died by the thousands.[7] Benny described the pristine mangrove inlets where we were about to fish as littered with the carcasses of bloated, rotting snook. Other species were killed, including tarpon, ladyfish, catfish, pinfish, and various members of the mojarra family. The only good thing about the arctic air, Benny pointed out, was that the cold killed off some of the invasive Burmese pythons[8] that, to this day, continue to breed and to devastate native mammals and birds in the Everglades. The pythons were introduced when a snake-breeding house was damaged by a hurricane, and the problem was exacerbated by a few pet owners looking for a place to illegally release their unwanted snakes.

Earlier that afternoon, Benny edged his boat up into a slough and removed a ten-foot-diameter bait-casting net with quarter-inch mesh from his boat box. With the throw line attached to his left wrist, Benny gathered the net up into a bundle. He took one of the egg-shaped weights along the edge of the net in his teeth, and holding the bulk of the bundled net in his left hand and a length of the weighted edge of the net in his right, he tossed the weighted edge while quickly following with the release of net from mouth and left hand. The net

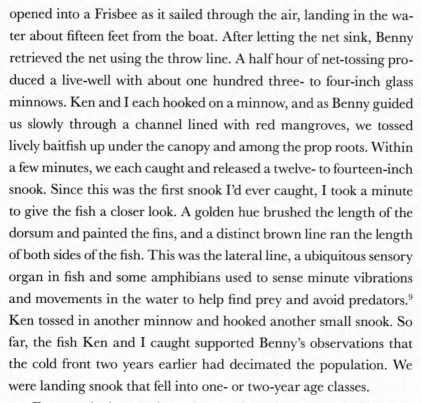

opened into a Frisbee as it sailed through the air, landing in the water about fifteen feet from the boat. After letting the net sink, Benny retrieved the net using the throw line. A half hour of net-tossing produced a live-well with about one hundred three- to four-inch glass minnows. Ken and I each hooked on a minnow, and as Benny guided us slowly through a channel lined with red mangroves, we tossed lively baitfish up under the canopy and among the prop roots. Within a few minutes, we each caught and released a twelve- to fourteen-inch snook. Since this was the first snook I'd ever caught, I took a minute to give the fish a closer look. A golden hue brushed the length of the dorsum and painted the fins, and a distinct brown line ran the length of both sides of the fish. This was the lateral line, a ubiquitous sensory organ in fish and some amphibians used to sense minute vibrations and movements in the water to help find prey and avoid predators.[9] Ken tossed in another minnow and hooked another small snook. So far, the fish Ken and I caught supported Benny's observations that the cold front two years earlier had decimated the population. We were landing snook that fell into one- or two-year age classes.

Fortunately, it turned out that our hypothesis that all the snook waiting to ambush our minnows in the prop roots were less than two years of age was false. A tremendous strike on my rod erased any doubt that at least one fish had survived the deadly cold front. I'd read that snook are great fighting fish, and within the first minute of hooking my seven-pounder, I was convinced. "Keep it out of the mangroves!" Benny cautioned, and I managed to work the fish out of the prop roots and toward the center of the channel. Surrounded by mangroves, this was not the place to let a big snook run too much drag. Breaking off would almost be a certainty should the fish wrap me on a prop root. Fortunately, I was able to wear the snook down while keeping it in the middle of the channel. Benny leaned over the side of the boat and dipped a three-foot-diameter long-handled fishnet under the snook. "Nice fish," he chimed as he lifted the fish by the lower lip and handed it to me. The photo Ken snapped of me grinning and holding my thirty-six-inch Atlantic snook hangs proudly on my office door. Not quite the International Game Fish Association all-tackle record of fifty-three pounds and ten ounces,[10] but a nice fish all the same.

Early each morning at the Tortuga Lodge, before our students arose, Ken and I met for a cup of strong coffee and cast jigs off the lodge dock using the collapsible fishing rods we brought along in our suitcases. We caught a few tiny snook but were mostly rewarded with an abundance of feisty checkered puffer fish (*Sphoeroides testudineus*),[11] which are common in the area. The ten- to twelve-inch, tan-colored fish were covered with a square network of olive lines that spared only the white underside of the abdomen. Brackish, riverine waters such as the Rio Tortuguero in front of the Tortuga Lodge are among their favored habitats, although checkered puffer fish and other species can equally thrive in coastal marine and inland freshwater environments. The ability of puffer fish to rapidly adjust the amount of salt in their blood plasma gives the fish the flexibility to thrive in either fresh or saline water. Collectively, puffer fish share several key features, including platelike teeth adapted to crushing the clams, snails, crabs, barnacles, and small lobsters that make up their diets; the ability to inflate their bodies when threatened; and, should puffing up prove insufficient to intimidate a predator, an extremely potent nerve toxin. Ken and I enjoyed watching the checkered puffers swim. We coaxed them to the dock by tossing bits of food into the water and watched them combine rapid fin movements and a rudder-like tail to maneuver about like little helicopters. We discovered that while the checkered puffers typically swim slowly, they put up a brilliant fight when hooked, suggesting that the tail is quite capable of transitioning from rudder to engine.

What puffer fish are most recognized for in the popular press is the nerve toxin tetradotoxin.[12] Twelve hundred times more toxic than cyanide, the tetradotoxin in puffer fish is sequestered in the skin and liver where it is likely produced by various strains of *Vibrio* bacteria. A single adult puffer fish contains enough tetradotoxin to kill about thirty humans. The toxin is so potent that it gives the puffer fish the distinction of being one of the most deadly vertebrates on Earth. While puffer fish are not eaten by humans in Costa Rica, in some regions of Asia, and particularly in Japan, puffer fish meat (*fugu* in Japanese) is prized as a delicacy and prepared and served in restaurants. Every year, as many as fifty human deaths are ascribed to eating puffer fish that a cook has inadvertently contaminated with tetradotoxin from the fish's skin or liver. A restaurant patron suffering from the ingestion of a fatal dose of tetradotoxin first experiences numbness of the lips, tongue, face, hands, and feet; then exhibits excessive salivation, vomiting, diarrhea, stomach pain, and speech difficulties; and in the end displays seizures, paralysis, and death, the latter, in most cases, from respiratory failure.

In a few situations, however, ingestion of tetradotoxin need not be fatal. A recent BBC documentary film crew captured video images of young dolphins cautiously handling a puffer fish in their jaws. Each dolphin lightly squeezed the puffer several times and then passed it to another dolphin, who repeated the fish-mouthing behavior. The filmmakers suspected the dolphins were using tetradotoxin derived from puffer fish to "get high." According to the producers of the film, after mouthing puffer fish, the dolphins acted "stoned," including long bouts of staring at their own reflections on the underside of the surface of the water. "Dude, pass the pufferfish," quipped Ben Wolford, the author of a 2013 *International Science Times* article on the topic of dolphins and puffers.[13]

In a letter to the editor that appeared in the June 1988 issue of the prestigious journal *Science,* Canadian anthropologist Wade Davis reported that in the course of studying the ethnobiology of zombification in Haiti, he learned that sorcerers (*bokors*) included several marine fish in the ingredients of a prepared powder called *poud zombie*.[14] Independent chemical analysis of two samples of the powder revealed the presence of trace amounts of tetradotoxin in one of the two samples, suggesting to Davis that tetradotoxin might cause deathlike symptoms that in rare instances are reversible. In other words, the victim appears dead to others and is then revived. Davis argued that the result of such events would be so powerful from a sociological perspective that, even if such events occurred only rarely, this would be sufficient to support a cultural acceptance of the concept of zombies (reanimated human corpses). While Davis did not invoke puffer fish per se in his article on zombification, the fish would seem a likely candidate as a source of tetradotoxin. Many of Davis's postulates garnered considerable scientific criticism, but his tenet, that on rare occasion victims of tetradotoxin poisoning display deathlike symptoms and recover, has been supported by similar observations in some Japanese people who have consumed tetradotoxin-contaminated puffer fish.

One morning after breakfast, Ken instructed our students to gather on the Tortuga Lodge dock. Ken loved to share surprising animal behaviors with students, and the puffer fish he caught earlier and put in a bucket of water was just the ticket. The students circled Ken and leaned in to watch as he reached down and gently poked the puffer with the end of a stick. Nothing happened, so Ken poked the fish again. The third poke proved the charm, and the puffer inflated its body to almost three times its normal size. The students, clearly impressed, listened as Ken explained that puffers inflate themselves with water to discourage predators, and that it's not a good idea to stimulate a puffer to inflate out of water because the fish may become too buoyant to swim. Ken pointed out that to accommodate inflation puffers have flexible muscles and lots of stretchy belly skin that allows for expansive swelling of the abdomen. Ken knew some wonderful myths about puffers that he shared with our students. Puffers don't pop or explode if you prick them; they don't die once inflated, although puffing up is considered a stressful, last-ditch defense response, and they don't, like a balloon, zoom around backward as they deflate.

The day following our tarpon-fishing adventure with Eddie Brown was the last field day in the Tortuguero region before we headed home. Our Costa Rican guide planned to take the class on one last morning boat excursion in search of wildlife in Tortuguero National Park. Then, after lunch, we would ferry from the lodge across the Rio Tortuguero to hike a famous stretch of beach adjacent to the Archie Carr Center for Sea Turtle Research. Archie Carr, who died in 1987, was an eminent ecologist and pioneering conservationist whose work with sea turtles is legendary.[15] Instrumental in sounding the alarm, Professor Carr brought to the world's attention the fact that sea turtles were in dire straits due to excessive hunting and loss of coastal nesting habitat. We were at an epicenter for sea turtles. Leatherbacks, hawksbills, greens, and loggerheads have emerged from the Atlantic to lay their eggs on the beaches of Tortuguera for millennia.

Unfortunately, May was not the best time to see females crawl from the sea to dig holes and deposit their eggs or to see hatchlings scurry to the waves. And yet an outside chance existed for us to see something exciting, if only a turtle crawl—the tracks left on the beach by a turtle. Hiking along the wet sand the next day, we gazed offshore at the rollers coming off the Atlantic. The cold water, the strong rip currents, and the bull sharks known to prowl the shore preying on turtles and tarpon muted any temptation to go for a swim. Unfortunately, other than one turtle crawl that was barely visible in the sand, we didn't see any signs of sea turtles. What we did see, washed up along the high-water line, was marine litter: plastic bottles and jugs, pieces of nylon nets, fishing floats, chunks of Styrofoam, rubber gloves, flip-flops, tennis shoes, balls of fishing line, CDs, toys, and many other items.

I reached down to pick up a translucent-blue plastic bag about the size of a large kitchen wastebasket liner that was caught on a piece of beach driftwood. Several days earlier, our class had been given a tour of a Costa Rican banana plantation. We'd seen hundreds of acres of heavily irrigated and fertilized banana trees, each loaded with ripening banana bunches and each bunch wrapped in a blue plastic bag. "The plastic bags are drenched in insecticide to protect fruit from insects and also help hide it from birds, monkeys, and other wildlife," explained our Costa Rican guide. We watched field laborers work in pairs, using razor-sharp knives to cut the stalks of the banana bunches and attaching them to hooks suspended from a head-high cableway that disappeared between rows of banana trees. When enough bunches were hung, donkeys or humans pulled the parade of banana bunches along the cable to the open-air processing plant. Despite the blue pesticide bags being removed by workers at the plant before the bananas are floated in large rinse basins, loose plastic banana bags find their way into the countryside.

Wind-blown or carried by storm runoff into small streams and tributaries, the plastic banana bags release pesticides into freshwater environments, which serve as sources of drinking water for humans and as habitat for aquatic invertebrates and fish. One insecticide that is widely used in association with the banana bags is chlorpyrifos, a compound with neurotoxic properties in the organophosphate family of insecticides. Studies have found that children living near banana plantations have higher concentrations of chlorpyrifos in their bodies than children in other areas and are thus at risk for impaired cognitive function.[16] Among freshwater organisms, studies show that exposure to concentrated chlorpyrifos kills fish, insects, and crustaceans. During the rainy season, torrents of water sweep a parade of blue plastic banana bags downstream into rivers, where the bags are carried, ultimately, to the Pacific or Atlantic Ocean. By the time the bags reach the sea, the pesticides are likely diminished, but the bags remain far from harmless as sea turtles mistake the blue plastic bags for jellyfish, one of their natural prey. Once in the sea turtle's digestive system, the plastic bags get stuck in the intestines, blocking normal movements of food and causing death.

Studies over recent years have revealed that plastics in the world's oceans occur as large floating objects such as soda bottles and as small particles of plastic that can be divided into distinct size categories. Mesoplastics are plastics greater than about a quarter-inch in size that are easily seen by the naked eye; microplastics are less than about a fifteenth-inch and just barely visible to the naked eye, or easily visible under a low-resolution microscope, and nanoplastics

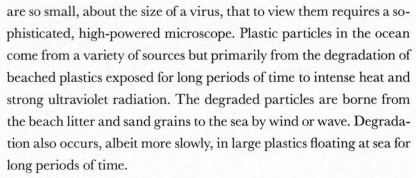

are so small, about the size of a virus, that to view them requires a so-phisticated, high-powered microscope. Plastic particles in the ocean come from a variety of sources but primarily from the degradation of beached plastics exposed for long periods of time to intense heat and strong ultraviolet radiation. The degraded particles are borne from the beach litter and sand grains to the sea by wind or wave. Degrada-tion also occurs, albeit more slowly, in large plastics floating at sea for long periods of time.

Today, massive whirlpools, or gyres, of plastics occur in various regions of the world's oceans. The most famous gyre is located in the northwestern Pacific Ocean and is known as the Great Pacific Gar-bage Patch.[17] Estimates of the dimensions of the garbage patch vary widely, depending on seasonal changes in ocean current patterns, but range from about a quarter million to over fifty million square miles.[18] Aerial photographs of the sea in the region reveal an endless skin of floating plastics as far as the eye can see.

Despite their small size, plastic particles can negatively impact marine life. In a 2014 journal paper published in the *Proceedings of the National Academy of Sciences* (*PNAS*), scientists reported that plastic par-ticles are increasingly finding their way into organisms that comprise trophic levels of midwater food webs.[19] Filter-feeding zooplankton, including tiny crustaceans such as copepods and euphausiids, are in-cidental consumers of microplastics, while predators of zooplankton, such as small, midwater fish, are also susceptible, having been found with guts containing significant amounts of plastic particles. The au-thors of the *PNAS* study estimate that at present the amount of plastic in the guts of oceanic midwater column fish is similar to the amount of plastics floating at the ocean's surface. While plastic particles do not constrict the intestines of fish like a plastic banana bag can in a sea turtle's gut, the tiny particles can absorb and transport harmful toxic chemicals and decrease the efficiency of food processing, thus compromising nutrition.

As our class turned to hike back down the beach to meet our waiting boats, the early evening sky displayed all the ingredients of a spectacular sunset—low-level stratus clouds and sky-to-horizon hues of yellow, orange, and rose. The students, disappointed we hadn't seen a sea turtle, walked silently, introspective, knowing the long week of exploring Costa Rica was coming to an end. A finger tap on my shoulder caught my attention. "Would it be OK for me to run over behind those sand dunes and relieve myself?" quietly asked one of our male students. "Sure," I said, continuing on my way. Suddenly, we heard a shout from the dunes, followed by the student's voice yelling, "Dr. McClintock and Dr. Marion, come here, come see!" The class heard the commotion and joined Ken and me as we zeroed in on the shout. Climbing over a small sand dune, we were greeted by the student and the sight of tiny flippers breaking through the sand. The flippers were soon followed by equally tiny heads then gray-green shells and tails. One by one, twenty loggerhead turtle hatchlings emerged, leaving behind the shells they had occupied for the past two months. The students watched intently as each baby turtle headed toward the ocean. Ten minutes later, the hatchlings had crawled over a dune, across the sand beach, and into the ocean. Faced with unbeatable odds, many of the hatchlings would succumb to small tarpon and sharks. Perhaps one female would make it to maturity and return to this very beach to lay her eggs, year after year, potentially growing to over six feet and more than a thousand pounds. "That was so cool," exclaimed one of our students, still reeling from the sight of the hatchlings crawling into the sea.

"We owe it all to a bladder," I said.

9

FRANCE

Anchovies

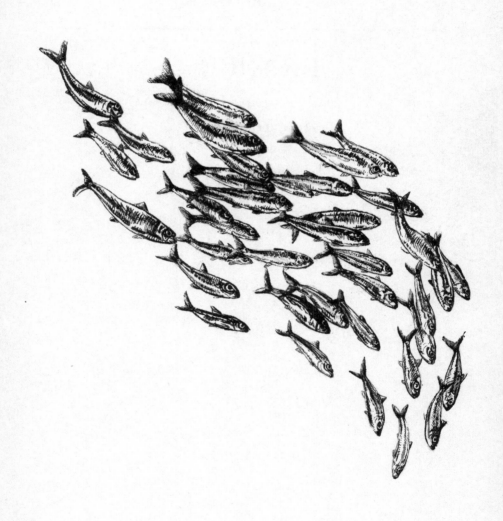

W ith her hair pulled back in a white hair net, the woman sat behind a sparkling-clean, stainless steel table. She wore a blue vinyl apron that hung to her knees and disposable plastic sleeves on her arms. In front of her were a half-dozen cookie-sheet-sized pieces of white parchment paper, each piece holding four neatly stacked columns of tiny, overlapping fish fillets. The inside of the old salting house was cool and damp and smelled of fish, of course. Long hours of sitting in the refrigerated air had taught the anchovy processor to bundle up, and she wore a heavy sweatshirt under her apron and a thick, orange knit scarf wrapped twice around her neck.

At one time an anchovy processing facility, Maison Roque, a coral-pink building, sat on a corner of Avenue du Général de Gaulle in the French Mediterranean town of Collioure. Downstairs, a market sold anchovies, and upstairs, where as many as thirty anchovy processors had once worked, a museum housed live demonstrations of anchovy processing. The company, Anchois Roque, was famous the world over for its anchovy products, having been founded almost a century and a half earlier as a small artisan company by Monsieur Roque.

My wife Ferne and I, and Dr. Anne-Marie Geneviève, our host and a biologist at the Banyuls-sur-Mer Oceanological Observatory, where I was carrying out a research sabbatical in the spring of 2014, watched as the woman demonstrated with her bare hands how anchovies are processed. A pile of about twenty five- to six-inch headless fish lay in front of her on the stainless steel table. The anchovies had been removed from one of several fifty-gallon barrels stacked against the wall, each tightly fitted with a plastic lid. Brine, formed from liquid leached from the fish, seeped out under the lid and down the upper sides of the barrel. When the top of one of the barrels was pried open, we saw, layered in brine, anchovies that had been packed fresh in salt for three to seven days, beheaded and gutted by hand (a twist of the head followed by a pull that removes both gut and head), rinsed in water, repacked in repeated layers of salt and fish, and cured in a cool warehouse for three to eight months. The curing ratio of salt to fish was half a pound of salt for every pound of fish. Following an age-old process, the expert lifted a headless anchovy from the pile on the table and, using her fingers in a deft, practiced motion, pulled the dorsal fin and peeled apart two fillets, one from each side of the backbone. She discarded the backbone and excess skin in a white plastic container and laid the two fillets at the bottom of the final column of fillets she had lined up on the parchment paper. With sufficient columns of fillets now complete, she moved on to the next step, hand-packing the anchovy fillets into fist-sized glass jars. When about a dozen jars were packed with fish, she carried them, on a tray, to a top-loading balance where she weighed each jar, adding or removing a fillet or two to reach the targeted weight. Later, the jars of anchovy fillets would be topped with vinegar or sunflower oil, sealed, and shipped around the world. At the main processing facility we visited later in the day, some anchovies were ground into a fine paste and combined with vinegar before being similarly packed and shipped.

Madame Malou Roque, general director of Anchois Roque, invited us into her upstairs office in the modern warehouse in an industrial section on the outskirts of town. "This region of France, and Collioure in particular, has a storied history of anchovy artisans,"[1] Madam Roque explained to us. She referred to a history dating back to medieval times when Collioure was the major commercial port on the Vermillion coast. Over the centuries, fishermen in small, single-mast Catalans (small sailing boats) headed out each morning to return later with netted anchovies. The brightly colored boats, painted in decorative combinations of light blue, yellow, and red, are still used today and proudly sailed on holidays. Ferne and I enjoyed watching people restore Catalan vessels in Banyuls-sur-Mer and other harbor towns.

Around the beginning of the twentieth century, as many as forty salt houses were still spread about the town of Collioure, employing hundreds of anchovy fishers, processors, and shippers. "Today, there are just two salting houses: ours, started by my great-grandfather in 1870, and Anchois Declaux, which was opened in 1903," explained Madame Roque, noting that her family's historic company was now in its fifth generation of *saleurs* (curers). Both of the remaining anchovy companies in Collioure pride themselves on upholding old traditions: hand processing the fish, using the same time-proven techniques, and seasoning and curing with the basic ingredients of salt, vinegar, and sunflower oil, the latter used instead of olive oil because it ages better.

"So where do your anchovies come from?" I asked Madame Roque as she shuffled through a stack of papers, looking for a brochure highlighting her company. I fully expected to learn which of the local port towns provided Anchois Roque its fresh anchovies for processing.

"Our anchovies don't come from the Mediterranean anymore," she responded, catching me off guard. Madame Roque explained that the anchovies were now shipped from the Atlantic coast where they are harvested between May and October. Mediterranean anchovies, she explained, suffered a dramatic decline beginning in 2001, and the few anchovy fisheries that remained were having problems netting enough fish to make ends meet. I asked her how many anchovies are shipped in from the Atlantic each year. "A hundred tons a year," she said. I pressed on and asked if it wouldn't make more sense to move her company to the Atlantic coast of France where the anchovies are being harvested? "No," Madame Roque replied quickly and went on to explain that the history of the anchovy in the region was too rich, too deep. Buyers around the world have come to expect the anchovies to originate from the "anchovy coast," a region of Catalonia, encompassing both the Vermillion coast of France and the Costa Brava of Spain. Clearly, the market value of this geographic branding was sufficient for the Roque family to stay rooted in its historic location. The scenario seemed analogous to discovering that Maine lobsters had vanished from the seafloor, and the famous New England lobster fishery shipped in lobsters from the Pacific to sustain the branding of a Maine product. Of course, this analogy is a hypothetical case in point, yet it echoes the dramatic nature of what has befallen the Mediterranean anchovy.

The European anchovy, *Engraulis encrasicolus,* was first described by the father of taxonomy, eighteenth-century Swedish botanist and zoologist Carolus Linnaeus. The small fish, no more than seven to eight inches, is best imagined swimming among a tight school of fellow anchovies where there is safety in numbers. Silver-green, the slender body with its single dorsal fin terminates in a forked tail, and the lower jaw is recessed below a protruding, pointy snout. The tiny mouths can open wide to filter planktonic copepods, amphipods, fish larvae, and other minute prey swimming or floating in the water column. The European anchovy ranges widely, its biogeographic distribution encompassing vast regions of the Mediterranean Sea and the Atlantic Ocean. Populations also used to be found in the Black Sea. Spawning occurs in the summer and early spring, mostly near river mouths where eddies and currents can distribute the eggs. Along the French Mediterranean coast, anchovies have historically spawned near the mouth of the Rhône River. Once fertilized, the clear, pencil-dot-sized eggs float in the upper water column, where development to a transparent larva takes only two days. The see-through nature of eggs and larvae is no accident but rather an adaptation found in many fish that render offspring invisible to predators that prowl the water column looking for prey. In anchovies, growth is fast and life is short, with longevity no more than three years.

"I finally found an anchovy fisherman!" Anne-Marie Geneviève exclaimed in her office in the Banyuls-sur-Mer Oceanological Observatory. For the past two weeks, Anne-Marie had been on

a crusade, calling friends and professional colleagues to see if anyone knew someone who still fished for anchovies for a living along the coast of the western French Mediterranean. We would drive over to the town of Port-Vendres the following week and meet the anchovy fisherman at the dock where he moors his boat, explained Anne-Marie.

"I'm going to have to sell my boat," grumbled Gabriel Diaz, a middle-aged French fisherman, as we stood with Anne-Marie on the edge of the bustling Port-Vendres harbor. Gabriel explained that when the moon was full and the sea calm he would motor his fifty-foot vessel out of the harbor and offshore to pull a big net, or trawl, after anchovies. Yet, like other fishers, his anchovy landings had been falling steadily for years, and, sadly, he'd watched as one after another of his fellow fishers sold their anchovy trawlers. Now, he was the last remaining anchovy fisher in Port-Vendres.

Anchovy purse seiners had also disappeared from Port-Vendres. Purse seining is a netting technique that employs a large "wall" of netting with floats attached to the top and a lead line strung along the bottom. Fishermen deploy the seine in a circle around a school of anchovies. A fisher cinches the bottom lead line and hand pulls, or winches, the purse-shaped net to the surface and up into the boat. Traditional anchovy purse seiners equipped their small boats with a *lamparo,* an acetylene lamp hung high over the bow, lighting the area within the net at night to attract anchovies to the sea's surface. Modern purse seiners string multiple electric lamps along the length of their boats. In ancient Greece, fishers in crude wooden boats cast nets over schools of small fish attracted to light from the flames of handheld torches.

I asked Gabriel why he thought the anchovy fishery in the Mediterranean was in such deep trouble. "The anchovies are not only scarce, but are now much smaller," he responded, holding out his thumb and forefinger, spread four inches apart, to emphasize what an average-sized anchovy harvested from the Mediterranean now measured. Gabriel explained that the fish he caught used to measure seven to eight inches in length. With the authority that comes from a life spent fishing the sea, Gabriel declared that Mediterranean anchovies had been "overfished" and for far too long. He explained that as fishers harvested even the small adult fish, they robbed the sea of mature fish capable of replenishing and sustaining the populations. Now, despite fewer anchovy fishers left to fish, the anchovy populations are still not recovering. In addition to suffering overfishing, anchovies in the Mediterranean faced additional problems. Probably the most significant of these is the invasive sea walnut *Mnemiopsis leidyi*, which literally wiped out anchovies in the Black Sea in the 1980s[2] and has, more recently, begun to take a toll on anchovy populations in the Mediterranean.

Sea walnut is a great descriptor of this walnut-sized and -shaped comb jelly, technically known as a ctenophore. Comb jellies look a little like jellyfish but differ in some important ways. Rather than using tentacles for propulsion, comb jellies have five rows of tiny hair-like cilia, called comb rows or ctenes, that beat in a synchronous fashion. Comb jellies also lack stinging bodies, or nematocysts, which are unique to jellyfish and can cause pain or even paralysis when touched by humans. Whenever I teach my invertebrate zoology course, I take my college students on a collecting trip in an eighty-foot ship owned and operated by the Dauphin Island Sea Lab near Mobile, Alabama. We collect comb jellies known as *Beroe* in plankton nets towed from the ship. I love plopping the freshly netted comb jellies in a quart-sized glass jar of seawater. Each student holds the jar of comb jellies up to the sun, watching the active comb rows generate rainbows of blues, greens, and reds, the result of their orchestrated cilia scattering wavelengths of light.

Watching these beautiful animals swimming in a sunlit jar, my students find it difficult to believe the comb jelly's close relative has a history of causing wholesale ecological disaster. Released from the ballast tanks of merchant ships that had loaded ballast water in the western Atlantic Ocean, the comb jelly was introduced to the Black Sea in the early 1980s. At the time, only a single native species of comb jelly existed in the entire Black Sea, and accordingly,

Mnemiopsis had virtually no competitors and plenty of resources to exploit. Comb jellies are voracious plankton predators that have a remarkable capacity to reproduce. A single adult *Mnemiopsis* can produce up to ten thousand eggs. Being a hermaphrodite, with both ovaries and testes, it is quite capable of self-fertilization. By 1989, the Black Sea was a soup of plankton-devouring *Mnemiopsis,* with densities as high as 270 comb jellies per cubic yard of seawater. In the face of billions of hungry *Mnemiopsis,* zooplankton, including the eggs and larvae of water-column fish, had little chance to survive. It didn't take long for the anchovy fisheries in the Black Sea to completely collapse. More recently, *Mnemiopsis* has found its way into a number of other large bodies of water, including the Mediterranean Sea, probably hitching a ride in the ballast water of a merchant or cruise ship. Fortunately, the conditions for the exponential population growth were not as favorable in the Mediterranean as in the Black Sea, but there is no doubt that the establishment of this invasive comb jelly complemented overfishing as a contributing factor in the decline of Mediterranean anchovies.

Further stressing the European anchovy, the Mediterranean Sea has rightly earned a reputation as one of the most polluted seas in the world.[3] Rivers and streams bring in agricultural fertilizer and insecticide runoff, and hotels and resorts line much of the coastline, home to an onslaught of tourists during the summer vacation season. The quaint, peaceful town of Banyuls-sur-Mer, where my wife and I spent our quiet spring living in a mostly empty beachfront apartment complex during my sabbatical, explodes into a sea of tourists in July and August. Locals told us that in the summer it becomes simply impossible to find an apartment or hotel or to even spread your beach towel on the sand. Tourists visiting for the day park their cars miles from town and walk in on dangerous, winding roads or, if they are more fortunate, park on the sand-bed of a river that enters the sea in the middle of town. In the summer, the riverbed is typically dry, but the garage-door-sized sign attached to the bridge spanning the river mouth warns tourists that in the event of a heavy summer rainstorm the town is not responsible for riverbed-parked cars swept to sea. The sewer pipes of Mediterranean beachfront properties dump directly into the sea, and the sewage is modestly treated, if at all. The summer burst of nutrient input from the sewage results in thick blooms of phytoplankton that reduce water clarity and diminish sunlight, stressing or killing vast meadows of the common sea grass *Posidonia oceanica*. The added nutrients also encourage tiny seaweeds to grow right on the blades of the sea grass, further reducing access to sunlight for photosynthesis. As a result, sea grasses die, their decaying roots and blades overloading the seafloor sediments with oxygen-demanding organic detrital particles; coastal regions can literally become oxygen-starved (hypoxic), stressing marine invertebrates and fish.

On most weekdays, weather permitting, I walked two blocks home from my office at the Oceanological Observatory to meet Ferne for a picnic lunch. Sometimes, we packed a baguette, Brie, salami, apples, and chocolate into a basket and drove north to a park halfway between Banyuls-sur-Mer and Port-Vendres. Paulilles Recreation Park was nestled on the Bay of Paulilles, a stunning pocket of the Mediterranean. The park was also famous for being the historic site of the French Nobel Dynamite Factory from 1870 to 1984. The factory was named for the Swedish chemist and industrialist Alfred Nobel, who patented the process of combining nitroglycerine and silica into a paste called dynamite. Nobel left an endowment that to this day funds the annual Nobel Prizes. In the small museum, captions tell how the dynamite factory workers coveted their unusually high salaries, retirement benefits, and excellent medical care. Presumably, these benefits offset the thirty explosions that killed fifty of the workers over the lifetime of the factory.

When we didn't go to Paulilles, we had our lunch at one of several wooden picnic tables perched along the edge of the Banyuls-sur-Mer harbor, just in front of our apartment building. When there was a breeze, which was often, the small bells affixed to the sailboat masts tinkled like chimes. One day while having lunch at a picnic table several weeks after we'd arrived in town, I noticed a gentleman fishing off one of the harbor's six concrete docks where motorboats and sailboats were moored. A second gentleman was biding his time, standing and chatting with his friend, keeping him company. Next to the fisher sat a white bucket, and every now and then, the fisher would lean over and do something with the bucket, but I was too far away to make out what he was doing or, possibly, catching.

After lunch, my curiosity got the better of me, and, leaving Ferne at the picnic table, I wandered out on the concrete dock. I'd been curious about fishing in the harbor ever since arriving. I smiled and greeted the two gentlemen with "Bonjour." With this formality complete, I took the liberty of edging in close enough to the men to look inside the bucket, which held fifty slim fish, ranging in size from three to six inches. Baitfish! I was sure the fisher was catching bait that he would later use to catch mackerel or some other game fish. In my broken French, I asked the fisher what he planned to fish for with the "petite" baitfish he was catching. His response confused me at first because I didn't fully understand his French but also because I hadn't in the least expected the answer he gave me. After several reiterations of his initial response, coupled with a bit of sign language, I was able to decipher that the little fish weren't intended for bait but rather were to be prepared for evening hors d'oeuvres. Later, I learned that the fish swimming in the bucket were juvenile *éperlan,* or European smelt (*Osmerus eperlanus*), which belong to the salmonid fishes. This gentleman was reeling in the world's smallest "salmon."

The European smelt is a dainty coastal fish with silvery sides and a greenish-colored dorsum and split tail fin.[4] The fish school on shoals to filter-feed planktonic copepods, amphipods, and larval crabs, grazing on polychaete worms among the sandy sediments and, in estuaries, chasing down and eating their own offspring and other larval fish. Smelt are well known for remarkable reproductive output, with one female producing as many as forty thousand eggs. When it's time to spawn in the spring, large schools of European smelt migrate up rivers, gathering in areas where currents are slack to enhance the likelihood of sperm meeting egg, and then the sticky, fertilized eggs attach to the sand or gravel. After spawning, life for most smelt is over, as they die of old age after two to three years. Adult fish, particularly the males, die en masse, although a few individuals survive to ensure the eggs of females are fertilized the following year.

Peering off the dock and into the crystal-clear water, I watched the French gentleman's fishing rod move slowly up and down. Below was a school of smelt, perhaps several hundred, clearly attracted to the tiny jigs attached to a *sabiki* rig (also called a *piscatore* rig). Sabiki is a Japanese fishing technique that involves vertically jigging for baitfish. Throughout fishing history, live baitfish have been recognized as more effective than artificial baits in attracting game fish. The sabiki rig is composed of a series of about a dozen tiny, feathered lures, one above the next, and its effectiveness can save the day when baitfish are swimming too deep to be caught in a cast net. Every two to three minutes, a silver flash on the sabiki rig signaled a catch. A mouth-hooked éperlan darted rapidly back and forth, its bright silver flanks flashing, the green dorsum no longer providing camouflage protection. Reeling in the sabiki rig and laying it on the wooden dock, the fisher bent over and gently removed the BB-sized hook from the fish's lip and plopped the fish into his bucket of seawater. "How do you prepare the fish?" I asked in my awkward French. Appreciative of my efforts to speak the native language, the fisher methodically explained the preparation of éperlan, emphatically enunciating each sentence. "First, scale the fish," he said, picking up a dead fish floating in his bucket to demonstrate how to pull a knife blade against the direction the scales lay along the flank. "Then gut the fish, and you are ready to cook," he continued. "What about the head and the bones?" I inquired. "Leave them," he replied, his friend clearly amused by the image of trying to de-bone a three-inch fish.

Pausing to remove another smelt from his sabiki rig, the fisher continued to explain that to cook the fish one should heat sunflower or olive oil in a fry pan and sauté some minced fresh garlic, dredge the tiny fish in white flour mixed with salt and pepper, and fry the coated fish in the hot oil until crispy. Of course, a glass of chilled white wine and a piece of freshly baked baguette should accompany the fried fish. Hearing this, I couldn't take any more. I had to experience this French tradition.

I hadn't packed my two-piece fishing rod and spinning reel for my stay in France, so the next day, Ferne and I poked around Banyuls-sur-Mer until we found the one store that sold fishing gear, L'Espadon. When I asked the owner, who had introduced himself to us by his first name, Fabien, about getting me set up to fish for éperlan in the harbor, he knew his stuff. We started with the selection of a rod and reel. This was easy, as there was only one rod that was collapsible and could be carried home to Alabama in my baggage. The medium-weight telescoping rod with a medium-sized Autain spinning reel was far too big for the task, but when catching fish that weigh a twentieth of an ounce, even an ultralight outfit is overkill. Next, the owner selected an extremely lightweight fishing line, two-pound test, and several small weights, one of which would be tied off at the base of the line. The sabiki rig consisted of twelve tiny yellow-and-red jig heads, each affixed to whitish, plastic wings and two luminescent rainbow tails. The owner suggested I buy a small packet of hooks and some live bait as a backup for the sabiki rig. The hooks were comically tiny, even smaller than the hook on a dry fly. The live bait was unique, too. From a small refrigerator, Fabien removed a plastic container labeled DURES with the subheading "*Vers de Mer Vivante*"—"Living Worms of the Sea." Fabien popped off the plastic lid, revealing a squirming mass of five-inch polychaete worms. Fabien lifted a worm out of the container, and Ferne and I watched it slither, snakelike, in the palm of his hand. "Cut off a tiny piece of the worm for bait," he said, grinning widely and probably imagining I might try to hook an entire worm to one of the microscopic hooks he'd just sold me.

After finishing lunch, Ferne and I headed out on the dock with my new fishing outfit, bait, tackle, and a plastic bucket I'd found among the cleaning supplies in our rental apartment. After filling the bucket with fresh seawater, I tied a fishing weight to the base of my sabiki rig and, lifting the bale of my spinning reel, released about ten feet of line, suspending the rig in the glass-clear water just above the sandy bottom. Slowly but surely, my presumptive evening appetizer formed a school around the tiny jigs. Soon, over a hundred smelt were all staring at my jigs as I bobbed them up and down. Nothing happened. Unlike the gentleman fisher the day before who'd landed a fish every two to three minutes on his rig, I fished for ten minutes without a bite. Puzzled, I experimented with different jigging patterns, slowing the rig down, speeding it up, and then varying the depth. Still, I caught no fish. Frustrated but unwilling to abandon my rig for hook and bait, I decided to see what would happen if I combined both. I removed a worm from the plastic container, laid it on the concrete dock, and, using a kitchen knife, sliced off three tiny pieces of one end of the worm. After delicately hooking each of the miniscule worm pieces to a tiny jig hook, I dropped the rig back into the water. The reaction of the fish was instantaneous as the smells from the worm permeated the water. A smelt hit one of my worm-baited jig hooks, flashes of silver signaling a catch. Had I not had a clear view of the fish, I wouldn't have known I had a fish on. I lifted the lively smelt from the water and, before removing the tiny hook, yelled to Ferne to come see my fish and take a picture. Capturing me proudly holding up my three-inch catch, my first European smelt, required snapping the photograph at close range. That evening, I scaled and cleaned fourteen tiny fish on a cutting board in our kitchen. Following the cooking instructions of my friends from the dock, I prepared our delicious éperlan hors d'oeuvres. The white, mildly fishy meat was nicely complemented by its seasoned crust.

This was not the first time in my life that I lived on a coast that had a once-burgeoning fishery. As a student at the University of California, Santa Cruz (UCSC), I studied marine biology, geology, poetry, and natural history. I read John Muir, Henry David Thoreau, Robinson Jeffers, and, especially, John Steinbeck. Fifty miles south of Santa Cruz, nudged up against the cold Pacific Ocean, lay the community of Monterey, whose sardine canneries were fodder for Steinbeck's *Cannery Row*,[5] set during the Great Depression. As a budding marine biologist, I identified deeply with Steinbeck's "Doc." Like Doc, I was intrigued with solving the puzzles of the mysterious marine invertebrates that lived in California's rocky tide pools. I imagined Doc's road trips to San Diego to collect small octopi beneath boulders on spring low tides. I soaked up the lore of parties hosted and beer milkshakes consumed in a ramshackle wooden marine lab perched over the ocean on Cannery Row. Knowing that Steinbeck's Doc was true to life (philosopher and marine biologist Ed Ricketts[6]) and not simply fictional made his untimely death at a railway crossing in Monterey all the more poignant. In that coming-of-age exploration of self that comes with a dash of the naïveté of youth, I took a break from college in the mid-1970s and moved across the bay to the city of Monterey.

My father generously provided me with funds for four years of college, with the caveat that I cover my own living expenses during summers. Living in Monterey for a three-month spring term was akin to a summer break, as far as my dad's financial contributions were concerned. Whether I consciously or subconsciously searched for employment near Doc's long-shuttered marine lab is hard to say. But in the end, the window of the restaurant kitchen on the end of Fisherman's Wharf, where I cleaned dishes and prepped squid and lobsters eight hours a day, looked out on the Pacific Ocean. I could walk from the pier north, past San Carlos Beach Park, past the San Xavier Cannery, and three more blocks to Doc's lab at 800 Cannery Row. When I got bored, I slid open my window and dropped squid entrails to a receptive family of sea otters that rafted just below my window. Each day, I spent hours watching the otters forage. When they surfaced with sea urchins—one of their favorite foods—they floated on their backs and cracked the spiny skeletons open against a smooth rock on their belly, relishing the ripe gonads. By including lots of sea urchins in their diet, sea otters play a keystone role in structuring nearshore Pacific kelp communities. Essentially, the otters keep sea urchin populations from exploding and rendering kelp forests into barren grounds. Otters, surfacing with crabs, chewed through the outer carapace to access the succulent meat; on occasion, otters ripped off the arms of sea stars and pulled the nutrient storage organs (pyloric caeca) and gonads from the body wall and ate them, no rock required.

A few years later, when I was a senior at UCSC, I became tangentially involved in a study involving abalone and sea otters at San Nicholas Island, one of the California Channel Islands off of Santa Barbara. My colleagues were taking part in a project documenting the intertidal and subtidal communities of the island in preparation for studying the impacts of releasing captured California sea otters. We flew to San Nicholas Island and spent a weekend in an old semi-truck container fitted with a heater, bunks, and a kitchen. Most of the time, we counted marine seaweeds and invertebrates along rope transect lines and in square quadrats made of PVC pipe. One day at low tide, we turned several of our study organisms into a meal, collecting seven-inch black abalone (*Haliotis cracherodii*) and four-inch limpets (*Lottia gigantea*) from the rocky intertidal, removing the thick shells and the tough foot used to suction the snails to intertidal rocks. We pounded the foot-meat soft with a wooden mallet, rolled the egg-dipped meat in flour, and pan fried the delicious snail steaks in butter and salt and pepper for dinner. In the mid-1980s, black abalone mostly vanished from the intertidal of the California coast and Channel Islands due to overfishing, illegal harvest, habitat destruction, and, largely, "withering syndrome," an infectious disease specific to the black abalone. The deadly disease is caused by a pathogen and is fatal because the abalone's foot shrinks or withers. Ultimately, the infected abalone can no longer use its foot to effectively grasp the rock surfaces that provide its habitat and encrusting seaweed food. The abalone is eventually washed free, and it starves or is consumed by scavengers. One hundred thirty-seven sea otters were collected from the Monterey and Big Sur region and introduced to San Nicholas Island a few years later. The attempt to establish an isolated sea otter population on the island as a reserve genetic stock to the mainland coastal population and as an extension of the breeding population to the south was, at least initially, a disaster. Many of the introduced sea otters immediately swam for the mainland or to a neighboring island. Some were found washed up onshore shot, probably by abalone or sea urchin fishermen who viewed the otters as a threat to their fishing operations. Today, a small number of sea otters still live in the waters surrounding San Nicholas Island, and Fish and Wildlife officials believe it is possible the population will persist.[7]

Early in the morning, before heading to work at the restaurant on the pier, I wandered the foggy streets and alleys of Cannery Row. I explored old factory buildings, the odds and ends of machinery and pipes abandoned in empty, grassy lots, and a mom-and-pop grocery store. These landmarks remained as testament to the burgeoning Monterey sardine fishery that sprung up around 1916, peaked in the mid-1930s (718,000 tons were harvested in 1936–37), and began a decline in the 1940s, when Steinbeck's Doc and "the boys" called Cannery Row home. A vastly depleted fishery continued on from the mid-1940s to the mid-1960s, at a level that was eighteen to thirty-five times below its peak.[8] At low tides, I pulled on hip-waders and wandered into the rocky intertidal behind Ed Ricketts's long-abandoned Pacific Biological Laboratories. The lab burned down in 1936 but was rebuilt and lived in by Ed soon after. In the seaweed-laden pools, I discovered small sculpins and blennies perched, like lizards, on their frontal pectoral fins. Orange and yellow sponges and tunicates coated the rocks. Reddish-purple sea slugs called nudibranchs, with their delicate gill-like cerata protruding from their backs, navigated carpets of deep-green sea anemones and purple sea urchins. Fat, ochre sea stars fed on mats of deep-black mussels, extruding their stomachs through the little gap between the tightly clamped shell halves. At the time I lived in Monterey in the mid-1970s, the world-famous

Monterey Bay Aquarium was still a dream of Julie Packard and her marine biologist boyfriend, who were both college students at UCSC a year or two ahead of me.

In 1984, Julie's parents, David and Lucille Packard, along with Julie and the young marine biologist she had met at UCSC, celebrated the opening of the aquarium and its brilliant architectural reformation of several former waterfront canneries. The opening of the Monterey Bay Aquarium, where today Julie continues to serve as the executive director, inspired the preservation and repurposing of several remaining historic sardine canneries.[9]

Many years after my spring in Monterey, still chasing Doc's spirit, I took my family to San Diego to visit my brother Pete and his wife and to search for small octopi that hide under the intertidal rocks at low tide. Pete researched the local tide tables, and at the break of dawn, we descended a flight of wooden stairs to a rocky platform smelling of seaweed below an affluent neighborhood in La Jolla. Sounds of the sea greeted us—the distant cracks of breaking waves, the initial smack of rolling surf meeting rock, followed by the subtle symphony of water flow as the incoming sea channeled toward us through myriad cracks and crevices and tidal pools.

We set to work, tipping rocks in search of octopi, returning each stone to its initial upright position to preserve the underlying, encrusted life. I puzzled over a circle of a dozen large green chitons I found under a boulder, arranged in perfect symmetry, their heads all centered as if attending a committee meeting. Pete found the first octopus, and to the delight of my two young children, we watched a walnut-sized body with eight one-inch arms twist and turn in the palm of his hand. More octopi followed, and by the time we were chased off the rocks by the incoming tide, we'd each fished an octopus out from under a rock.

The next morning, Pete and I rose early and drove to the San Diego Harbor where we boarded a half-day fishing boat we'd made reservations for the previous day. Rather than motoring offshore the captain headed the boat north, up the coast. Half an hour later, we pulled in tight under the cliffs of La Jolla, not far from where we searched for octopi the previous morning. As the captain and mate anchored our boat, I watched several fishers paddle by us in fishing kayaks laden with rods and reels. I, too, have kayak-fished, regularly renting an ocean kayak on our family's beach trips to Destin, Florida. I would paddle out at sunrise and sunset and cast for schooling lady-fish (commonly called poor man's tarpon), one time hooking a twenty-five-pound redfish that pulled my kayak so far offshore I disappeared over the horizon. My wife, no longer able to see me from the patio of our second-floor rental condo, had come close to calling the Coast Guard.

The twenty or so fishers aboard the half-day boat baited medium-weight rods with chunks of squid and fished among forests of the world's fastest-growing organism, the giant kelp *Macrocystis pyrifera*. For the first two hours we caught tasty, fifteen-inch kelp bass (*Paralabrax clathratus*), which hunt in small tight schools, attacking fish and squid all at once from different directions. The larvae of kelp bass spend a month developing in the plankton before, as early juveniles, taking up residence among the blades of giant kelp. Here, they exploit the canopy of the undersea forest to hide from predators and better ambush prey as they grow to adults. Later in the morning, the captain moved the boat a little farther up the coast. The first fisher's cast produced a loud cry of "Barracuda!" The captain had found us a hungry school of juvenile Pacific barracuda[10] running just along the seaward edge of the kelp forest. The local fishers on board who had brought along their own spinning rods quickly tied on lures. Soon, the boat was riddled with cries of "Fish on!" or "Another one!" as even those of us relegated to fishing with pieces of squid were rewarded with lively battles. Pacific barracuda, which range from Southern California to Panama, lack the distinct spots that characterize the species of barracuda I've caught in the Bahamas and are thinner and have more of a polished silver appearance. Reaching a little over three feet, the Pacific species doesn't get as large as its Atlantic and Caribbean relative. What the Pacific barracuda does share with its

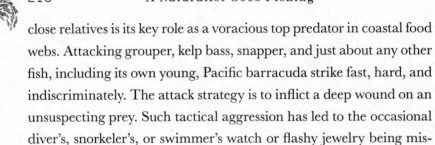

close relatives is its key role as a voracious top predator in coastal food webs. Attacking grouper, kelp bass, snapper, and just about any other fish, including its own young, Pacific barracuda strike fast, hard, and indiscriminately. The attack strategy is to inflict a deep wound on an unsuspecting prey. Such tactical aggression has led to the occasional diver's, snorkeler's, or swimmer's watch or flashy jewelry being mistaken for a small fish. Barracuda bites may require stitches or even reconstructive surgery.

During my breaks from work at the restaurant in Monterey, I stood on the end of the wharf and looked northeast along the Cannery Row waterfront and on to Point Cabrillo. I imagined the long-abandoned canneries clattering with the sounds of motorized machines and rife with the mixed stench of fuel exhaust and the process of "reducing" many of the sardines to fish meal or oil byproducts. According to Michael Kemp, a Cannery Row historian, the odor of the fish was responsible for the saying "Carmel-by-the-Sea, Pacific Grove by God, and Monterey by the smell."

From 1930 until the crash of the fishery in the late 1940s, sardines were harvested by fishers using purse seine nets, similar in construction and design to those described earlier for netting anchovies in France. Prior to this period, the nets used to catch sardines were lamparas, round haul nets that functioned a little like a purse seine but with less efficiency. Lamparas measured about 960 to 1,200 feet long and 110 to 210 feet deep and had shallow wings on either end that deepened toward the center of the net, or bag, that served as a pocket to concentrate and trap the fish as they were rapidly encircled. When the occasional sea lion was encircled in a net, the sardines and sea lion would panic and escape—the latter leaving behind a large hole in the net.

The forty-five-foot lampara launch was crewed by eleven to fourteen men and powered by a thirty- or forty-horsepower engine. The launch would tow a slightly smaller boat called a lighter, which was used to load up to fifty tons of netted sardines. During the height of the sardine fishery, hundreds of lampara boats—and later, purse seine boats—set sail each evening from Monterey Bay, taking advantage of the propensity of sardines, similar to anchovies, to school in surface waters at night to feed on zooplankton. Schools can reach up to ten million individuals. Sardine fishers often reported that schools could be spotted at night because of a luminescence they generated in the water. My guess is that the luminescence is caused by waterborne single-celled dinoflagellates that are known to be stimulated to glow when physically disturbed. During the height of the fishery, the availability of sardines in Monterey Bay and neighboring coastal regions seemed bottomless, and during World War II, the small silver fish provided 25 percent of America's catch of fish. Importantly, the war effort benefited because the third of the sardines that were not ground, baked, or squeezed into fertilizer, oil products, or fish meal were canned and could be shipped and stored without refrigeration.

When the lampara boats towing sardine-laden lighters returned each morning to Cannery Row, the fish were shoveled from the lighters into buckets hoisted to a cannery. By the time purse seiners had replaced lamparas in 1930, it was possible to vacuum the sardines from the boats up to the cannery using a suction hose. Once the sardines entered the cannery to be processed, fish were selected for size, washed, and the heads, tails, and entrails removed by hand. Then the fish, skin on, were spread on wooden slats, or flakes, to dry. Dried fish were placed in metal baskets and boiled in peanut oil and then drained and hand-packed into cans. Lastly, the lids of the cans were hand-soldered closed, and the cans of sardines were labeled and boxed for shipment.

Eighteen species of sardines exist worldwide, but the species that was the focus of Monterey's once active canneries is the Pacific sardine, *Sardinops sagax*.[11] The species is widely distributed along the Pacific coast from northern Mexico to southeastern Alaska and is known to be highly migratory, moving to seasonal spawning grounds. In contrast to the anchovy, which thrives in cooler temperatures, sardines are considered a warm-water species that prefers to spawn at night at temperatures between fifty-nine and sixty-five degrees Fahrenheit.

The typically seven- to nine-and-a-half-inch fish is silver on its belly and spotted on its sides, and its dorsum can be blue or green. Adult females spawn as many as sixty-five thousand eggs and can do so three times each year. Juveniles reach a length of an inch and a half after three months and about four inches after a year, feeding on phytoplankton and zooplankton. Pacific sardines generally live five to eight years, most succumbing to predators or environmental factors.

Similar to anchovies in the Mediterranean, Atlantic, and elsewhere, sardines play an important role in the flow of carbon and energy within ocean food webs, in part because they consume phytoplankton and zooplankton and produce waste that provides nutrients to a host of organisms living in the water column and on the seafloor. Sardines also provide a nutritional resource for a variety of seabirds, fish, and mammals. In a 2005 study of Pacific sardines in the Pacific Northwest, fisheries biologists peered into the stomachs of a variety of predatory fish and sharks and determined that sardines were important in the diets of juvenile and adult Chinook and Coho salmon, jack mackerel, Pacific hake, and three species of shark.[12] The list of seabirds that take advantage of the surface schooling behavior of Pacific sardines to capture a rich, oily meal is long and varied, including terns, seagulls, and pelicans. Marine mammals such as the California sea lion also prey on sardines. The Dall's porpoise and the Pacific white-sided dolphin chase down schooling sardines, and whales get in on the action, filtering schooling sardines using their feathery sieve-like baleens. Both the humpback whale and the Sei whale are sardine predators, the latter called *Iwashi kujira* in Japanese, meaning "sardine whale."

Like the European anchovy fishery in the French Mediterranean, overfishing appears to have contributed to the crash of the California Pacific sardine in the 1940s and 1950s. Fishery biologists, however, believe the precipitous decline in the Pacific sardine was also related to changes in ocean temperature that were linked to ocean regime changes or changes in climate. Ocean temperatures of the California Current were warmer during the 1930s and early

1940s and thus more favorable to sardines than the cooler water temperatures that followed during the 1950s to 1970s. Further evidence that warm sea temperatures enhance the sardine's spawning success was garnered when the California Current warmed again in the late 1970s, the late 1980s, and in both 2003 and 2004. In these instances, ocean warming correlated with increased numbers of young Pacific sardines. Despite a recent abrupt decline in populations of sardines along the West Coast of North America, fisheries biologists believe that as climate change results in warmer climates and oceans, the Pacific sardine may increasingly spawn successfully and thus establish more robust populations.[13] For now, the canneries of Cannery Row remain silent. Pacific sardines that are currently harvested are shipped to the Philippines, where cheap labor and large canning factories make processing the small fish cost-effective. Ironically, the canned sardines are then shipped back to North America where they are marketed. Recently, a California entrepreneur, Daren Warnick, established the Cannery Row Sardine Co.,[14] a business built from a partnership with several local sardine fishers in the Monterey Bay region and the owner of one of the few small canneries in the area. The company produces a boutique product line of California-coast sardines (boneless and skinless!) packed in pure olive oil. Warnick, in a nod to the rich history of Cannery Row, wraps his company's canned sardines with labels similar to those used during twentieth-century boom times—a cherry-red oval with a painting of a silvery fish, its lively tail flipped upward.

10

FISHING FOR SOLUTIONS

O ur planet's streams, rivers, lakes, estuaries, bays, and oceans have been fished ever since early man first crafted crude spears, hooks, weirs, and nets. Fishing pressure was sufficiently low, ensuring fish populations remained sustainable. As humankind expanded, so did the numbers of fishers, the sophistication of fishing techniques, and the potential for overfishing. Additional pressures on fish and their habitats surfaced with the onset of the Industrial Revolution, primarily though sedimentation from development and aquatic pollutants, including toxic metals from mining, pesticides from agriculture, and airborne chemicals from industrial smokestacks. Today, fish are confronted with several new stressors: rising temperatures and, in the marine realm, ocean acidification. Both of these stressors owe their origin to increased levels of greenhouse gases.

Ocean acidification, the outcome of a series of chemical reactions that occur when seawater absorbs atmospheric carbon dioxide,[1] is particularly problematic. With the exception of fish living in polar seas, most fish can tolerate moderate temperature increases, and if not, many may migrate to cooler waters. In contrast, acidification of seawater—the essential medium in which marine fish respire, feed, grow, reproduce, and perceive their environment—has the potential to cause widespread deleterious effects on the health and, ultimately, survival of fish. Scientists have conducted ocean acidification studies that indicate tropical fish lose their ability to find their home reef[2] or even become attracted to, rather than repelled from, predatory fish.[3]

With environmental pressures mounting, biologists are carrying out studies to characterize how given species of marine invertebrates or fish respond to multiple stressors. Investigators conduct controlled laboratory studies, exposing fish to different combinations of potential stressors. Such multifactor studies are timely because they more accurately mirror the natural environment. The outcomes of these experiments have, in some instances, been surprising. In rare cases, one of two stressors may actually have a subtractive effect, negating the negative effect of the other stressor. For example, in some marine invertebrates, the development of embryos may be slowed by exposure to ocean acidification but accelerated to a normal rate of development by elevated temperature.[4] More commonly, the impacts of multiple stressors are either additive or synergistic.

To picture additivity and synergism, imagine an experiment carried out by fish biologists with three equal-sized groups of Antarctic fish, with one group exposed to a thermal stress (elevated temperature), another to ocean acidification stress (increased seawater acidity), and a third to the two stressors at the same time. In this example, imagine that 10 percent of the fish in the group exposed to elevated temperature die over a month, while 15 percent of the group of fish exposed to increased acidity die over a similar amount of time. If 25 percent of the final group of fish exposed to both increased temperature and increased acidity die over a month's time, then the two stressors have an additive effect on fish survival. If, on the other hand, half the fish die over a month, the two stressors have caused a synergistic effect on fish survival. It is this latter, synergistic example that is of particular concern, as fish weakened by one of the stressors have become more vulnerable to the second stressor. By understanding which environmental stressors have subtractive, additive, or synergistic outcomes, fisheries biologists are better able to develop effective mitigation strategies to promote fish conservation.

Fish habitats are also experiencing increased environmental disturbance. Yet, despite these challenges, promising stories exist of successful efforts to preserve and in some instances restore or even enhance fish habitat. The first story is one of habitat preservation, originating in my hometown of Birmingham, Alabama. The story is testament to the quintessential nature of effective communication and cooperation. The characters include an environmental organization and a state agency in charge of highway construction.

Birmingham's Cahaba River Society (CRS)[5] was established in 1988 as a nonprofit organization to promote and ensure the sustainable health of the Cahaba River, the longest free-flowing river remaining in Alabama. One of the unique attributes of the CRS is that over the years members of the board of directors have increasingly been selected to represent a full spectrum of community stakeholders, including CEOs and executives of land development companies, real estate firms, banks, law firms, and energy companies. Corporate leaders serve alongside freshwater biologists and environmentalists.

Board members of the CRS became concerned when they learned that the Alabama Department of Transportation (ALDOT) planned to build a three-mile section of highway northeast of Birmingham. The short section of highway would establish a foothold for a controversial northern beltway around the city of Birmingham. The fifty-two-mile beltway would ultimately cross all five upper tributaries of the Cahaba River. The construction project, near the town of Pinson, Alabama, would not directly impact the Cahaba River, but the four-lane highway, designed to expand to six lanes in the future, would be in close proximity to Self Creek, a tributary that ultimately feeds into the Black Warrior River, a 178-mile river in west-central Alabama. Accordingly, the highway's construction near the creek posed risks to fish habitats, both through sediment deposition and runoff carrying asphalt toxins. The creek and the river it feeds provide habitat for native darters and redeye bass, spotted and largemouth bass, and a host of other aquatic plants, invertebrates, and fish. In large part because of the corporate nature of the CRS board, an objective "best practices" document developed by the board was delivered to ALDOT, rather than a legal challenge to the state transportation agency over the need for an environmentally sound mitigation strategy. What followed was remarkable. The director of ALDOT invited CRS board members to meet with his leadership team and forge a statement outlining collaborative aims to protect Self Creek and its downstream waters. A culture change was under way.

"I couldn't believe what I saw!" exclaimed Randy Haddock, field director for the CRS, describing his reaction to touring the mid-construction phase of ALDOT's highway project near Self Creek. Barry Fagan, the ALDOT environmental compliance engineer, walked Randy and Beth Stewart, executive director of the CRS, over to the edge of one of the detention ponds that had been built by construction workers to mitigate sediment runoff and asphalt pollutants from the banks and road surface of the highway. Randy explained that Barry had proudly shown them a pond that was two to three times larger than a normal detention pond and uniquely shaped to retain the brunt of waterborne sediments at its deep end nearest the highway. Finer sediments settled out as the water slowly moved the length of the pond. Water flowing into the pond first moved across swales—gently sloping, grassy drainage areas—which facilitated absorption of water by the soil. Water draining out of the pond flowed over a water-level spreader, a device that dispersed water across a wide, relatively flat slope, further facilitating soil absorption and sediment settlement before water entered Self Creek.

Randy Haddock explained to me that to accommodate the swales and detention ponds, ALDOT, in an unprecedented action, had purchased additional land prior to highway construction. The state agency had also established an on-site team to monitor runoff near Self Creek during storms and provided a $40,000 bonus to the highway's contractor for each month of road construction completed without a storm-water violation. Randy and Beth were convinced that the aggressive mitigation efforts by ALDOT had significantly enhanced protection of fish habitat in Self Creek and river waters farther downstream. The successful culture change also owed considerable credit to ALDOT's compliance officer, Barry Fagan, who'd become passionate about the development and promotion of what he'd coined ALDOT's "Five Pillars," which include the management of communication, work, water, erosion, and sediment.[6] "ALDOT's previous focus had been only the last two pillars," Barry explained to me over the phone. The adoption of the other three pillars had been essential in convincing the CRS board that aquatic habitat could be protected in concert with highway construction. Should plans to build a northern beltline come to fruition, there's now hope for sustaining water quality and fish habitat in the Cahaba River and its tributaries. I could tell by Barry's tone he was proud of recent invitations from a variety of agencies to speak about his Five Pillars approach to managing road construction in environmentally sensitive areas.

The second story is a cautiously optimistic tale that centers on recent signs of environmental recovery in mountain lakes of the northeastern United States that were ravaged by acid rain in the 1960s and 1970s. First described by Yale and Dartmouth ecologist Herbert Bormann in 1971, acid rain is generated when sulfur dioxide and nitrate oxides, released from industrial smokestacks, combine with ammonia and infiltrate rain droplets. The sulfuric- and nitric acid–laden rain falls to earth and ultimately ends up acidifying creeks and streams that feed lakes. The result is the establishment of chronically low pH "acid lakes." Unfortunately, the mineralogy of soils in the northeastern United States does little to buffer the acidity of lake water. Under acidifying conditions, soils surrounding acid lakes release toxic forms of aluminum and mercury, heavy metals that, in combination with acidity, can be harmful or even deadly to fish and other aquatic organisms. A few species of fish can survive in moderately acidic lakes, while others such as brook trout are sensitive to acidity. Even fish that survive acidic waters often display damaging sublethal effects such as slow growth and small adult body size, factors that reduce the ability of the fish to compete effectively for food and habitat. In some lakes, however, the water becomes so acutely acidic that, no matter how carefully fisheries biologists search, there's not a living fish to be found. The bottleneck that prevents fish from surviving such conditions is often some aspect of their reproductive cycle.

In 1995, the federal government established the Acid Rain Program.[7] The program set limits on major emissions of sulfur dioxide and nitrogen oxides originating primarily from industrial combustion of fossil fuels. During the seven-year period from 2005 to 2012, sulfur dioxide emissions in the United States were reduced by over three million tons. Although acid rain is certainly not a thing of the past, the environmental consequences of reducing emissions have been promising. Indeed, environmental scientists have documented tangible benefits to game fish living in some, but not all, of the acid lakes of the northeastern United States.

Brooktrout Lake is an example of a lake that has undergone a remarkable recovery from the impacts of acid rain. Located in a heavily forested region of the Adirondacks near the town of Speculator in upstate New York, the lake, shaped like an upside-down Louisiana, is a deep, blue gem. Leila Mitchell, who works for the state Department of Environmental Conservation, extols the region's beauty in her 2014 article titled "Coming Full Circle," published in the *New York State Conservationist*.[8] Mitchell knows the Brooktrout Lake area well, having grown up visiting the Adirondacks on family vacations. When Mitchell searched the literature, she discovered a 1950 report by Martin Pfeiffer, a biologist who praised the lake's bounty of fish. Martin's evidence of a bountiful fishery included his hiking the seven miles in to the lake and catching sixty brook trout that ranged from seven to fourteen and a half inches. In his report, Martin declared the brook trout population "self-sustaining." Sadly, over the next three decades, fish surveys carried out in the increasingly acidic waters of Brooktrout Lake revealed a steady decline in brook trout, until in 1984 not a single fish was sampled by fisheries biologists. The lake had essentially become fishless. In 1990, concerned about the three thousand mountain lakes and ponds sprinkled across the Adirondacks, New York state politicians passed the country's first law regulating acid rain: the Acid Deposition Control Act. Mitchell reflects in her article that by 2005 the acidity of Brooktrout Lake had largely dissipated and that water quality was sufficient for the New York Department of Environmental Conservation to restock the lake with a couple thousand young brook trout fingerlings. Brooktrout Lake was restocked with fingerlings in each of the three subsequent years, and in 2010, national media outlets heralded stories of success when the first offspring of a stocked trout was collected. When I caught Mitchell at her desk at the Department of Environmental Conservation in April 2015, she told me over the phone that today Brooktrout Lake remains a success story. Natural reproduction has risen to a sufficient level that restocking is no longer necessary, and it's possible once again to cast a dry fly or spinner from the bank and catch brookies.

The third story recounts the history of the successful enhancement of marine fish habitat in a state with the largest artificial reef program in the United States. The seafloors of the Gulf of Mexico off the coast of Alabama are largely sand and don't offer much in the way of structural habitat for game or commercial fish. The few ancient, low-lying carbonate reefs remaining from the Pleistocene are covered on and off by storm-driven sands. "It all started in 1959 when the Alabama Department of Marine Conservation [ADMC] poured concrete in the center-shafts of old car tires," Dr. John Dindo, a longtime friend and assistant director of the Dauphin Island Sea Lab, explained to me from his office. The tires were wired together and dropped to the seafloor. It didn't take long for the ADMC to figure out that the tire-reefs didn't work. Hydrocarbons leaching from the rubber prevented the development of the bacterial biofilms and the encrusting algae and invertebrates that attract fish. The next attempt came in the early to mid-1960s when ADMC sank some old cars, buses, and trucks. Once again, there were problems, this time from the leaching of residual oil and transmission and brake fluids. This issue was addressed by marine conservation staff painstakingly removing every drop of fluid before the vehicles were sunk. Yet soon another problem surfaced. By the time the vehicles had become overgrown enough to attract a healthy population of fish, two to three years, the corrosive seawater had rotted the vehicles away.

"Pieces of concrete pipes!" exclaimed John, in his usual excited way. The intact pipes, about twenty feet long and two feet in diameter, were broken up into smaller sections and tested as artificial reefs by the ADMC in the mid-1960s. The broken pipes were so successful that half a century later they are still being piled on the seafloor for artificial reefs. Concrete is conducive to reef construction because it doesn't leach toxic chemicals and is heavy enough to stay put on the seafloor during hurricanes. Concrete also provides an excellent surface for the rapid development of biofilms that lead to the recruitment of coralline and fleshy algae, sponges, moss animals (bryozoans), and sea squirts (tunicates). Soon, crustaceans, sea urchins, and brittle stars arrive, and small fish take up residence in cracks and crevices of the concrete. The smaller fish and larger invertebrates attract schools of resident fish, including snapper, grouper, trigger fish, and sheepshead.

In the mid-1970s, the ADMC initiated a program to create artificial reefs by sinking retired ships. Mothballed Liberty ships that had been used by the U.S. Navy to transport American troops to Europe during World War II were used first by the Department of Marine Conservation. John explained that everything above deck on the 130-foot transport ships was stripped off by navy personnel. The topless ships were towed offshore by tugboats and sunk in eighty-five feet of water using explosives set off by navy demolition experts. Soon, the sunken ships attracted marine life, including schooling game fish. An unexpected gold mine of reef construction material became available when Hurricane Frederick slammed into Dauphin Island in 1979. The mile-long bridge connecting the island to the mainland collapsed in the heavy seas and hurricane-force winds, breaking into sections. Piece by piece, the ADMC barged the fragmented bridge offshore, creating a series of fish reefs in designated no-trawl zones avoided by shrimp boats pulling nets. The new hurricane-proof bridge took over a year to build, and Dauphin Island locals, relegated to using small boats or a car ferry to get back and forth from the mainland, still speak fondly of being cut off from the rest of the world.

John collaborated with several colleagues at Dauphin Island Sea Lab on an artificial reef project funded in the mid-1980s by the Mississippi-Alabama Sea Grant Consortium. Four flower-shaped, trawl-proof artificial reefs were constructed by John and his colleagues out of Nalgene plastic, each measuring fourteen feet across and six feet tall. The five petals or arms, each drilled with holes of varying size to attract and accommodate fish, projected from a central region poured in concrete. After the concrete was added, each artificial reef weighed three thousand pounds, enough to ensure the structure stayed in place on the seafloor. As hoped, the unique flower design allowed shrimp trawls to pass over the artificial reef without getting caught. However, the Nalgene plastic, perhaps because it leached toxic chemicals or had too smooth a surface, did not fare well in developing a biofilm and the ensuing communities of small marine organisms that attract fish. John lamented that in retrospect concrete would have probably fared better: "Fish love concrete."

Ever searching for innovative artificial reefs, the ADMC in 1999 sought and received permission to sink stockpiled U.S. Army tanks that had been used in the Korean War. "They sealed the hatches first," noted John, explaining that before submerging each tank the hatch was welded shut to ensure that adventurous scuba divers didn't slip inside the tank and get trapped. ADMC carried out experiments to compare the diversity and abundance of game fish attracted to reefs composed of individual tanks or clusters of tanks. Not surprisingly, the clustered tank design turned out to be more popular with the fish, signifying that when it comes to fish reefs bigger is often better. In 2006, the age-old bigger-is-better axiom was pushed to the extreme when the retired U.S. aircraft carrier USS *Oriskany* was sunk as an artificial reef off the panhandle of Florida near Pensacola. The carrier weighed thirty thousand tons and measured 880 feet. Today, divers fondly refer to the massive sunken vessel as the Great Carrier Reef.

Another genre of massive artificial reefs came about unintentionally and from a somewhat unexpected source. As anyone who has gazed offshore along the northern Gulf of Mexico can testify, natural gas and oil rigs litter the horizon. The submerged legs of the superstructures both attract game fish and provide important habitat for juvenile fish that seed neighboring waters. I've had the good fortune of experiencing the bounty below one of these Gulf rigs. Long ago, John took me and Ken Marion out onto the Gulf of Mexico on a calm fall day in his twenty-foot wooden skiff. We fished below a towering natural gas rig several miles south of Dauphin Island. Rig machinery hummed above our heads as we tied on hooks and admired flocks of cormorants and brown pelicans skimming above the water. We were treated to thick schools of hard-fighting Spanish and king mackerel, their silver backs slicing the frothy surface. We reeled in red snapper, landed several cobia, and cursed the bulldog-strength of jack crevalle that broke our lines. Ken taught me how to catch spadefish, two- to three-pound saucer-shaped fish that tightly schooled up under the rig. The fish, painted with vertical black bands, flipped onto their sides as they fought, bending our ultralights to the breaking point. The highlight of my day of rig fishing was hooking a twenty-five-pound king mackerel and working the fish up along the boat three times before the fish broke free. Had I landed the big mackerel, I suspect I'd have broken the world record for a king mackerel caught on a closed-reel Zebco rod and reel.

In the United States, natural gas and oil rigs operate on a twenty-year federal site lease. At the end of two decades, the massive rigs' legs have been transformed into diverse ecosystems, encrusted with marine invertebrates and swimming with schools of fish. The companies that own the rigs are required, by law, to remove all traces of the rig from the drilling site at the end of the lease. In 2013, a controversy erupted among rig owners, recreational and commercial fishers, and marine resource managers when a natural gas company, following its lease guidelines, blew up a natural gas rig and thousands of dead snappers and groupers floated to the surface. One promising approach to avoid squandering these de facto fish reefs is the U.S. Rigs-to-Reefs program.[9] Owners of natural gas or oil rigs can apply to this program and be granted permission to convert their rig into an artificial reef. Despite the potential deterrent of the owners having to cover the costs of rig-to-reef conversion, the program has been a success. Rigs are either toppled over onto the seafloor or the superstructure cut off below water level. Today, over 150 natural gas and oil rigs in the Gulf of Mexico have been converted into artificial reefs that support large populations of fish.

Whether wild populations of fish are ultimately sustainable—given the growing pressures of recreational and especially commercial fishing—is fodder for debate among fisheries biologists, recreational fishers, and commercial fish harvesters. Arguments about the world's oceans have become heated; the accuracy of annual catch data being reported to the United Nations Food and Agricultural Organization (FAO) has been brought to question by some fisheries scientists. Alarming studies led by Dr. Daniel Pauly at the University of Columbia in Vancouver indicate that fish landings in many countries may be at least twice as great as those being reported to the FAO, and in some instances much higher.[10] For example, China's annual catch may actually be thirteen times higher than that being reported. To address overfishing in the world's oceans, Pauly advocates stepping up enforcement of catch limits, phasing out the discarding of by-catch (incidental fish that come up in the trawl net), creating new policies to protect biodiversity, and paying greater attention to large fleets of industrial fishing vessels operating in the unprotected waters of third world countries. I'd add that fish with life histories requiring multiple years to reach reproductive maturity, such as the Chilean and Antarctic toothfish addressed in chapter 5, are in serious danger of being overharvested to the point of a collapse in the fishery. Moreover, those species of fish so prized for their fillets that commercial fishers have placed a high price on their fatty belly-meat may be doomed without immediate intervention. Bluefin tuna, a species capable of commanding hundreds of thousands to over a million dollars for a single fish, as detailed in chapter 4, is a sad case in point.

Despite a global fisheries crisis largely driven by overfishing, promising examples of sustainable fisheries certainly do exist. The coastal blue cod fishery of New Zealand is one example. Blue cod are hand-caught with drop lines or using baited pots (traps) rather than being harvested by vessels pulling bottom trawls. These low-impact catch techniques, combined with annual quotas set jointly by representatives from both the government and fishing industry, help ensure the blue cod fishery is managed for the long term while avoiding the pitfalls of trawl by-catch. Particularly troubling pitfalls include the high mortality of the by-catch returned to the sea and the global overexploitation of by-catch to produce fish meal used to farm fish.[11]

The herring fishery in coastal Alaska has also stood the test of time because it is meticulously managed. I learned firsthand about the fishery from Alaskans—Erika Knox and her husband—at a picnic at the Chelsea, Alabama home of my good friend Carol Odess. Carol is an avid fisher, and her love of salmon fishing drew her to Sitka, Alaska, where she now spends her summers. Carol befriended Erika and Peter in Sitka and invited them down to Alabama. Erika explained to me that you have to see the Sitka herring fishery in action to truly appreciate its management. When herring are ripe with roe, they command top dollar in Japan. Each year, when the spawning schools arrive near Sitka, herring experts sent from Japan sample the herring to decide when the timing to harvest the fish is just right. The trick is to harvest the herring a day or even a few hours prior to the spawn, so the fish are almost bursting with roe. Prior to each year's herring season, Alaska State Fish and Wildlife experts analyze catch data from past seasons to establish the tonnage of herring that can be harvested from a given location in a given year. Harvest is set at 20 percent of "exploitable" or "mature biomass," a conservative level when compared to commercial fish with similar life histories. The herring season at any given location is short, often just a few days, and millions of dollars can ride on a single day's fishing. Fishers must possess a state herring license; according to Erika and Peter, if you're lucky enough to find one for sale, the asking price is half a million dollars, so it's little surprise that family-owned herring licenses are passed down from generation to generation.

When a fishery official gives the go-ahead over the radio, a parade of seine boats and their supporting tenders storm off from their starting positions toward thick schools of herring located earlier in the day by small spotter planes. Erika explained that fishery officials keep close tabs on the tonnage of herring being netted and transferred into the holds of the tenders. With the targeted tonnage imminent, fishers' radios bark out "Fifteen minutes left to fish!" The tenders, riding deep with herring, sail directly to the docks of the Sitka fish-processing plant. Here, the fish are flash-frozen by fish processors and stacked tight into cardboard boxes marked "keep frozen" for shipment to Japan.

Another sustainable fishery, more recreational in its nature, is that of the largemouth bass (*Micropterus salmoides*). Native to North America, largemouth originally occupied the eastern half of the United States along with portions of Ontario, Quebec, and northern Mexico. Today, largemouth are stocked in every U.S. state except Alaska, as well as most of southern Canada and in a number of other countries in Europe, Asia, and Central and South America. One reason the largemouth bass fishery has a history of sustainability is that the species is highly adaptable, exploiting a variety of habitats and surviving large swings in temperature. Indeed, the competitive nature of introduced largemouth can at times be problematic for native species of fish as resources become constrained. Largemouth bass are readily raised in hatcheries, where mature fish are sequestered in culture ponds to reproduce and the young removed and grown in separate ponds (adults eat their young). Mature fish can also be spawned and larval fish reared artificially. Ponds and lakes stocked with largemouth bass are enhanced by adding fertilizers and various prey. My colleague and fishing buddy Adam Vines has managed a small private reservoir in Alabama for largemouth bass for over a decade. Adam is convinced that bass management is a combination of science, art, and luck. The removal of small bass is one key to a successful fishery, as is an abundance of underwater structure to provide bass with cover. Adam told me he removes fifteen pounds of sixteen-inch-and-under fish per acre per year, and to enhance structure, he's sunk hundreds of weighted Christmas trees in the reservoir to supplement rocks and tree falls. Each year when I fish at Dream

Lake, a small private reservoir in northwest Alabama loaded with five- to ten-pound largemouth bass, I'm fishing in a body of water that receives as much attention as a spoiled child. A variety of aspects of the lake's water chemistry are measured regularly and pelletized lime added to elevate pH as needed; fertilizers are periodically added to adjust the nitrates and phosphates that nourish the phytoplankton that sustain zooplankton, and on up the line, ensuring a rich, dependable food chain. An abundance of crayfish, shad, and tilapia are purchased and added each year as bass forage. Because so many fish are of considerable size, the Dream Lake largemouth bass fishery also benefits from a strict catch-and-release policy.

My favorite sustainable fishery doesn't involve fish. The claw-centric stone crab fishery of Florida has a history of resilience, despite an occasional down year caused by storms, cold fronts, or too many octopi crawling into traps to eat the crabs. The stone crab trapping season is limited to the winter and spring, and crabbers, by law, must return live crabs to the sea.[12] Moreover, if one of the claws falls below a minimum size, as is often the case, it must be left attached to the crab. The key to the fishery's resiliency is that the stone crabs live to see another day. Experimental studies have revealed that crabs released bearing a single claw fare well, foraging capably on clams, snails, and carrion while effectively warding off competitors and predators. The stone crab's considerable regenerative capacity results in the rapid growth of a new claw. By the time the next harvest rolls around, the crab is ready to make another donation.

In a recent paper in the journal *Science,* fisheries biologists from the University of California, Santa Barbara, and the University of Washington make a strong case that despite serious declines in worldwide fisheries overall, with a few notable exceptions, major fisheries in developed countries have yet to collapse, and many—especially smaller, severely depleted fisheries in third world countries—could recover given proper management.[13] The authors report that of the ten thousand fishing areas on Earth only a fifth has currently managed fisheries. They point out that larger fisheries within the maritime borders of developed countries have benefited from scientifically based management strategies, keeping these fisheries in reasonable shape. Accordingly, the authors argue, considerable potential exists to apply the same management strategies to the depleted fisheries of third world countries. They recommend two specific management tools that could prove particularly fruitful: establishment of fishing quotas that permit local fishers to own a tradable portion of the over-all catch (deemed catch shares in developed countries) and provision of territorial rights to fishing grounds to better guard against outsiders poaching fish. With any luck, this approach would sidestep the conundrum of a shared environmental resource being overexploited and eventually depleted, a scenario spelled out eloquently in Garrett Hardin's "Tragedy of the Commons."

In addition to establishing practices to assist third world fisheries, promising collaborative programs are under way in developed countries to repopulate threatened or endangered fish. One such program was initiated in Tennessee in 1998 with the ambitious goal of restoring the lake sturgeon (*Acipenser fulvescens*) to its native waters within the Tennessee River Basin[14] and, more recently, the Cumberland River. The working group overseeing this twenty-five-year-long program includes expert fish biologist and friend Dr. Bernie Kahajda of the Tennessee Aquarium. The Tennessee Lake Sturgeon Reintroduction Working Group is broad and diverse, including representatives from the aquarium and the U.S. Fish and Wildlife Service, U.S. Geological Survey, University of Tennessee, Tennessee Technical University, Tennessee Valley Authority, Tennessee Clean Water Network, and the World Wildlife Fund. One of the earmarks of a successful reintroduction strategy is the up-front establishment of clearly articulated goals. The working group stepped up to this challenge by defining six achievable goals to deem the lake sturgeon restoration effort successful. Goals for each river included observations of natural reproduction, survival of young fish at levels sufficient to sustain populations, the existence of individuals among the fish populations older than fifteen years, suitable habitats within management areas occupied by fish, population sizes of at least five hundred fish, and sustainable recreational harvests.

Lake sturgeon are torpedo-shaped, gray-green fish whose sides bear distinct rows of bony plates.[15] Looking like they swam right out of the Upper Cretaceous 136 million years ago, the fish live a long time—up to 50 years in males and 150 years in females. Slow to reach sexual maturity, male sturgeon can take ten to thirteen years to mature and females fifteen to thirty years. Bernie pointed out me that the warmer waters of Tennessee will almost certainly reduce the time sturgeon take to reach sexual maturity. For a fish that can reach a length of eight feet and weigh over two hundred pounds, the sturgeon's foraging habits are surprising. Prey consists of aquatic insects, worms, crustaceans, and small fish. To help locate such small food items, the fish's snout is equipped with ampullary organs that detect electrical signals emanating from prey, and the lower lip bears whisker-like barbels that "taste" prey odors.

Vast populations of lake sturgeon used to ply the river and lake waters from the northeastern to the southeastern United States. Commercial fishers first considered the lake sturgeon by-catch and deliberately killed the fish to prevent them from damaging fishing gear. Later, the fish's tasty eggs and fillets helped spawn a large fishery during the latter third of the nineteenth century. Overfishing, coupled with water pollution, destruction of habitat, and the construction of dams that prevented lake sturgeon from reaching their natal spawning grounds all contributed to the collapse of the fishery over the first half of the twentieth century. Today, the species is listed as either threatened or endangered in nineteen of the twenty states that encompass its natural range in the United States.

Bernie answered my phone call as he drove north on Highway 59, bound for Chattanooga, Tennessee after participating in a conference on fish biology in Birmingham, Alabama. "We decided on lake sturgeon for several reasons," he explained. The primary reason was aesthetics—the fish just fascinate people. "They're living dinosaurs swimming in our midst," said Bernie, explaining that the body design of the lake sturgeon has essentially remained unchanged since the fish were first fossilized. The second reason is the fish are "exciting to catch," Bernie said. Environmental conditions were also ripe for reintroduction of lake sturgeon in Tennessee. The Clean Water Act of 1972 greatly improved water quality, and in the late 1980s, the Tennessee Valley Authority reconstructed dams to improve water flow and elevate oxygen levels. Now, when sturgeon spawn in the waters below dams, their embryos and larvae have a good chance of surviving. And techniques to raise captive lake sturgeon have greatly improved. The young sturgeon released by the members of the Tennessee working group come from adults caught in the Wolf River in Wisconsin. The eggs and "milk" are stripped by clasping the fish and gently applying pressure as the hand is pulled down the length of the fish to the genital opening. Fertilized embryos are shipped to Warm Springs, Georgia, where larval fish are raised on a diet of live brine shrimp and then, as juveniles, switched to a diet of chopped blood worms and krill. When the juvenile fish reach an inch, a thousand or so are shipped to each of several member organizations of the lake sturgeon reintroduction project, including the Tennessee Aquarium. Here, the fish are grown to six to eight inches and then released.

"We're catching two- to four-foot lake sturgeon we released long ago into the Tennessee River," said Bernie. "We use trotlines to catch them, baited bottom lines attached to floats and left overnight. Then we surgically insert an acoustic tag inside the body cavity," Bernie explained. The lake sturgeon reintroduction program has, to date, tagged, released, and followed about fifty to sixty fish. The tagging program is allowing the Tennessee working group to evaluate distances the fish move and locations of key spawning grounds. The ultimate goal is to grow the lake sturgeon fishery to the point where an angler may keep one fish. "This goal is still decades away," Bernie reassured me. Today, fishers are allowed to catch a lake sturgeon in Tennessee but are required by law to release the fish. The fishers know that if they inform the Tennessee Wildlife Resources Agency of their catch, they'll be sent a certificate of appreciation. This recreational catch information provides Bernie and his working group with important data for assessments of the size of the sturgeon population.

The success of the sturgeon reintroduction program can be attributed to its broad inclusion of key constituents. Each participating organization brings to the table its own unique suite of resources that contribute to the project, including key personnel, contributions of funds, and individually tailored promotional and educational outreach programs. Importantly, the players all come together every year at the Tennessee Aquarium to participate in a collaborative workshop. The working group engages in discussion sessions to carve out plans to sample lake sturgeon in the coming year; the group tweaks the stocking numbers, explores ideas to raise additional funds, and makes plans for new educational outreach programs. It's amazing how much these face-to-face meetings have inspired the program, Bernie said, happy that our discussion had delivered him halfway to Chattanooga.

Given the vastness of the oceans, reintroduction of threatened or endangered marine fish is considerably more challenging than raising and releasing fish into streams, rivers, and lakes. My friend and colleague Professor E. O. Wilson invited me to join with other members of the E. O. Wilson Biodiversity Foundation Advisory Board to participate in a conference on biodiversity and conservation at Duke University in April 2015.[16] One of the invited speakers, Professor Callum Roberts of the University of York in Great Britain, a leading international expert on marine conservation, gave a timely keynote presentation. Roberts highlighted the growing problem of "fishing down the food web," whereby marine fisheries first quickly remove the largest predatory fish and then progress, step by step, to remove smaller and smaller species of fish.[17] Unfortunately, even the fish at the bottom of the food chain, once considered "trash fish," are now profitable on the global market, which, of course, is a recipe for overfishing. At the biodiversity conference, E. O. Wilson announced his forthcoming book, *Half Earth: Our Planet's Fight for Life*, which calls for humanity to preserve half the Earth. In the spirit of E. O. Wilson,

Roberts recommended humanity should similarly set its sights on preserving half the world's oceans. Roberts defended his recommendation by pointing out that, at present, a meager 1.5 percent of the world's oceans are sheltered in marine protected areas.[18] Despite what might at first appear a draconian leap in the level of protection, Roberts indicated to the conference audience that the "half ocean" goal is largely attainable in one simple step—protect the world's open seas. By protecting all the waters that extend beyond national two-hundred-mile offshore fishing limits, the international fishing community would immediately stop removing the vast production stock of the open seas. Fish populations in the open seas would quickly rebound to levels that would seed coastal waters with larval, juvenile, and adult fish and, not inconsequentially, I might add, countless larvae of marine invertebrates. Both small-boat fishing operations in developing countries and large high-tech fishing fleets in developed countries would benefit from increased fish production along their coasts.

A catch-and-release conservation ethic has taken root in many of today's most popular sport fisheries. I've practiced this ethic on streams, rivers, and lakes, fishing with friends for rainbow, brook, brown, and lake trout; for largemouth, spotted, and redeye bass; and for gar, pike, walleye, catfish, and bream. On oceans, my fishing partners and I have caught and released bonefish, ladyfish, hard tails, needlefish, and hundreds of speckled trout and redfish with slot limits that made them either too small or too big to keep. Some fishers argue that fish rarely survive being caught and released, but most experimental studies would suggest otherwise. Of course, the incidence of mortality that results from catch and release depends on the species of fish and how a given fisher handles a fish once it is caught. I've caught delicate brook trout that I leave submerged as I gently cup the fish's belly and tease the fly or spinner from the lip with a pair of needle-nose pliers. I've also caught hard-fighting, tail-slapping ladyfish that have slipped out of my hands and bounced off my kayak and back into the water and recaught the same fish later as full of fight as ever. A study conducted by the Florida Fish and Wildlife Conservation Commission that followed survival of rod-caught tarpon by tagging individual fish concluded that tarpon are hardy fish with a high probability of survival after being hooked and released, with survival levels ranging from 83 to 93 percent.[19] When potential effects of predation by sharks are removed, tarpon survival after being hooked rose to 95 percent. In a study published in the *North American Journal of Fisheries Management,* fisheries biologists found that survival of brook trout after catch and release was moderately high, about 70 percent or higher when trout were caught on passive baits or lures.[20] When brook trout were caught and released on a single-hook fly, survival rose to 95 percent.

I find it remarkable that the catch-and-release ethic has wrapped itself around so many large sport fish, including the quintessential blue marlin. I suspect marlin fishing guides helped plant the seeds of conservation in the psyches of their clients. As the numbers of blue marlin in the world's oceans tumbled from intense commercial and recreational fishing, guides must have realized their livelihoods were endangered. In 1986, The Billfish Foundation (TBF) was established and quickly became the leading global organization dedicated to conserving billfish—the twelve species of fish with bills, including blue marlin, sailfish, and swordfish.[21] One of TBF's greatest accomplishments has been engaging anglers in a tag-and-release program to assess and monitor the state of the world's billfish populations. This program empowers billfish fishers with the satisfaction of personally contributing to the conservation of an endangered fishery and has made the task of guides convincing their clients to release billfish that much easier. Fortuitously, at about the same time as tag and release was becoming popular, the art and technology of mounting game fish transitioned from taxidermists using actual parts of the fish to companies specializing in crafting lifelike fiberglass replicas of fish. Yet as deeply ingrained as Ernest Hemingway's prose, the act of catching a big billfish had a long and storied big-game history that encompassed a triumphant return to harbor and "hoisting of the fish." Guides and marlin tournament officials came up with a brilliant plan. Marlin boats with clients that had caught and released a big marlin were permitted to hoist a flag with a picture of a marlin to signify the catch, a flag for all to see, celebrate, and envy. Today, approximately 97 percent of blue marlin landed in the recreational fishery are measured, photographed, and released.

Elements of the catch-and-release ethic extend beyond the sustainability of a given species of fish. Each time fishers watch their catch swim away, the moment serves as a subtle reminder of the intrinsic value of what humankind collectively labels "nature" or "the creation." Coupled with a lifelong respect for the natural environment and the inarguable triumph of the catch so deeply rooted in a human genome shaped by hunting, fishers have long been ardent conservationists. Fly fishers and deep-sea fishing enthusiasts sit equally on boards of corporations and environmental organizations, soliciting funds to battle water pollution and to purchase wetlands to preserve fish habitats. Fishers organize river and ocean cleanups, participate in philanthropic fishing tournaments, and join national fishing organizations such as the Bass Angler Sportsman Association, Trout Unlimited, and the Coastal Conservation Association that support various fishing related conservation and educational activities. Most important, fishers play an essential role in fostering the next generation of fishers (and conservationists) by volunteering to support youth fishing events sponsored by organizations like the Take a Kid Fishing Foundation for disadvantaged youth and children with special needs or by climbing into a canoe, bass boat, or a Boston whaler with a niece, nephew, godchild, grandchild, son, or daughter to go out fishing.

My daughter, now twenty, recently touched my heart by suggesting that our family go kayaking during a spring trip to New Orleans. Where other young people would want to shop and hit the major tourist attractions, Jamie searched online and found a tour company that takes people on half-day kayak trips in the local waters. I remembered earlier water adventures with Jamie that must have helped form her appreciation of boating and fishing and established the underpinnings of a conservation ethic that will last a lifetime.

On one such trip long ago, Jamie bounded into our aluminum Bass Tracker Panfish 16 with all the unbridled energy of a seven-year-old. "Squeeze the rubber ball on the gas line," I told her. Once the outboard engine started, I nudged the motorboat away from the wooden dock of our boathouse and accelerated down Pennamotley Cove. We were off to fish the banks of Lake Mitchell, one of several large reservoirs that combine to form the Coosa River chain in central Alabama. On a typical summer day, the bass fishing in Lake Mitchell is slow. I wasn't expecting to catch much of anything, maybe a bass if we were lucky, but more likely I'd switch to an ultralight rod and cast a rooster tail to see if I could entice a small bream or two. Exiting the mouth of the cove, I swung the boat into Hatchet Creek and headed toward the main body of Lake Mitchell. A quarter mile later, I slowed up and, steering the boat within fifteen feet of the creek bank, cut the engine and dropped the trolling motor's prop into the water. Lifting my spinning rod off the boat's carpeted floor, I unhooked the plastic green pumpkin-seed worm from a rod eyelet and swiveled in my seat to promise Jamie that she'd get to reel in any fish. Three casts later, I felt a strong tug as I bounced the worm along the lake floor. A quick skyward whip of the rod set the hook. "Hold on tight," I advised, handing Jamie the rod. Jamie smiled nervously and gripped the handle like the rod might literally leap from her hands. "Turn the handle on the reel like this," I said, leaning over and rotating the handle a few times in the right direction. With the base of the rod snugged up under her armpit, Jamie cranked away, giving a yell of delight when a small spotted bass sprung from the water. "Take it off, Dad!" she exclaimed, still grinning. With the bass unhooked and released, I depressed the foot pedal of the trolling motor and continued down the bank, casting along the edge of the weed beds. Another quick tug followed by a hook set and Jamie reeled in her second fish and then, quickly, a third. All told, over the next hour, Jamie reeled in ten bass. When we got back to the boathouse, Jamie was beaming, just itching to tell her mom and brother about her fish.

Two years later, when Jamie was nine, I took her on an overnight campout on a tiny island in the middle of Lake Mitchell. The two of us set off from our boat dock on a late summer afternoon, our motorboat loaded with a camping tent, Coleman stove, sleeping bags, fishing gear, pots and pans, food and water, toiletries, and a boombox. The football-field-sized island was covered with a thick stand of tall pines, but someone had cleared out a nice campsite on the end of the island where the ground was level. Jamie did her fair share of setting up camp, lugging rocks to secure the tent's guy lines, holding tent poles erect as I attached the cloth tent, arranging rocks for a campfire pit, collecting firewood, and picking up trash left behind by the last campers. The camp completed, we stood on the bank fishing, reeling in a few bream as the late afternoon sky turned crimson with the setting sun. Jamie helped me make spaghetti, and soon we were roasting marshmallows on sticks held over the open flames of our campfire. Later, as the fire died down, we discovered why there's nothing quite like spending the night in the middle of a lake under a clear, moonless sky—the stars above us were spectacular. I pointed out to Jamie the paintbrush stroke across the sky that is our own Milky Way galaxy and explained how she could line up the two stars at the base of the Big Dipper to locate the North Star. Before retreating to the tent, I picked up an oldies station on the boombox, and Jamie and I danced under the stars to the music of Michael Jackson, the Beach Boys, and the Beatles.

At fifteen, my daughter settled into the front seat of our wellworn, fourteen-foot Mad River canoe. Earlier in the morning on our back driveway, I'd gathered and surveyed all of the gear for our canoe trip. I didn't want to repeat the time my son and I forgot the paddles. Among our fishing rods, tackle kit, bottles of water, float bag, and life jackets rested my felt-bottomed river boots. I wondered if Jamie sensed in the boots, like I did, the river adventure about to take place. It was a struggle to get the heavy canoe off the van and down a steep path to the concrete slab that served as a canoe launch, but there were no complaints from my teenager. Canoe loaded, we set off to paddle a five-mile section of the Cahaba River not far from our home in Birmingham. A little before noon, Jamie and I pulled off the river and had a picnic on the sun-drenched bank. Our conversation turned from the redeye bass she caught, which she had insisted I unhook and release, to the red-eared slider we'd spooked off a river-washed log and to the great blue heron we'd adopted as our mascot. Jamie was intrigued by the huge blue-gray bird, soaring ahead of us for the past hour, as if leading us downriver, from one branched roost to the next. Maybe I, like our blue heron, have helped lead Jamie, one cast at a time, toward a healthy respect and appreciation for our natural world. One thing is for certain: Jamie's children, my grandchildren, will fish.

ACKNOWLEDGMENTS

This book came about, in part, because of a nudge from my great friend, academic colleague, and fishing buddy Adam Vines, an outstanding poet and professor of English at the University of Alabama at Birmingham (UAB). Adam was the first to read and review each chapter, and his editorial input was an essential element of the book. I thank my literary agent, Katherine Flynn, of Kneerim, Williams & Bloom, who, as with my first book, *Lost Antarctica,* was enthusiastic about the proposed narrative from the start and provided encouragement and guidance in securing an outstanding publisher. My friend, colleague, and fellow Alabamian Edward O. Wilson, Pelegrino University Professor at Harvard University, continues to encourage and inspire me to write about nature and the environment for a general audience. I thank Paula Ehrlich, president and CEO of the E. O. Wilson Biodiversity Foundation, for her support.

I thank my editor at St. Martin's Press, Elisabeth Dyssegaard, for her editorial expertise, patience, and, upon receipt of each chapter, her growing excitement about the book's potential to reach a broad audience. I wish to thank others at St. Martin's Press, including Donna Cherry, Christine Catarino, David Rotstein, Gabrielle Gantz, and Laura Apperson. Bill Warhop, an independent contractor, did a superb job as copy editor and had a keen eye for detail and creative insights. I engaged the services of artist and UAB student Annabelle DeCamillis to create the illustrations of fish featured in the ten chapters. Annabelle's illustrations not only came to life, but convinced me that she is a superb student of art. I wish her, and fully anticipate, a most successful professional career in the arts. Another talented artist, professional photographer Beth Maynor Young, captured the image of me fishing in my canoe on the Cahaba River. Beth is a friend and talented naturalist whose stunning photographs of the Cahaba River have graced many magazines and books. I am grateful to friends and family who edited, reviewed, and fact-checked the book, especially my wife Ferne McClintock, my friend and research associate Margaret Amsler, and my friend Dr. Joseph Shepherd. Those who provided expertise on aspects of fish biology, fishing, and other relevant topics include my friends and colleagues Professors Emeriti Ken Marion and Rob Angus, Department of Biology (UAB); Rick Remy (Southern Research Institute, Alabama); Professor James Brown, Department of History (Samford University); Dr. Randall Haddock (Cahaba River Society, Alabama); Dr. John Dindo (Dauphin Island Sea Laboratory, Alabama); Professor Emeritus Joseph Eastman, Department of Biological Sciences (Ohio University); Professor John Janssen, School of Freshwater Sciences (University of Wisconsin Milwaukee); Professor Emeritus John Pearse, Ecology and Evolutionary Biology (University of California, Santa Cruz); Professor Emeritus Mike Barker, Department of Marine Science (University of Otago, New Zealand); Associate Professor Miles Lamare, Department of Marine Science (University of Otago, New Zealand); Leila Mitchell (New York State Department of Environmental Conservation); Dr. Anne-Marie Genevière, Oceanological Observatory (Banyuls-sur-Mer, France); Dr. Bernie Kahajda (Tennessee Aquarium); Tommy Campbell (Sixmile, Alabama); Barry Fagan (Alabama Department of Transportation); Malou Roque (Anchois Roque, Collioure, France), Gabriel Diaz (Port-Vendres, France); Fabien (L'Espadon–Peche, Plage, Plangue; Banyuls-sur-Mer, France); and of course my Chandeleur Islands fishing partners.

My Antarctic marine biological research and educational outreach efforts have been generously supported by the Office of Polar Programs at the National Science Foundation and by a gift from the Robert R. Mayer Foundation, Birmingham, Alabama, which funds the UAB Endowed Professorship in Polar and Marine Biology. I appreciate the support of the chair of the Department of Biology at UAB, Professor Steven Austad. Additional educational outreach funding has been provided by the Abercrombie &

Kent Foundation, Jorie Kent (A&K philanthropy chair), Geoffrey Kent (A&K chair and chief executive director), and Bob Simpson (vice president for product operations and small ships). I thank the individuals in the media who feature aspects of my biological research in national and international newspapers, science magazines, radio programs, and television productions. The societal value of media-based educational outreach on matters of science is tremendous.

I wish to recognize and thank fishing guides, not just those experts who took me fishing in the Bahamas, Costa Rica, Florida, Manitoba, and New Zealand, but fishing guides the world over. These individuals spend countless hours on our streams, rivers, lakes, and oceans. They are born naturalists whose knowledge spans aspects of fish behavior, reproduction, feeding, and ecology, and a much broader natural history. Even better, most guides are deeply rooted in a conservation ethic, and the value of their profession in this regard should not be underestimated.

I thank my wife Ferne, my son Luke, and my daughter Jamie, for their love, encouragement, and patience during the year I spent writing this book. Finally, I thank my mother, Helen Muriel Ganopole, to whom I dedicate this book and who, through her considerable literary talents, inspired in me both a respect and love for the written word.

NOTES

CHAPTER 1: CHANDELEUR ISLANDS

1. Breton National Wildlife Refuge, www.fws.gov/breton/.
2. "Brown Pelican, *Pelecanus occidentalis*," U.S. Fish & Wildlife Service, November 2009, http://fws.gov/home/feature/2009/pdf/brown_pelicanfactsheet 09.pdf.
3. Harry Blanchet et al., "The Spotted Sea Trout Fishery of the Gulf of Mexico, United States: A Regional Management Plan," publication no. 87 (Ocean Springs, MS: Gulf States Fisheries Commission, March 2001), http://www .gsmfc.org/publications/GSMFC%20Number%20087.pdf.
4. Marie P. Fish and William H. Mowbray, *Sounds of the Western North Atlantic Fishes* (Baltimore: John Hopkins University Press, 1970).
5. J. Read Hendon et al., "Movements of Spotted Seatrout (*Cynoscion nebulosus*) in Mississippi Coastal Waters Based on Tag-Recapture," *Gulf of Mexico Science* 2 (2002): 91–97.
6. Michael Saucier and Donald M. Baltz, "Spawning Site Selection by Spotted Seatrout, *Cynoscion nebulosus*, and Black Drum, *Pogonias cromis*, in Louisiana," *Environmental Biology of Fishes* 36 (1993): 257–72.
7. Steven Beddingfield and James McClintock, "Environmentally-Induced Catastrophic Mortality of the Sea Urchin *Lytechinus variegatus* in Shallow Seagrass Habitats of Saint Joseph Bay, Florida," *Bulletin of Marine Science* 55 (1994): 235–240.
8. Anne Magurran, "The Adaptive Significance of Schooling as an Antipredator Defence in Fish," *Annales Zoologici Fennici* 27 (1990): 51–66.
9. "Hurricane Katrina. Before and After Photo Comparisons: Chandeleur Islands," U.S. Geological Survey, http://coastal.er.usgs.gov/hurricanes/katrina /photo-comparisons/chandeleur.html.
10. "Sea Oats: *Uniola paniculata*," Natural Resources Conservation Service, U.S. Department of Agriculture, http://plants.usda.gov/factsheet/pdf/fs_unpa .pdf.
11. "Seagrass Habitat in the Northern Gulf of Mexico: Degradation, Conservation and Restoration of a Valuable Resource," U.S. Geological Survey, http:// gulfsci.usgs.gov/gom_ims/pdf/pubs_gom.pdf.
12. "Salt Marsh Habitats," Smithsonian Marine Station at Fort Pierce, http:// www.sms.si.edu/irlspec/Saltmarsh.htm

13. Peter Hogarth, *The Biology of Mangroves* (Oxford, UK: Oxford University Press, 1999).

14. "Magnificent Frigate Bird, *Fregata magnificens*," Audubon Guide to North American Birds, http://www.audubon.org/field-guide/bird/magnificent-fri gatebird.

15. "What Is Ocean Acidification?" National Oceanic and Atmospheric Administration, http://www.pmel.noaa.gov/co2/story/What+is+Ocean+Acidi fication%3F.

16. Cecilia Brothers and James McClintock, "The Effects of Climate-Induced Elevated Seawater Temperature on the Covering Behavior, Righting Response, and Aristotle's Lantern Reflex of the Sea Urchin *Lytechinus variegatus*," *Journal of Experimental Marine Biology and Ecology* 467 (2015): 33–38.

17. Roberta Challener et al., "Effects of Reduced Carbonate Saturation State on Early Development in the Common Edible Sea Urchin *Lytechinus variegatus:* Implications for Land-Based Aquaculture," *Journal of Applied Aquaculture* 25 (2013): 154–175.

18. "Red Drum," Gulf Coast Research Laboratory, University of Southern Mississippi, http://www.usm.edu/gcrl/public/fish/red.drum.php.

19. "Executive Order: Protection of Striped Bass and Red Drum Fish Populations," White House press release, October 20, 2007, http://georgewbush -whitehouse.archives.gov/news/releases/2007/10/20071020-4.html.

20. Asbury Sallenger et al., "Extreme Coastal Changes on the Chandeleur Islands, Louisiana, During and After Hurricane Katrina," in D. Lavoie, ed., *Sand Resources, Regional Geology, and Coastal Processes of the Chandeleur Islands Coastal System—An Evaluation of the Breton National Wildlife Refuge:* U.S. Geological Survey Scientific Investigations Report, 5252 (Reston, VA: U.S. Geological Survey, 2009), 27–36.

21. Douglas Brinkley, *The Great Deluge: Hurricane Katrina, New Orleans, and the Mississippi Gulf Coast* (New York: William Morrow, 2006).

CHAPTER 2: MANITOBA

1. "Neultin Lake," Natural Resources Canada, http://www4.rncan.gc.ca /search-place-names/unique/OALYK.

2. "Native Languages of the Americas: Cree," http://www.native-languages .org/cree.htm.

3. The story of sailing home with Ralph was published as an essay titled "Captain Ralph" in the Ponder section of the September/October 2013 issue of *Sierra* magazine, http://www.sierraclub.org/sierra/2013-5-september-october /ponder/captain-ralph.

4. Brian J. Shuter et al., "A General, Life History Based Model for Regional Management of Fish Stocks: The Inland Lake Trout (*Salvenlinus namaycush*) Fisheries of Ontario," *Canadian Journal of Fisheries and Aquatic Sciences* 55 (1998): 2161–2177.

5. "Record Fish Canada," http://www.recordfishcanada.com/lake-trout8 .html.

6. Ibid.

7. Xanthe Walker and Jill Johnstone, "Widespread Negative Correlations Between Black Spruce Growth and Temperature Across Topographic Moisture Gradients in the Boreal Forest," *Environmental Research Letters* 9 (2014), http:// iopscience.iop.org/1748-9326/9/6/064016/article.

8. "Frontiers in Understanding Climate Change and Polar Ecosystems," National Academy of Sciences, 2011, http://dels.nas.edu/resources/static-assets /materials-based-on-reports/reports-in-brief/Frontiers-Climate-Change -Report-Brief-Final.pdf.

9. Glenn Juday, "Boreal Forests and Climate Change," in Andrew Goudie and David Cuff, eds., *Oxford Companion to Global Change* (Oxford University Press, 2009), 75–84.

10. Richard H. Waring and William H. Schlesinger, *Forest Ecosystems: Concepts and Management* (Orlando, FL: Academic Press, 1985).

11. Mark Johnston et al., "Vulnerability of Canada's Tree Species to Climate Change and Management Options for Adaptation: An Overview for Policy Makers and Practitioners," Canadian Council of Forest Ministers, http:// www.ccfm.org/pdf/TreeSpecies_web_e.pdf.

12. "Arctic Grayling, *Thymallus arcticus*," *FishBase*, http://www.fishbase.org/sum mary/Thymallus-arcticus.html.

13. "Northern Pike, *Esox lucius*," *FishBase*, http://www.fishbase.org/summary /SpeciesSummary.php?id=258&AT=pike.

14. Ted Hughes, "Pike," Boyle Poetry (blog), https://russellboyle.wordpress.com /2013/10/02/pike-by-ted-hughes/.

15. Susan Morse, "Ghost Moose: Winter Ticks Take Their Toll," *Northern Woodlands* (Spring 2012), http://northernwoodlands.org/articles/article/ghost -moose-winter-ticks-take-their-toll.

16. John Pastor et al., "Moose Browsing and Soil Fertility in the Boreal Forest of Isle Royale National Park," *Ecology* 74 (1993): 467–480.

CHAPTER 3: CAHABA RIVER

1. "Snake Bites," U.S. National Library of Medicine, http://www.nlm.nih.gov /medlineplus/ency/article/000031.htm.

2. "Cahaba River National Wildlife Refuge," U.S. Fish and Wildlife Service, http://www.fws.gov/refuges/profiles/index.cfm?id=43665.

3. Herbert Boschung and Richard Mayden, *Fishes of Alabama* (Washington, D.C.: Smithsonian Books, 2004).

4. Theresa Thom et al., *Water Resource Inventory and Assessment (WRIA): Cahaba River National Wildlife Refuge Bibb County, Alabama*(Atlanta, GA: U.S. Fish and Wildlife Service, Southeast Region, 2013), http://www.fws.gov/southeast /IMnetwork/pdfs/Cahaba_River_WRIA_Narrative_2013.pdf.

5. Monte Burke, *Sowbelly: The Obsessive Quest for the World-Record Largemouth Bass* (New York: Penguin, 2005).

6. Winston H. Baker et al., "The Alabama Bass, *Micropterus henshalli* (Teleostei: Centrarchidae), from the Mobile River Basin," *Zootaxa* 1861 (2008): 57–67.

7. Frank Jordan and D. Albrey Arrington, "Weak Trophic Interactions Between Large Predatory Fishes and Herpetofauna in the Channelized Kissimmee River, Florida, USA," *Wetlands* 21 (2001): 155–159.

8. James McClintock et al., "*Plestiodon fasciatus* (Five-Lined Skink). Predation by Fish," *Herpetological Review* (in press).

9. "Cahaba Bass, *Micropterus cahabae*," *FishBase*, http://www.fishbase.org/sum mary/67133.

10. Michelle Nijhuis, "The Cahaba: A River of Riches," *Smithsonian Magazine*, August 2009, http://www.smithsonianmag.com/ist/?next=/science-nature /the-cahaba-a-river-of-riches-34214889/.

11. "Longnose Gar, *Lepisosteus osseus*," *FishBase*, http://www.fishbase.org/summary/1076.

12. Jim Brown et al., "River Redhorse and the Seasonal Snaring Thereof in Alabama," *Tributaries* 9 (2006): 9–26.

13. Ibid.

14. Lydia Avant, "Alabama Sturgeon on the Brink of Extinction," *Tuscaloosa News*, November 12, 2008, http://www.tuscaloosanews.com/article/20081112/NEWS/811120276.

15. "Cahaba Shiner, *Notropis cahabae*," The IUCN Red List of Threatened Species, http://www.iucnredlist.org/details/14884/0.

16. Cahaba River Society, http://www.cahabariversociety.org/.

17. "Water Quality," Cahaba River Society, http://www.cahabariversociety.org/programs/water-quality/.

CHAPTER 4: GULF OF MEXICO

1. "Blackfin Tuna, *Thunnus atlanticus*," *FishBase*, http://www.fishbase.org/summary/144.

2. "Yellowfin Tuna, *Thunnus albacares*," *FishBase*, http://www.fishbase.org/summary/Thunnus-albacares.html.

3. Ben Romans, "IGFA Record 427-Pound Yellowfin Tuna Wins Angler $1M Prize from Mustad," *Field and Stream* (September 18, 2012), http://www.fieldandstream.com/articles/fishing/2013/03/igfa-record-427-pound-yellowfin-tuna-wins-angler-1m-prize-mustad.

4. David Barstow et al., "Deepwater Horizon's Final Hours," *New York Times*, December 25, 2010, http://www.nytimes.com/2010/12/26/us/26spill.html?pagewanted=all&_r=0.

5. Scott Zengel and Jacqueline Michel, "Deepwater Horizon Oil Spill: Salt Marsh Oiling Conditions, Treatment Testing, and Treatment History in Northern Barataria Bay, Louisiana," U.S. Department of Commerce, NOAA Technical Memorandum NOS OR&R 42 (2013): 74 pages, http://docs.lib.noaa.gov/noaa_documents/NOS/ORR/TM_NOS_ORR/TM_NOS-ORR_42.pdf.

6. Steven Murawski et al., "Prevalence of External Skin Lesions and Polycyclic Aromatic Hydrocarbon Concentrations in Gulf of Mexico Fishes, Post-Deepwater Horizon," *Transactions of the American Fisheries Society* 143 (2014): 1084–1097.

7. Debbie Elliott, "5 Years after BP Oil Spill, Effects Linger and Recovery Is Slow," *NPR*, April 20, 2015, http://www.npr.org/2015/04/20/400374744/5-years-after-bp-oil-spill-effects-linger-and-recovery-is-slow.

8. Fabien Brette et al., "Crude Oil Impairs Cardiac Excitation-Coupling in Fish," *Science* 343 (2014): 772–776.

9. John Incardona et al., "Deepwater Horizon Crude Oil Impacts the Developing Hearts of Large Predatory Pelagic Fish," *Proceedings of the National Academy of Sciences* 111 (2014): E1510–E1518, http://www.pnas.org/content/111/15/E1510.full.pdf.

10. "Atlantic Bluefin Tuna, *Thunnus thynnus*," *FishBase*, http://www.fishbase.org/summary/147.

11. Kenneth Brower, "Quicksilver," *National Geographic*, March 2014, 67–87.

12. Anna Mukai and Yuki Yamaguchi, "Japan Sushi Chain Pays Record $1.76 Million for Tuna at Auction," *Bloomberg*, January 6, 2013, http://www

.bloomberg.com/news/articles/2013-01-06/japan-sushi-chain-pays-record
-1-76-million-for-tuna-at-auction.

13. "Bluefin tuna, *Thunnus thynnus,*" IGFA Online World Record Search, http://
     wrec.igfa.org/WRecordsList.aspx?lc=AllTackle&cn=Tuna,%20bluefin.

14. "Plan to Save Bluefin Tuna," *Science* 345 (2014): 1435–1436, ftp://ws5.chitose
     .melsa.net.id/pub/EBooks/Science-September.19.2014.pdf.

15. Brian Silliman et al., "Degradation and Resilience in Louisiana Salt Marshes
     after the BP-Deepwater Horizon Oil Spill," *Proceedings of the National Academy of
     Sciences* 109 (2012): 11234–11239.

16. Erik Stokstad, "Oil Contamination of Crab Larvae Could Be Widespread,"
     Science, July 2, 2010, http://news.sciencemag.org/2010/07/oil-contamination
     -crab-larvae-could-be-widespread.

17. Matt Smith, "Empty Nets in Louisiana Three Years After the Spill," *CNN,*
     April 29, 2013, http://www.cnn.com/2013/04/27/us/gulf-disaster-fishing
     -industry/.

18. Robbie Brown, "Fishermen Sign On to Clean Up Oil," *New York Times,* April
     30, 2010, http://www.nytimes.com/2010/05/01/us/01marsh.html.

19. Mark Schrope, "Still Counting Gulf Spill's Dead Birds," *New York Times,* May
     6, 2014, http://www.nytimes.com/2014/05/06/science/still-counting-gulf
     -spills-dead-birds.html.

CHAPTER 5: ANTARCTICA

1. Arthur DeVries and D. Wohlschlag, "Freezing Resistance in Some Antarctic
    Fishes," *Science* 163 (1969): 1073–1075.

2. Arthur DeVries et al., "Decline of the Antarctic Toothfish and Its Predators
    in McMurdo Sound and the Southern Ross Sea, and Recommendations for
    Restoration," *CCAMLR* (2008) Doc WG-EMM 08/xx.

3. "Antarctic Toothfish, *Dissostichus mawsoni,*" FishBase, http://www.fishbase
    .org/summary/7039.

4. Joseph Eastman, "The Evolution of Neutrally Buoyant Notothenioid Fishes:
    Their Specializations and Potential Interactions in the Antarctic Marine
    Food Web," in W.R. Siegfried et al. (eds.) *Antarctic Nutrient Cycles and Food Webs*
    (Berlin: Springer-Verlag, 1985).

5. DeVries et al., "Decline of the Antarctic Toothfish.".

6. Bruce Knecht, "Chasing the Perfect Fish," *Wall Street Journal,* May 4, 2006,
    http://www.wsj.com/articles/SB114670694136643399.

7. Amanda Mascarelli, "Seafood Suffers from Fishy Eco-Labelling," *Nature,*
    August 22, 2011, http://www.nature.com/news/2011/110822/full/news.2011
    .496.html.

8. Marco Favero et al., "Estimate of Seabird By-Catch Along the Patagonian
    Shelf by Argentine Longline Fishing Vessels, 1999–2001," *Bird Conservation
    International* 13 (2003): 273–281.

9. Palmer Station, National Science Foundation, https://www.nsf.gov/geo/plr
    /support/palmerst.jsp.

10. "Black Rockcod, *Notothenia coriiceps,*" FishBase, http://www.fishbase.org/sum
    mary/4702.

11. James McClintock, *Lost Antarctica: Adventures in a Disappearing Land* (New York:
    Palgrave Macmillan, 2012).

12. "What Is Ocean Acidification," National Oceanic and Atmospheric Administration, http://www.pmel.noaa.gov/co2/story/What+is+Ocean+Acidification%3F.

13. Victoria Fabry et al., "Ocean Acidification at High Latitudes: The Bellwether," *Oceanography* 22 (2009): 160–171.

14. Richard Aronson et al., "Climate Change and Invasibility of the Antarctic Benthos," *Annual Review of Ecology, Evolution, and Systematics* 38 (2007): 129–154.

15. Philip Munday et al., "Ocean Acidification Impairs Olfactory Discrimination and Homing Ability of a Marine Fish," *Proceedings of the National Academy of Sciences* 106 (2009): 1848–1852.

16. Wen-Sung Chung et al., "Ocean Acidification Slows Retinal Function in a Damselfish Through Interference with $GABA_A$ Receptors," *Journal of Experimental Biology* 217 (2014): 323–326.

17. So Kawaguchi et al., "Will Krill Fare Well Under Southern Ocean Acidification?" *Biology Letters* 7 (2011): 288–291.

18. So Kawaguchi et al., "Risk Maps for Antarctic Krill Under Projected Southern Ocean Acidification," *Nature Climate Change* 3 (2013): 843–847.

19. N. Bednaršek et al., "Extensive Dissolution of Live Pteropods in the Southern Ocean," *Nature Geoscience* 5 (2012): 881–885.

CHAPTER 6: NEW ZEALAND

1. "New Zealand Blue Cod, *Parapercis colias*," *FishBase*, http://www.fishbase.org/summary/Parapercis-colias.html.

2. Mark Kurlansky, *Cod: A Biography of the Fish That Changed the World* (London: Penguin, 1997).

3. Garrett Hardin, "The Tragedy of the Commons," *Science* 162 (1968): 1243–1248.

4. "NOAA Fisheries Announces Temporary Gulf of Maine Cod and Haddock Management Measures," *Greater Atlantic Region Bulletin*, November 10, 2014, https://www.greateratlantic.fisheries.noaa.gov/nr/2014/November/14gomhaddockcodphl.pdf.

5. James Prosek, "Trout Fishing, a Taut Line to Our Past," *New York Times*, April 18, 2015, http://www.nytimes.com/2015/04/19/sports/trout-fishing-a-taut-line-to-our-past.html.

6. "Rainbow Trout, *Oncorhynchus mykiss*," *FishBase*, http://www.fishbase.org/summary/239.

7. Dave Kelly, "The Evolutionary Ecology of Mast Seeding," *Trends in Ecology and Evolution* 9 (1994): 465–470.

8. "*Didymosphenia geminata*," *AlgaeBase*, http://www.algaebase.org/search/species/detail/?species_id=S7d7294c1563cfb25.

9. Alexander Flecker and Colin Townsend, "Community-Wide Consequences of Trout Introduction in New Zealand Streams," in Fred B. Samson and Fritz L. Knopf, eds., *Ecosystem Management* (New York: Springer, 1996), 203–215.

CHAPTER 7: BAHAMAS

1. "Free Diving and Shallow Water Blackout," Diving Medicine Online, http://www.scuba-doc.com/latenthypoxia.html.

2. Gerace Research Centre, http://www.geraceresearchcentre.com/.

3. Melissa Friedman et al., "Ciguatera Fish Poisoning: Treatment, Prevention and Management," *Marine Drugs* 6 (2008): 456–479.

4. "Coral Reef Conservation Program," U.S. National Oceanic and Atmospheric Administration, http://coralreef.noaa.gov/conservation/status/.

5. Jennifer Smith et al., "The Effects of Top-Down Versus Bottom-Up Control on Benthic Coral Reef Community Structure," *Oecologia* 163 (2010): 497–507.

6. "Bonefish, *Albula vulpes*," *FishBase*, http://www.fishbase.org/summary/228.

7. Jimmy Buffett, *A Pirate Looks at Fifty* (New York: Random House, 1998).

8. "Johnson Sea Link (JSL) I and II," *Ocean Explorer*, National Oceanic and Atmospheric Administration, http://oceanexplorer.noaa.gov/technology/subs /sealink/sealink.html.

9. William Ausich and Charles Messing, "Crinoidea: Sea Lilies and Feather Stars," Tree of Life web project, http://tolweb.org/Crinoidea.

10. "Blue Marlin, *Makaira nigricans*," *FishBase*, http://www.fishbase.org/summary /216.

CHAPTER 8: COSTA RICA

1. La Selva Biological Station, Organization for Tropical Studies, http://www .ots.ac.cr/index.php?option=com_content&task=view&id=162&Itemid =348.

2. "Tarpon, *Megalops atlanticus*," *FishBase*, http://www.fishbase.org/summary/ Megalops-atlanticus.html/.

3. "Tarpon *(Megalops atlanticus)*," IGFA Online World Record Search, http:// wrec.igfa.org/WRecordsList.aspx?lc=AllTackle&cn=Tarpon.

4. Laurence Dodds, "The Darwin Awards: 20 Years of Lethal Stupidity," *Telegraph*, December 12, 2014, http://www.telegraph.co.uk/news/newstopics /howaboutthat/11288563/The-Darwin-Awards-20-years-of-lethal-stupid ity.html.

5. "Common Snook, *Centropomus undecimalis*," *FishBase*, http://www.fishbase.org /summary/345.

6. David A. Blewett et al., "Feeding Habits of Common Snook, *Centropomus undecimalis*, in Charlotte Harbor, Florida," *Gulf and Caribbean Research* 18 (2006): 1–13.

7. "2010 Florida Fish Kill," Snook and Gamefish Foundation, http://www .snookfoundation.org/news/38-general/212-2010-florida-fish-kill-.html.

8. Frank Mazzotti et al., "Cold-Induced Mortality of Invasive Burmese Pythons in South Florida," *Biological Invasions* 13 (2011): 143–151.

9. Horst Bleckmann and Randy Zelick, "Lateral Line System of Fish," *Integrative Zoology* 4 (2009): 13–25.

10. "Atlantic Snook *(Centropomus undecimalis)*," IGFA Online World Record Search, http://wrec.igfa.org/WRecordsList.aspx?lc=AllTackleLength&cn =Snook,%20Atlantic.

11. "Checkered Puffer Fish, *Sphoeroides testudineus*," *FishBase*, http://www.fishbase .org/summary/1242.

12. "Tetrodotoxin: Biotoxin," Centers for Disease Control and Prevention, http://www.cdc.gov/niosh/ershdb/emergencyresponsecard_29750019.html.

13. Ben Wolford, "Do Dolphins Get High? BBC Cameras Catch Dolphins Chewing on Pufferfish Toxins," *International Science Times*, December 30, 2013, http://www.isciencetimes.com/articles/6595/20131230/dolphins-high-bbc -cameras-catch-chewing-pufferfish.htm.

14. Wade Davis, "Zombification," *Science* 240 (1988): 1715-1716.
15. Frederick Davis, *The Man Who Saved Sea Turtles: Archie Carr and the Origins of Conservation Biology* (New York: Oxford University Press, 2007).
16. Berna van Wendel de Joode et al., "Indigenous Children Living Nearby Plantations with Chlorpyrifos-Treated Bags Have Elevated 3,5,6-trichloro-2-pyridinol (TCPy) Urinary Concentrations," *Environmental Research* 117 (2012): 17–26.
17. "Great Pacific Garbage Patch," Marine Debris pProgram, National Oceanic and Atmospheric Administration, http://marinedebris.noaa.gov/info/patch .html.
18. Charles Moore, "Choking the Oceans with Plastic," *New York Times*, August 26, 2014, http://www.nytimes.com/2014/08/26/opinion/choking-the -oceans-with-plastic.html.
19. Andrés Cózar et al., "Plastic Debris in the Open Ocean," *Proceedings of the National Academy of Sciences* 111 (2014): 10239–10244.

CHAPTER 9: FRANCE

1. Christopher Hall, "Homage to the Anchovy Coast," *Smithsonian Magazine*, May 2005, http://www.smithsonianmag.com/travel/homage-to-the-anchovy -coast-78374133/?no-ist.
2. Temel Oguz et al., "Invasion Dynamics of the Alien Ctenophore *Mnemiopsis leidyi* and Its Impact on Anchovy Collapse in the Black Sea," *Journal of Plankton Research* 30 (2008): 1385–1397.
3. Ludovica Iaccino, "World Oceans Day 2014: World's Most Polluted Seas Revealed," *International Business Times*, June 8, 2014, http://www.ibtimes.co.uk /world-oceans-day-2014-worlds-most-polluted-seas-revealed-1451638.
4. "European Smelt, *Osmerus eperlanus*," *FishBase*, http://www.fishbase.org/sum mary/1334.
5. John Steinbeck, *Cannery Row* (New York: Viking, 1945).
6. Eric Enno Tamm, *Beyond the Outer Shores: The Untold Odyssey of Ed Ricketts, the Pioneering Ecologist Who Inspired John Steinbeck and Joseph Campbell* (New York: Four Walls Eight Windows, 2004).
7. Brian Hatfield and Tim Tinker, "Spring 2014 California Sea Otter Census Results," *U.S. Geological Survey*, September 22, 2014, http://www.werc.usgs .gov/ProjectSubWebPage.aspx?SubWebPageID=24&ProjectID=91.
8. John Radovich, "The Collapse of the California Sardine Fishery: What Have We Learned?" *CalCOFI Report* 23 (1982): 56–77.
9. "Our History," Monterey Bay Aquarium, http://www.montereybayaquar ium.org/about/our-history.
10. "Pacific Barracuda, *Sphyraena argentea*," *FishBase*, http://www.fishbase.org/sum mary/3678.
11. "Pacific Sardine, *Sardinops sagax*," *FishBase*, http://www.fishbase.org/sum mary/1477.
12. Robert Emmett et al., "Pacific Sardine (*Sardinops sagax*) Abundance, Distribution, and Ecological Relationships in the Pacific Northwest," *California Cooperative Oceanic Fisheries Investigations* 46 (2005): 122–143.
13. Ethan Deyle et al., "Predicting Climate Effects on Pacific Sardine," *Proceedings of the National Academy of Sciences* 110 (2013): 6430–6435.
14. Cannery Row Sardine Co., http://www.canneryrowsardineco.com/.

CHAPTER 10: FISHING FOR SOLUTIONS

1. "What Is Ocean Acidification?" National Oceanic and Atmospheric Administration, http://www.pmel.noaa.gov/co2/story/What+is+Ocean+Acidification%3F.

2. Philip Munday et al., "Ocean Acidification Impairs Olfactory Discrimination and Homing Ability of a Marine Fish," *Proceedings of the National Academy of Sciences* 106 (2009): 1848–1852.

3. Maud Ferrari et al., "Putting Prey and Predator into the CO_2 Equation: Qualitative and Quantitative Effects of Ocean Acidification on Predator-Prey Interactions," *Ecology Letters* 14 (2011): 1143–1148.

4. Maria Byrne, "Impact of Ocean Warming and Ocean Acidification on Marine Invertebrate Life History Stages: Vulnerabilities and Potential for Persistence in a Changing Ocean," *Oceanography and Marine Biology: An Annual Review* 49 (2011): 1–42.

5. Cahaba River Society, http://www.cahabariversociety.org/.

6. Barry Fagan, "The Five Pillars of Construction Stormwater Management Workshop," presentation prepared for the 2011 annual meeting of the International Erosion Control Association, February 23, 2011, http://www.geosynthetica.net/Uploads/IECA_Fagan_FivePillars.pdf.

7. Acid Rain Program, U.S. Environmental Protection Agency, http://www.epa.gov/AIRMARKETS/programs/arp/.

8. Leila Mitchell, "Coming Full Circle," *New York State Conservationist*, August 2014, http://www.dec.ny.gov/pubs/98204.html/.

9. "Rigs to Reefs," Bureau of Safety and Environmental Enforcement, http://www.bsee.gov/Exploration-and-Production/Decomissioning/Rigs-to-Reefs/.

10. Daniel Pauly et al., "Fisheries: Does Catch Reflect Abundance?" *Nature* 494 (2013): 303–306.

11. Rosamond Naylor et al., "Effect of Aquaculture on World Fish Supplies," *Nature* 405 (2000): 1017–1024.

12. "Commercial Regulations for Stone Crab," Florida Fish and Wildlife Conservation Commission, http://myfwc.com/fishing/saltwater/commercial/stone-crab/.

13. Christopher Costello et al., "Status and Solutions for the World's Unassessed Fisheries," *Science* 338 (2012): 517–20.

14. Cantrell et al., "Evaluation of the Tennessee Lake Sturgeon *(Acipenser fulvescens)* Reintroduction and Management Plan," 2013, https://www.was.org/documents/MeetingPresentations/AQ2013/AQ2013_1229.pdf.

15. "Lake Sturgeon, *Acipenser fulvescens*," *FishBase*, http://www.fishbase.org/summary/2591.

16. Biodiversity Days Videos, E. O. Wilson Biodiversity Foundation, http://eowilsonfoundation.org/tag/nicholas-school-of-the-environment-at-duke-university/.

17. Callum Roberts, *The Ocean of Life: The Fate of Man and the Sea* (New York: Penguin, 2012).

18. Benjamin Halpern, "Conservation: Making Marine Protected Areas Work," *Nature* 506 (2014): 167–168.

19. "2005–2006: Tarpon Catch-and-Release Study—Tampa Bay," Florida Fish and Wildlife Conservation Commission, 2006, http://myfwc.com/research/saltwater/tarpon/catch-release/tampa-bay-study/.

20. Robert DuBois and Richard Dubielzig, "Effect of Hook Type on Mortality, Trauma, and Capture Efficiency of Wild Stream Trout Caught by Angling with Spinners," *North American Journal of Fisheries Management* 24 (2004): 609–616.
21. Izumi Nakamura, "Vol 5. Billfishes of the World," FAO Species Catalogue (Rome: Food and Agriculture Organization of the United Nations, 1985), ftp://ftp.fao.org/docrep/fao/009/ac480e/ac480e00.pdf.

INDEX